SIMPSON

IMPRINT IN HUMANITIES

The humanities endowment
by Sharon Hanley Simpson and
Barclay Simpson honors
MURIEL CARTER HANLEY
whose intellect and sensitivity
have enriched the many lives
that she has touched.

The Pierogi Problem

CALIFORNIA STUDIES IN FOOD AND CULTURE
Darra Goldstein, Editor

The Pierogi Problem

COSMOPOLITAN APPETITES AND THE
REINVENTION OF POLISH FOOD

Fabio Parasecoli, Agata Bachórz, and Mateusz Halawa

UNIVERSITY OF CALIFORNIA PRESS

University of California Press
Oakland, California

© 2025 by Fabio Parasecoli, Agata Bachórz, and Mateusz Halawa

All rights reserved.

Cataloging-in-Publication data is on file at the Library of Congress.

ISBN 978-0-520-39905-1 (cloth : alk. paper)
ISBN 978-0-520-39906-8 (pbk. : alk. paper)
ISBN 978-0-520-39907-5 (ebook)

Manufactured in the United States of America

GPSR Authorized Representative: Easy Access System Europe,
Mustamäe tee 50, 10621 Tallinn, Estonia, gpsr.requests@easproject.com

34 33 32 31 30 29 28 27 26 25
10 9 8 7 6 5 4 3 2 1

*The publisher and the University of California Press
Foundation gratefully acknowledge the generous support of the
Simpson Imprint in Humanities.*

CONTENTS

Acknowledgments ix

Introduction 1

1 · Poland and Its Food in History 22

2 · The Social Life of Polish Food 39

3 · People 66

4 · Place 88

5 · Time 109

6 · Materiality 140

Conclusions 177

Appendix. Exploring Food in Poland: Literature and
Autoethnographic Reflections 187
Notes 197
References 203
Index 235

ACKNOWLEDGMENTS

First and foremost, I would like to thank my coauthors Agata Bachórz and Mateusz Halawa for this collaborative process. In this case, "I could not have done it without them" is not a platitude: it is a reflection of reality. They patiently guided me towards understanding Polish culture, society, and politics in ways that would not have been otherwise possible. We went through a few rough patches, but we made it!

I would also like to thank my family, who were not always happy that I spent my summers in Poland rather than in Rome. I am glad they had the opportunity to visit and see what all the fuss was about. Thanks as always to Doran Ricks for his unwavering support.

I will not even try to thank all the people who welcomed me in Poland and allowed me to get to know them. Over the years, many have collaborated with me on various projects that I hope will continue in the future. Some have become close friends, an outcome that I was not expecting from an academic research project. It is because of them that I can say I feel at home in Poland. I also want to thank Barbara Kirshenblatt-Gimblett for suggesting my name to Monika Kucia, who then invited me to visit Poland in 2016. That is where this project began. . . .

The indispensable Karolina Kosiura, Anna Węgiel, and Zofia Rohozińska supported me at different times in my efforts to learn and improve my Polish. Without them, I would not have been able to do half of the work I did.

My colleagues at the Institute of Philosophy and Sociology at the Polish Academy of Science provided a supporting and stimulating working environment. I especially want to express my gratitude to Andrzej Rychard, Danilo Facca, Marcin Serafin, Marta Olcoń-Kubicka, Justyna Straczuk, and Ruta Śpiewak. Enormous thanks go to Grażyna Drążyk for her help in navigating the intricacies of Polish bureaucracy. I am honored and humbled to be now a member of the institution.

Innumerable Polish scholars have generously shared their knowledge and have proven fundamental in offering the intellectual excitement that sustained me along the research. In no special order, I'd like to thank Jarosław Dumanowski, Łukasz Łuczaj, Andrzej Kuropatnicki, Marcin Rebes, Mirek Filiciak, Zofia Boni, Feliks Tuszko, Renata Hryciuk, Dorota Koczanowicz, Aleksandra Kleśta-Nawrocka, Gabriel Kurczewski, Dorota Dias-Lewandowska, and Marta Sikorska. Ihor Lylo, Marianna Dushar, and Oleksii Sokyrko in Ukraine, as well as Rimvydas Laužikas in Lithuania and Diana Mincyte in New York, also helped me better understand adjacent culinary cultures that I was not familiar with. Also thanks to my colleagues at The New School and later at New York University for making my work life pleasant and engaging.

I would also like to show sincere appreciation on my and the coauthors' behalf to Natasha Bunzl not only for editing the book manuscript but also for making it much more pleasant to read.

Fabio Parasecoli

I would like to thank my coauthors, Fabio Parasecoli and Mateusz Halawa, for inviting me on the incredible adventure of participating in this project that they planned and started. I especially express my gratitude to Fabio for opening up the field of food studies to me, but also for trusting me, being open to my ideas, accepting my background as it is and—last but not the least—patiently polishing my "Polish" English.

I thank Dorota Rancew-Sikora and Anna Horolets for the best "academic friendship" I could imagine and human support when it was needed. I also warmly acknowledge my colleagues from Polish Food and Drink Research Network (especially Ruta Śpiewak, Wojciech Goszczyński, Renata Hryciuk, Ewa Kopczyńska, and Justyna Straczuk)—I am grateful for this academic environment, in which I could feel comfortable and grow. I would also like to thank my home institution, the University of Gdańsk, for formal support that enabled me to work with Fabio and Mateusz.

I thank my parents for their constant support: my mother Aleksandra, who not only makes wonderful Polish *pierogi,* but also knows how to go beyond them, and my father Stanisław, who is the best mushroom picker in the world.

Agata Bachórz

The research for this book was made possible by grant DEC-2017/27/B/HS2/01338 provided by the National Science Centre, Poland; logistic support from the Institute of Philosophy and Sociology of the Polish Academy of Sciences; and the startup fund provided to Fabio Parasecoli by New York University, Steinhardt School of Culture, Education, and Human Development. Support from the Institute of Sociology of the University of Gdańsk enabled Agata Bachórz to finance and conduct part of her research on food career changers that was also useful for the project.

Parts of our preliminary fieldwork and arguments that led to this book have appeared on Gambero Rosso International (https://www.gamberorosointernational.com) and Fabio Parasecoli's blog (fabioparasecoli.com).

Elements of the research (which have been edited and reorganized for the book) have been previously published as follows:

Agata Bachórz, "*Rzuciła pracę w korpo i zajęła się . . . gotowaniem.' Praca z jedzeniem, nieoczywiste transformacje zawodowe i poszukiwanie alternatywnej relacji ze światem*" ["'She quit her job in corporate and took up . . . cooking': Working with food, unobvious professional transformations and the search for an alternative relationship with the world"], *Studia Socjologiczne* 1 (2023): 59–86.

Agata Bachórz and Fabio Parasecoli, "Why Should We Care? Two Experiences in the Politics of Food and Food Research," *Ethnologia Polona* 41 (2020): 13–31.

Agata Bachórz and Fabio Parasecoli, "Savoring Polishness: History and Tradition in Contemporary Polish Food Media," *Eastern European Politics and Societies and Cultures* 37, no. 1 (2023): 103–24.

Mateusz Halawa and Fabio Parasecoli, "Designing the Future of Polish Food: How Cosmopolitan Tastemakers Prototype a National Gastronomy," *Gastronomica* 22, no. 3 (2022): 8–18.

Fabio Parasecoli, *Gastronativism: Food, Identity, Politics* (New York: Columbia University Press, 2022).

Eszter Krasznai Kovács, Agata Bachórz, Natasha Bunzl, Diana Mincyte, Simone Piras, Fabio Parasecolil, and Mihai Varga, "The War in Ukraine and Food Security in Eastern Europe," *Gastronomica* 22, no. 3 (2022): 1–7.

Introduction

AT THE ROOTS, an upscale bar in Warsaw, a young, bearded bartender in suspenders tells us about the vodka he is meticulously pouring. In contrast to mass-produced labels—commonly made from industrial rye, served ice-cold, and downed in one go from shot glasses—the product presents itself not just as a rarer potato-based distillate, but as an altogether unique and artisanal drink. Its label, emblazoned *Młody Ziemniak* (Young Potato), features the handwritten serial number of this bottle, part of a small batch. It even lists the place and time of harvest. Instead of the typical shot glasses, the bartender serves the spirit in a long-stemmed snifter. Instructed to slowly sip it at room temperature, we are coached through different aroma notes in a manner not unlike that used when tasting single-malt whisky. The language highlights the upscale sensory characteristics of the spirit. The bartender frequently uses the word *wyrafinowane* (literally, refined, and figuratively sophisticated) when describing the aromatic characteristics of the vodka.

Around the corner, the Muzeum Wódki (Vodka museum) showcases artifacts that represent the cultural and economic significance of the drink in Poland since the eighteenth century. Next door, at Elixir by Dom Wódki restaurant, specialty vodkas are served in creative pairings with contemporary interpretations of traditional Polish dishes like pierogi and the fermented rye soup *żurek*. The portions are not as abundant as in common bistros or bars, the flavors are at times unusual, and the presentation distances itself from how such traditional specialties would appear on domestic tables, with more curated arrangements on the plate and the addition of colorful elements.

It is not only vodka that is getting a makeover. All sorts of ingredients, products, and dishes are undergoing a similar process. Throughout the country, potatoes, the main ingredient in many traditional vodkas, are also being classed up. In 2018, chef Joanna Jakubiuk published the book *Ziemniak* (The potato), which has achieved national visibility. Potato-centric cookbooks existed in the past, but they used to make virtue out of necessity, providing a starchy fix to prewar poverty or scarcity under state socialism. Jakubiuk, instead, appeals to an audience with a hedonistic approach to food and focuses on the sensual pleasures of consuming the staple in all interpretations. The subtitle of her book is significant: "Everything you don't know about potatoes and 60 brilliant recipes." At farmers' markets and organic stores in large cities around the country, different premium-priced heirloom potatoes are also increasingly available. In these spaces, vendors explain to shoppers the best uses for each varietal—knowledge unknown or forgotten by many consumers in contemporary Poland. These vendors find enthusiastic students in shoppers who want to educate themselves and become better home cooks and hosts.

The elevation and refinement of a staple that used to be an icon of unremarkable plainness throughout Central and Eastern Europe (Ries 2009) is only one instance of a much broader process of reimagining local food and drink in contemporary Poland. The country now aspires to present itself as offering products that are not only better than similar ones from neighboring countries, but that can hold their own on the global market as uniquely Polish. A central component in this transformation is the new role that chefs, experts, and entrepreneurs have been playing in the last decade or so in reshaping the culinary scene.[1]

We argue that a novel and major shift has been taking place from the early 2010s. 2012 seems to mark a particularly significant moment. In that year, the beginning of the Polish edition of *MasterChef* and the highly publicized Cook it Raw Poland—a visit bringing internationally renowned chefs, including Danish star René Redzepi, together with local chefs and food writers—contributed to moving Poland into the cosmopolitan circuit of gastronomy (Del Secco 2012; *Kuchnia* 2012). Part of the Polish food world was plugging itself into the global circulation of culinary cosmopolitanism, while taking stock of the domestic state of affairs. Actors on the local scene often refer to these events as the beginning of the "foodie revolution" in Poland. Following Johnston and Baumann (2010, 2), we will use the term "foodie" to refer to "somebody who thinks about food not just as biological sustenance, but also as a key part of their identity, and a kind of lifestyle." Often with snobbish and faddish connotations, the term foodie indicates "a

2 · INTRODUCTION

disposition one brings to food—a subject for study, aesthetic appreciation and knowledge acquisition" (Johnston and Baumann 2010, 57). In the past decade, a foodie culture that interacts with global trends, values, and practices has emerged in Poland, and with it a new generation of professionals and experts.

These shifts in the culinary landscape are not unique to Poland. Growing interest in food as a topic worthy of media attention, public debate, economic investment, and national pride is visible in Central and Eastern Europe (Caldwell, Dunn, and Nestle 2009), allowing chefs to reach new levels of fame (Tominc 2023). Just like everywhere on the global culinary scene (Parasecoli 2017), connoisseurs and enthusiasts in former socialist countries show renewed interest in local food and traditions (Caldwell 2002; Drace-Francis 2022; Joffe 2012; Makharadze 2020; Vezovnik and Tominc 2019). The current aspirations toward refinement and elevation differ from forms of engagement with artisanal and traditional ingredients and dishes that had emerged during previous decades, often ideologically motivated to display the existence—or rather the continuation—of cultural diversity and multiculturalism within the socialist bloc (Jacobs 2022; Koenker 2018; Shkodrova 2018; Scott 2012). These shifts, however, raise the question of who in each country claims authority to decide what is worth highlighting, how they built their legitimacy, and what their motivations are.

Stakeholders with very different access to power negotiate the terms of such culinary revaluations; as a result, marginalized communities and their foodways risk being excluded from the limelight or tokenized as anthropological curiosities. In Poland, debates about what counts as Polish food are frequent and heated, especially when taking in consideration class differences. Not only experts and professionals, but cooks and eaters are making noticeable efforts to define Polish cuisine, while trying to distinguish it from that of neighboring countries even though they share ingredients, dishes, techniques, and practices.

The process of defining a national Polish cuisine is inevitably influenced by both domestic politics and international events emerging against the background of specific circumstances that distinguish it from other countries in the area: a tortuous history (including its partition among invading empires for two hundred years, followed by a difficult unification process), over thirty years of postsocialist transformation,[2] an extremely rapid and sustained economic development,[3] and the country's sheer size.[4] Moreover, the renewed interest in Polish cuisine was weaponized by the conservative governments in power from 2015 through 2023, which often embraced chauvinistic tones in contrast with a widespread sense that the country has been unjustly separated from the West, to which it rightfully belongs.

Fascinating because of its social and political distinctiveness, the Polish case contributes to a deeper understanding of the dynamics of global phenomena such as cosmopolitan foodie-ism and its supposedly democratic aspirations; the growing interest in lesser-known culinary traditions' most artisanal, "authentic" manifestations; and the worldwide scramble to define national cuisines, playing them up for diplomatic, commercial, and geopolitical goals (Parasecoli 2022). It also allows us to observe the dynamics that shape the emergence of a cultural field in which a set of actors aspire to achieve legitimacy, authority, and autonomy while vying for positions of influence within the field itself (Bourdieu 1993). The concept of a dynamic and complex system of institutions, agents, rules, and practices has already been used to study gastronomy as an industry and the network of people engaged in and communicating about food. Priscilla Ferguson looked at gastronomy in nineteenth-century France as a cultural field (1998), while Raul Matta built on this Bourdieuan concept and analyzed the expansion of gastronomic field in terms of socio-politics (2019). Following this tradition, we have decided to use the term culinary field.[5]

For these reasons, this book is not especially focused on what makes Polish cuisine unique in terms of flavors, specialties, and customs, and what differentiates it from the gastronomic traditions of neighboring countries. We rather try to reflect on how and why so much effort is dedicated to its definition and to the identification of ingredients, dishes, techniques, and customs that can be recognized as unequivocally Polish. Our goal is to understand the mechanisms through which perceptions about local, artisanal, and traditional foods have changed, and how their production has acquired growing visibility. We intend to explain why delineating a Polish national cuisine has become a priority and how its understanding has changed, who are the actors involved, why they engage in rebuilding the gastronomy field, how they narrate what they perceive as assets, and what cultural and social tensions find expression in these shifts in the culinary landscape.

FOLLOWING A CHEF

The emergence of a chef like Joanna Jakubiuk, the author of the above mentioned *Ziemniak* (potato) cookbook, reflects these recent developments.

Born and raised in the gastronomically distinctive region of Podlasie, in the east of the country, she received her professional training by working in the local culinary scene during her studies in pedagogy. Unlike many of her peers, she did not hone her trade abroad. Nevertheless, she fits into this story because she has benefited from the support and esteem of culinary and media-savvy experts who are respected in the cosmopolitan foodie circuit. She now enjoys national recognition not as an executor of fancy dishes in elegant restaurants, but as a soulful interpreter of popular, often rural, customs and flavors.

We met chef Jakubiuk several times, including on the occasion of a 2017 dinner planned by Monika Kucia, food writer and event curator, for a group of foreign food writers and scholars on an exploratory trip to discover Polish cuisine.[6] Guests also included local food professionals, ranging from media personalities to festival organizers. In the lead-up to the dinner, chef Jakubiuk kept herself busy making pierogi and *kartacze,* also known as *cepeliny* (zeppelins, as they look like blimps), one of the specialties of her native Podlasie. These oval-shaped, four-to-five-inch long dumplings, made by mixing grated raw potatoes, their starch, and potato flour, are filled with seasoned ground meat (at times with the addition of cabbage or mushrooms) and served with bacon bits and sauteed chopped onion. The event showcased traditions that tickled the curiosity of foreigners whose knowledge of the local specialties was mostly limited to what is available abroad: pierogi dumplings, kiełbasa sausage, and borscht (*barszcz,* in Polish).

We crossed paths with chef Jakubiuk again during the 2018 edition of the Flavor Festival (Festiwal Smaku) in Gruczno, a rural village in the northwest of Poland. Jakubiuk was making *pączki,* a fried dessert in the shape of a flattened ball, usually filled with jam, frosted or sprinkled with powdered sugar, and decorated with candied orange or lemon peel. The chef was not preparing the wheat flour version of the confectionery that can be found in pastry stores all over Poland; instead, she mixed potatoes into the dough, highlighting the particular varieties that the booth where she was working promoted. Chef Jakubiuk's visibility sought to elevate the profile of those potato varieties and to underline their connection with valuable culinary traditions, such as their use in flavorful *pączki.*

We came across the chef again in November 2018 at an event devoted to Polish cuisine in New York at the Museum of Food and Drink (MOFAD), located in Brooklyn.[7] Jakubiuk was of course cooking, displaying her skills for curious and enthusiastic American foodies (some of Polish descent). The menu included herring with a potato salad; an apple, celery, thyme, and sea buckthorn soup; duck with sauerkraut, beetroot, kale, and carrot; and a dessert of dried plums, nuts, honey, and butter. Jakubiuk also made pierogi together with the Pierogi Boys, a duo of young Poles who have made a name for themselves in New York City. The active participation of both foreigners and Polish expats provided an external perspective that is emblematic of the dynamics between the domestic food landscape and the globalized circulation of things, ideas, practices, and people. For instance, a new batch of English language writers (both expats and within Poland) have recently produced cookbooks meant to change widespread perceptions of the Polish culinary world, such as *Polska: New Polish Cooking* (2016) and *Pierogi* (2022) by Zuza Zak, as well as Michał Korkosz's *Fresh from Poland: New Vegetarian Cooking from the Old Country* (2020a) and *Polish'd: Modern Vegetarian Cooking from Global Poland* (2023).[8]

Several times during the dinner, the hosts remarked that the food maintained its uniqueness and authenticity. All the dishes, from appetizers to dessert, were presented as a concentrate of unadulterated Polish flavors and textures, whose cultural specificity was likely to appeal to an audience seeking to explore an exciting food tradition, often unfamiliar in this form even to Polish-descent audience members. The starchiness of potatoes, the sourness of pickles, and the pungency of fermented foods were presented as specifically Polish. The emphasis on these sensory "Polish" traits constitutes one of the recurring strategies in the redesign of contemporary Polish cuisine and in the attempts to elevate its status on the international scene. The Brooklyn event sought to combat the notions that many Americans may entertain about Polish food as meat-centered, dull, and heavy.

Similar ingredients—salted, dried, smoked, pickled, fermented, turned into jams, macerated in alcohol, or otherwise manually processed and stored—are also common in nearby countries including the Czech Republic, Ukraine, Belarus, Lithuania, and Russia, where historically both farmers and low-income city folks were used to planning for lean times. Under the socialist regimes, these foods acquired emotional and social value as they allowed cooks to provide for themselves and their families, surviving in spite of the frequent food scarcities. Demographic shifts and growing urbanization both during the socialism years and the postsocialist transformation have turned these products, often received as gifts in *słoiki* (jars) from relatives in the countryside, into ambivalent symbols of both nostalgic comfort and the rural background new urbanites were eager to erase (Caldwell, Dunn, and Nestle

2009). In recent years, these homemade products have been taken out of domestic pantries to be reinterpreted by famed chefs, produced by skilled artisans, and sold at premium prices.

The story of Joanna Jakubiuk's budding fame is a reflection of the broad changes taking place in Polish culinary circles, which are the main focus of this book. The recipes she cooks, the techniques she employs, and the ingredients she uses are far from exotic for Polish consumers. In fact, they tend to be quite familiar as domestic fare and as staples in modest eateries such as working-place canteens (*stołówki*), school cafeterias, and *bary mleczne,* the affordable "milk bars" (so called because they offered various dairy-based dishes) that became a mainstay during the socialist decades. Over the past few years, private and public efforts have been dedicated to raising the prestige of these dishes, especially if made lighter, healthier, and more creative, or presented in intentionally iconoclastic vegetarian and vegan versions. Overall, Poles seem to be torn between conservative food habits and a budding desire for culinary innovation, between pride and a variously articulated sense that their fare is bland, uninteresting, heavy, and somewhat backward. This ambivalence was voiced both by the professionals and the consumers we met in our fieldwork.

Many of the stakeholders in the new approaches to Polish food are eager to showcase to the world ingredients and dishes beyond the mainstays that are well known outside of Poland. As Tomasz Duda, then chef at the Polish Embassy in London, told us during a 2019 event in which we presented our research project to a largely expat community of Polish food enthusiasts, Poland may have a "pierogi problem:" the dumplings are often the only dish that foreign consumers may be familiar with, frequently available in low-quality interpretations. In addition to its artful alliteration, the chef's reflection stuck with us because it fully conveys the conundrum facing those who want to redesign and elevate Polish gastronomy: the desire to cherish traditional fare and yet the fear that it may not be good or interesting enough, not only for foreign foodies, but also for refined local consumers.

Such quandaries are magnified by questions about the role of Polish culture in Western civilization and a postcolonial syndrome Poland seems to suffer in regard to modernity and the West (Brzostek 2015; Buchowski 2006; Leszczyński 2017; Sosnowska 2004; Zarycki 2016). As Larry Wolff (1994) suggests, since the Enlightenment the very concept of Eastern Europe is the result of cultural strategies aiming at identifying a nearby otherness meant to provide contrast to the progress of modern Western Europe. In the words of

Siegfried Huigen and Dorota Kołodziejczyk (2023, 2), "The inbetweenness of the region has been inherently contradictory: on the one hand, founded on the strong identification with Europe, and, on the other, driven by the anxiety of incomplete belonging and into ranking high enough to merit the status of Europeanness."

The Europeanization process after 1989 provided an opportunity to manifest these contradictions: the inclination to imitate and catch up with the West while trying to stand out as a "good student," looking down on the eastern neighbors or the popular classes (Buchowski 2006; Dunn 2004; Kuus 2004), together with the reflection on the place of Europe in Polish identity (Horolets 2006). Such debates were rekindled during the 2015 migration crisis, which saw clashing attitudes and policies on the issue adopted by Western and Eastern European countries, with the latter stigmatized for their "un-European," more rigid, and seemingly exclusionary positions (Gille 2017). The place of the East in Europe is further complicated by forms of post-communist nostalgia in the West, which at times generate patronizing and moralizing criticism (Todorova and Gille 2010) or more sympathetic but not less orientalizing appreciation (Bach 2017). Participating in ongoing political debates in civic society, Polish scholars discuss whether their country is a semi-periphery or a full-blown periphery (Zarycki 2016). Positioned between East and West, Poland appears torn between the changes that have transpired since its accession to the European Union in 2004 and the recurring backlashes against these developments, especially in terms of a perceived subordination to other European countries.

These often unexpressed anxieties play a central role in the revaluation of local food, the renewed appreciation for artisanal products, and the rediscovery of old practices and traditions. Through the analysis of these local phenomena, our research goes beyond the Polish case to address broader tensions in the cultural relations between center and peripheries, revealing the underlying hierarchies within the global culinary field—in the postindustrial societies of the Global North, but increasingly also in countries like Brazil, India, and China (Parasecoli 2017; Parasecoli and Halawa 2021). The dynamics at play in Poland question the seeming homogeneity and egalitarianism of culinary cosmopolitanism, originating from omnivorousness rather than snobbery but still built on connoisseurship and other forms of cultural capital. While the recent developments within the culinary field apparently blur any neat correspondence between consumers' positions in the social stratification and their practices (Bourdieu 1984), not all Poles feel equally comfortable with the forms of consumption promoted by culinary innovators. The power relations and the distribution of financial capital within the emerging food scene are less democratic than they appear.

Taste turns into an arena in which countries marked as second- and third-tier vie for a limelight whose access rules have been set by a handful of (mostly Western and secondarily East Asian) actors (Cappeliez and Johnston 2013; Ray 2016; Trandafoiu 2014). Such dynamics are further complicated by the fact that what is increasingly cosmopolitan—and shared by many local food movements around the world—is not only the openness to and familiarity with foreign cuisines but also the fascination with the food traditions of one's own region or country. However, such interest is filtered through preferences and values that may be established elsewhere, a phenomenon that Hao-Tzu Ho (2020) has referred to as cosmopolitan locavorism.

TASTEMAKERS AND MATERIALITY

Not everybody has the same access to cultural tools that allow them to enjoy forms of omnivorousness ranging from low to highbrow (Ferrant 2018; Peterson and Kern 1996). As Poles engage in the revaluation of their culinary landscape, often through processes of elevation and refinement of what would otherwise be judged as plain and dull, they find themselves negotiating tensions between large cities and peripheral areas, as we elaborate in chapters 3 and 4. This process intersects with contrasts between urban and globalist elites on the one hand, and the working class or rural dwellers on the other. Local and traditional foods that until recently were marked as banal or low-class have now a place in the experiences and aspirations of those who imagine themselves as upwardly mobile, reframed in ways that reflect their preferences and aspirations. The transformations in the Polish culinary landscape, however, cannot be understood as random and spontaneous, or the natural and inevitable outcome of the current situation. These shifts are taking place because cultural intermediaries are intentionally introducing, supporting, narrating, and shaping them.

Our book follows these intermediaries, or "tastemakers" (Sax 2015), to uncover how they construct materials, spaces, narratives, and practices around culinary tradition and locality. They increasingly do it through digital storytelling, by participating in the global circulation of things, skills, and sensibilities that constitute the emerging omnivorous culinary cosmopolitanism

(Dürrschmidt and Kautt 2019), and by intentionally imagining the future of Polish food through modalities that can be interpreted as forms of design interventions.

They operate not only at a discursive level, but also at a material and practical one by creating new objects, social arrangements, marketplace connections, and value chains, while displaying applied ingenuity and practical skills that are highly appreciated in the professional market. They introduce sensory practices, interpretive frameworks, and aesthetic categories that are already prevalent in the global circles of food professionals and enthusiasts, including elaborate tasting rituals and the vocabularies that come with them (Tsigkas 2019). These forms of culinary cosmopolitanism—often developed through tastemakers' lived experiences of migration and apprenticeship in world cities like London—are applied to elements that are rooted in the local context, like potatoes in vodka and fermented rye flour in a *żurek* soup.

These tastemakers include food producers, chefs, journalists, bloggers, entrepreneurs, marketers, event organizers, and academic historians. Although in very different ways, chef Joanna Jakubiuk, the vendors of heirloom potato varieties at farmers' markets, and the makers of the *Młody Ziemniak* vodka all belong to this varied and growing category of tastemakers. Their roles morph depending on the context. A chef may write an article for a culinary magazine, manufacture ingredients for sale, become a landscaper and interior designer, and participate in a vodka tasting to hone their knowledge of the spirit. We will examine this fluidity in chapter 3. Tastemakers are focused on good food, negotiating what eating well means aesthetically, ethically, and politically. Crucially, they also concern themselves with *other* people: what they eat, and how they should eat. Although they vary in terms of educational and social backgrounds, tastemakers share significant commonalities in terms of attitudes and life projects. Many of them belong to the intelligentsia, self-invested with a distinctly regional "mission to civilize" (Zarycki 2009, 2019; Zarycki, Smoczyński, and Warczok 2017). Their centrality in the current Polish food scene manifests itself in their influence on media, marketing, and at times on government policies.

Our interactions with intermediaries in the Polish food landscape has led us to consider their role and function and to ask more broadly how the Polish culinary field is organized, engineered, designed, and structured. As a group crucial to the expertise regimes of postindustrial societies, intermediaries have become the object of growing interest in sociology and anthropology (Bourdieu 1993; Negus 2002; Smith Maguire and Matthews 2014) in terms of the socio-technical networks they establish (Moor 2012), the imaginaries they generate within creative industries (O'Connor 2015), the evaluation canons they contribute to establish (Lane and Opazo 2023), and their participation in the emergence and solidification of new fields (Byrkjeflot, Pedersen, and Svejenova 2013; Gomez and Bouty 2011; Svejenova, Mazza, and Planellas 2007). In other words, much research has addressed tastemaking as a process that operates on narratives, meanings, and relationships among those involved (Bouty and Gomez 2013; Messeni Petruzzelli and Savino 2014). We also look into the affective qualities that tangible elements seem to embody, eliciting emotional responses in those who interact with them (Chumley and Harkness 2013; Fehérváry 2013; Gal 2013; Harkness 2015; Munn 1986).

Tastemakers innovate by transforming ingredients, dishes, built environments, and landscapes, from hills that are planted with vineyards to farms that are transformed into organic productions of heirloom varieties of vegetables and old barns repurposed as locations for upscale, farm-to-table wedding banquets. As we will see in chapter 6, they work with actual stuff: plants, flesh, fungi, soil, mortar. They consider materials, their physical traits, and the way they interact with each other and with us (Ingold 2007).

We argue that their preoccupation with materiality can be better understood through the lens and the conceptual language of design, not only as a feature of objects, spaces and experiences, but also as a particular approach to understanding and interacting with reality. In doing so, we build on design anthropology (Clarke 2018; Gun, Otto, and Smith 2013; Smith et al. 2016) and design theory (Atzmon and Boradkar 2017; Walker et al. 2018), especially in their examination of the relationships between makers and materialities. By framing the tastemakers' practices through categories of design—and we are fully aware that they often do not intentionally operate as designers—we interpret design as a mode of action where thinking and making, or "head" and "hand," are collapsed into one (Sennett 2008). To design, perhaps especially when it comes to food, is not to pull things out of thin air. As sociologist Bruno Latour (2008) observed, to design is always to redesign, working the old together with the new through an ethos of open-ended experimentation, tinkering, and bricolage. It is to reassemble "preexistent objects, which [the designer] identifies, decontextualizes, and reinterprets modifying their meaning and some of the details," as design theorist Enzo Manzini (2019, 50) suggests.

Tastemakers attempt to place themselves outside of the routine and the conventional in order to rearrange what is familiar in novel formations. The reintroduction of almost extinct breeds of potatoes, the launch of a pop-up restaurant, or the refinement of vodka-making techniques can turn those spearheading such initiatives into local heroes and models for others. The realities of such projects necessarily involve a great deal of improvising and tinkering, amateurism and failure, going through several more or less successful iterations. This is at times due to the novelty of tastemakers' approaches within the existing culinary landscape, and other times to their inexperience, which is counterbalanced by enthusiasm. As we will see in chapter 3, the tastemakers we interviewed are often career-changers and have moved to food because they were attracted by the potential of the culinary field in terms of entrepreneurship, success, and self-realization.

THE EXPERIENCE OF TIME

Situated in what they perceive as the periphery of global food trends, tastemakers in Poland at times find themselves emulating others, a move sometimes narrated in temporal terms as "catching up" or "making up for lost time," or in related spatial terms as Westernization, an integration with core circuits of taste and prestige (Krastev and Holmes 2020). They may endeavor to define themselves as proponents of progress who—in alleged contrast to the rest of society—maintain connections with Western hubs, thereby claiming an understanding of future developments. Because the tastemakers we observe in our ethnography are often culturally and socially privileged, despite their small numbers their voices are relatively powerful in deciding how to tell stories and establish narratives about Polish food, its past, and its future. Their visions reflect valuable entrepreneurial investments, individual passions, and aesthetic inspirations that rely on the growth and success of specific cultural or social trends. Although uncertain, tastemakers' hopes and dreams have very real effects in the present, from decisions on what kinds of restaurants to open, to choices about what crops to farm.

Business strategies, cultural outlooks, and social attitudes do not only depend on expectations about what is to come, but also draw deeply from a sense of shared history. They do not happen in a void, but rather in a present that is heavily influenced by the past. In order to make sense of their complex national story and its current predicaments, Poles refer regularly, although selectively, to both recent and remote events, drawing from the Christianization of the country in the Middle Ages to its social and political golden age in the early modern period. This is a trait shared with other Central and Eastern European countries, where historical events seem to be mentioned in contemporary political and cultural discourse with great emotional intensity (Svašek 2006).

In defining the worldview they promote, tastemakers appeal to history and memory as collective interpretations of the past and tradition that are constantly negotiated. Following polymath Michael Polányi (1962) and historian Eric Hobsbawm (Hobsbawm 1983), by "tradition" we mean not only the social mechanisms that identify, select, use, and interpret fragments of the past, but also the results of such activities: new, often "invented," cultural formations that respond to the needs of the present. The protagonists of our ethnography tend to identify tradition with this second aspect, focusing on specific ingredients, dishes, or customs rather than on the often implicit cultural dynamics that allow these materials to be experienced as traditional. In any case, tradition should be understood as a process, an ongoing endeavor in the present rather than an established set of historical references. Taking into consideration tastemakers' attitudes and practices, we extend Hobsbawm's argument into the future: "invented traditions" may emerge not only as a response to current concerns but also as tools in a kit of design-inflected projects that leverage the past in order to imagine what is yet to come. These futures of Polish food are far from abstract. Tastemakers work to bring them about in tangible objects, spaces, and experiences, from the opening of a restaurant in the cellar of a castle to the planting of vineyards in areas where they had disappeared.

The very cultural environment in which Polish tastemakers operate is a space of aspiration, potentiality, and openness to the future. Due to Westernization and the country's swift economic development, Poland is often hailed as a model for other Eastern European nations (Halawa 2015). As we will illustrate in chapter 2, in the often traumatic transformations that followed the end of the socialist regime, the opportunities to improve one's conditions and standards of living were unevenly distributed, leaving clear winners and losers. Not all citizens were receptive towards the attempts at transforming them into risk-taking, self-regulating, entrepreneurial subjects embracing the "habits, tastes, and values of postmodern flexible capitalism" (Dunn 2004, 6). Some were better equipped than others to take advantage of the shifting circumstances, often amassing noticeable wealth.

Against this background, tastemakers' aspirations are constantly conciliating local approaches, heavily steeped in historical debates and Western, supposedly cosmopolitan perspectives. Such dynamics at times generate pushback against the progressive outlooks that several of the tastemakers we interacted with appear to embrace. Conservative and nativist leaders elaborate counternarratives that are presented not as the expression of specific political and economic interests, but rather as the voice of those who were left behind during the postsocialist transformation, if not as manifestations of true Polishness. These critiques resonate with large swaths of the Polish electorate, especially in the east of the country and in rural environments. For many in Poland the transformational processes that have followed the socialist regime are not concluded yet. As such, they are still contested. Invented traditions, claiming to originate from legitimate versions of the past, assume different meanings and values according to the context in which they are put together and experienced. They are never politically neutral, but rather reflect values and priorities meant to shape what the future might, or should, be.

History and traditions—in this case those concerning food and foodways—constitute arenas in which social actors establish connections between their understanding of the past, their experiences in the present, and their projections for the future (Koselleck 2004; Gvion 2009; Mische 2009). Through these interactions, individuals and communities articulate their social identity not only by positioning themselves in time but also by evaluating time periods as positive or negative, desirable or undesirable, and often filtering them through the lens of nostalgia (Boym 2007; Pickering and Keightley 2006).

Political polarization fuels heated debates that examine and evaluate Poland's complicated development as a nation, the fall of socialism, the integration in the European Union and, more recently, the resurgence of Russia as an existential threat. Disputes about the legitimacy of those who took advantage of the postsocialist transformation and how the resulting power balance should be renegotiated are especially bitter. Tensions also flare when pride for the nation and national culture clashes with forms of nationalism that can acquire xenophobic features. The PiS (*Prawo i Sprawiedliwość,* "Law and Justice") party, which controlled the government, the judiciary, and the lower chamber of the Parliament from 2015 to 2023, embarked on a profound and divisive reinterpretation of Polish history that posited religion and traditional family values at the core of Poland's future (Korycki 2017; Kuisz 2023; Nizinkiewicz 2017). At the time of this writing, it is still too early to assess the approaches of the new, more pro-European government towards these issues.

14 · INTRODUCTION

NEGOTIATING THE VALUE OF FOOD

Against this background, the value of things, places, and practices is not static but rather constantly negotiated. Value should be understood not only literally as pricing, but also as a moral and symbolic category that is socially constructed and, as such, subject to changes. Looking at processes of value formation and changing ideas about what is valuable can provide a good vantage point to understand the current transformations of the Polish culinary field and the negotiations taking place among its stakeholders.

Tastemakers participate in valuation processes by elevating or refining previously lowly things (and, conversely, by belittling beloved and widespread culinary practices), by arranging new relationships between things previously disconnected (like pierogi and the criteria of the Michelin guidebook), or by attempting to create new valuation schemes altogether. In doing so, they mobilize broader and older cultural hierarchies while reacting to the "Western gaze" and embracing narratives of modernization. At the same time, they claim legitimacy and prestige for the culinary field as a whole, in particular vis-à-vis the segments of society that tend to dismiss it as faddish and inconsequential.

The reinterpretation of folk, simple, and pragmatic elements as valuable reflects the mechanisms highlighted by sociologist Luc Boltanski and Arnaud Esquerre (2017) in their analysis of the *économie de l'enrichissement,* the postindustrial "enrichment economy" that presupposes the blurring of the material and the symbolic through the relevance attributed to the narratives and stories attached to products. Through the appropriation and concurrent gentrification of traditional low-class and countryside food, old stuff is repackaged and made available for new, supposedly elevated forms of consumption. The new valuation brings about not only economic outcomes, as producers can charge premium prices for experiences and things that consumers are willing to pay for, but also revisions of aesthetic categories of food appreciation, which will be examined in chapter 6.

Our research agrees here with economists Hans Kjellberg and Alexandre Mallard (2013, 13–14) when they observe "an erosion of the traditional standards supporting evaluation, and the rise of arenas where valuation processes tend to integrate new aesthetic dimensions" that include sensory features and flavors, skills, and embodied experiences. In Poland, however, the traditional standards themselves are not clear-cut; in fact, they are at times imagined. Stakeholders' interpretations of authenticity are also far from univocal: references to supposedly objective history and considerations about products' origin and genuineness get linked to more personal and contextual approaches (Bendix 1997; Zukin 2008, 2011). In the case of Polish tastemakers, rather than focusing on authenticity, we should draw attention to the authentication processes they activate to attribute legitimacy to their pursuits, to claim authority in determining values, and to elevate their status, as is often the case in the global circles of cosmopolitan foodies (Mapes 2021; Olszanka 2022).

Through these negotiations of value, traditional and manual activities that were previously limited to the working classes turn into gentrified cultural and creative industries. Just like sociologist Richard Ocejo (2017) observed in the US context, in Poland it is not uncommon for the children of the contemporary urban middle classes and adult career-changers to fantasize about rural life and manual craft. This would have been hardly acceptable a generation ago. However, when urban professionals decide to quit their office or corporate occupations and undertake a job in gastronomy or move to the countryside to produce food, they do it bringing with them ideas and practices that they may have picked up during their travels or prolonged stays abroad.

They may present the fruits of their activities as traditional rural products, but they do so using urban and cosmopolitan points of view (Goszczyński 2023), citing references and inspiration from abroad or international movements like Slow Food. They frequently plan their work and organize it as they did in their previous careers, leveraging knowledge they gained in other lines of business. They use marketing strategies and sophisticated methods to build their brands. They can talk to their urban customers in a language that makes sense to them and reflects their aspirations and desires. Tastemakers may have next-door neighbors who make products that are as tasty as those they manufacture or promote and might have done so for much longer. But their style of communication and economic strategies, perceived as backward, are at odds with those of their cosmopolitan would-be clients, who often do not share the same values and priorities. This mismatch frequently prevents producers in the countryside from promoting what they do, unless they turn to tastemakers as intermediaries who translate their rural products for city customers.

AN INTERDISCIPLINARY APPROACH

The phenomena on which this book focuses are so diverse, complex, and closely interconnected, that it was necessary for us to employ a wide range of interpretive tools. Our research project is situated within food studies, a field of research that engages with food as a complex social fact by analyzing the biological, cultural, social, economic, technical and political issues concerning the production, distribution, preparation, consumption, and disposal of food in its material and immaterial aspects (Albala 2013; Belasco 2002; Miller and Deutsch 2009; Nestle 2010).

Over time, food studies has developed a keen interest in the fraught and complex connections between lived bodies, imagined realities, and structures of power built around food (Williams-Forson 2006). Due to the nature of its interests, food studies has emerged as an inherently multidisciplinary field, constantly striving towards interdisciplinarity (Bentley, Parasecoli, and Ray 2024). Researchers have often borrowed theories and methods from anthropology, sociology, history, economics, political science, geography, gender studies, race and ethnicity studies, and media studies, to mention just a few (Bestor 2004; Parkhurst Ferguson 2004; Trubek 2009). The field is also in dialogue with the culinary arts (Zhen 2019), design (Parasecoli 2018), and other applied practices. As happens in other multidisciplinary fields, it is the context and the characteristics of the specific objects of investigation that suggest what theories and methods are the most apt to explore it.

In our research we have used ethnographic qualitative methodologies such as observation of cultural practices (mostly participant observation) and in-depth interviews (Johnston and Baumann 2010; Julier 2013; Ray 2016) to support other well-established food studies approaches, such as culinary analysis of ingredients and dishes, investigation of material culture (objects and spaces), as well as discourse and visual analysis (Frye and Bruner 2012; Parasecoli 2008). We conducted over seven years of fieldwork not only in large cities such as Warsaw, Kraków, Poznań, Bydgoszcz, Wrocław, Gdańsk, and Lublin, but also in smaller centers like Toruń and Olsztyn, as well as in rural areas. Our fieldwork includes over sixty interviews with people involved in the transformation of the Polish food scene, from short chats on the sidelines of events to more formal in-depth interviews over coffee, drinks, or food. We selected some interviewees based on their visibility or relevance in the field. Others we identified through snowball sampling and introductions offered by other interviewees. In some cases, professional interviewees reached out to us after hearing about our research project.

We also formally interviewed five domestic cooks (selected by a specialized agency) in Warsaw and Gdańsk, shadowed them in their grocery shopping, and informally interacted with numerous others in their kitchens and on various food-related occasions. During our ethnographic fieldwork, we observed tastemakers in their professional practice and public appearances, participating with them in public and private events. We visited their places of work and, at times, interacted with them in their homes. The conversations took place in English and in Polish.

We also conducted five expert panels in three cities, four focus groups that included men and women from different income brackets and from different parts of the country, a design workshop with eight young chefs, and made a great many visits to restaurants (both the front and the back of the house), markets, specialty grocery stores, farms, and domestic kitchens. We attended events such as tastings, food festivals, panel discussions, academic conferences, food and beverage competitions, and professional meetings. We participated in initiatives ranging from government-led projects to the establishment of a food academy, among other things. We also observed our interlocutors' social media activities: posts, public discussions and private chats all contributed to better understanding how the stakeholders think, operate, express themselves, and relate to each other in those contexts (Leer and Strøm Krogager 2021). Given the increased trend towards vernacular uses of photography in the food world, we also extended our analysis to include visual online environments such as Instagram and video platforms. These experiences have confirmed for us the growing importance of digital and virtual spaces in ethnographic research, an aspect that was even more important during the COVID-19 pandemic.

Our analysis is based on transcripts of our interviews, as well as descriptive and analytical field notes from observation (including sensory notes on meals and dishes). We have used a strategy of open coding, identifying key themes and issues and iteratively deepening them as the fieldwork went on. We have also kept an archive of photographs and audio recordings taken in the field and clippings from relevant online publications and social media interactions. The evocative power of the visual material we gathered has proved useful in reminding us of the sensory elements of our research, from flavors and smells to moods and built environments, which we were able to cross-check with our own notes and the ephemera we collected over the years.

In addition, we analyzed the food discourse in Polish media such as video, TV, books, and magazines, in particular regarding food that is perceived as Polish—local, artisanal, and traditional (Bachórz and Parasecoli 2023). We hope our research contributes to the expanding research on the role of media in shaping contemporary foodscapes and the discourses surrounding them in Central and Eastern Europe (Daniel, Kavka, and Machek 2015; Tominc 2017). Building on Alan Warde's (1997, 199–200) caveat on the "limits to the capacity of food to express personal identity," which reminds us that not everybody is interested in food as self-expression and as a feature in popular culture, we do not make any assumptions about what Polish people actually do with food representations offered by the media, unless they can be observed in ethnographic research. However, food studies and media scholarship suggest that, by indicating desirable forms of consumption and aesthetics, representations in food media often offer quasi-pedagogical and aspirational depictions of the good life and contribute to the negotiations through which categories of good taste are established (LeBesco and Naccarato 2008; Leer and Povlsen 2018; Phillipov 2017). We build on the idea that food media, which cocreates discourses about buying, cooking, and eating, contains elements of a "life project" and visions for the future in its repetitive message (S. Rousseau 2012; Tompkins 2012).

Although coauthor Fabio Parasecoli started exploring food in Poland in 2016, the research project that led to this book was formally launched in 2018 thanks to a grant from Poland's National Science Centre, with Mateusz Halawa and Agata Bachórz as co-researchers, which found its home in the Institute of Philosophy and Sociology of the Polish Academy of Sciences in Warsaw. The fieldwork ground to a halt in spring 2020, due to the spread of the COVID-19 pandemic. Not only was it no longer possible to interact with tastemakers in person (we did continue online) or visit relevant locations; the whole culinary landscape entered a period of temporary crisis, especially in the realm of hospitality and fine dining.

After a few months the outlook for gastronomy improved, as the country imposed a relatively short lockdown policy and a great number of Poles showed resistance to abiding by strict measures, which explains the intensity of the following waves of the pandemic in the fall of 2021 and the winter of 2022 (Drinóczi and Bień-Kacała 2020). Although some restaurants closed, new ones opened. Furthermore, the delivery business boomed, not only for stores and markets, but also for brick and mortar eateries. At the time of writing, the culinary scene has been suffering from the steep inflation that gripped the country until the spring of 2024, making customers less willing to spend in restaurants or to go out, while rising costs of energy and materials squeeze the income of food producers, retailers, and restaurant owners.

THE STRUCTURE OF THE BOOK

Our examination of the existing literature on Polish food (see the appendix for more details) indicates that there is no full-length monograph in English that deals with Polish contemporary gastronomy from a cultural and social point of view. Nor is there one that looks in particular at how current trends in the country connect with a global "foodie" landscape from the points of view of practices, discourse, media, and materiality. Our book fills this gap, not only engaging with current food dynamics in Poland, but also focusing on segments of the populations—the upwardly mobile middle classes, and especially tastemakers—that have shown growing discursive and material influence.

After this introduction, this book is structured into six chapters. Chapter 1 provides background information about the history of Poland and how food contributed to social and economic changes. Chapter 2 focuses instead on contemporary Poland, setting the stage for the exploration of the emergence of the culinary field, the current incarnation of cosmopolitanism, and their entanglements with current political debates. Chapter 3 focuses on tastemakers and other social actors in the field of gastronomy, examining their individual and shared trajectories in redesigning "good food." They are a very colorful bunch, often career-changers or returning migrants, articulating and performing their vision of an aspirational future. Chapter 4 looks at how tastemakers prototype and iterate innovative approaches to reimagining Polish cuisine through place-based dynamics at different scales and through various lenses. They explore placemaking, *terroir*, locality, urban and rural rearrangements, as well as Poland as a nation on the regional, European, and global arena. In this chapter we describe peripheral anxieties and complexes as they mix with imperial nostalgia and aspirations. In chapter 5 we turn to time, also on different scales, focusing on the uses of the past as a resource for retelling of history and the invention of tradition. We see tastemakers navigate the definition of heritage in progressive categories of openness, inclusion, and multiculturality, but also the more conservative idea of canon. Tastemakers make the past and history tangible—and above all edible—through the materiality of culinary expertise, shared meals, and hospitality entrepreneurship. These practices, seemingly aiming at reshaping the present, reveal the tastemakers' designerly aspirations at future-making.

Chapter 6 explores the material stuff entangled in tastemaking, focusing on practices around sourcing ingredients, from farming to foraging, and processing them to reveal or negotiate sensory qualities that Poles acknowledge as expression of their culinary identity, like sourness or heaviness. Here, we pay attention to processes such as fermentation, brewing, infusion, or smoking, while also examining the transmission of knowledge and skill necessary to successfully master these techniques. In our conclusion, we offer a few closing reflections on our work and its contributions to the study of cultural and social trends in the global food landscape, their political implication, and the role of tastemakers in such dynamics; at the same time, we identify themes for future research. Finally, in the appendix, we discuss the literature we built on during our research, the methodologies we used, and the politics of fieldwork; in particular, we examine the dynamics of collaboration and coauthorship between Fabio Parasecoli as food insider but cultural outsider; Mateusz Halawa, a food outsider and cultural insider; and Agata Bachórz, a Polish food scholar. This work would have not been possible without our ongoing reflection on the dynamics of power and prestige in which we constantly found ourselves entangled. In some ways, our team had to overcome some of the tensions arising from the aspirations, shared by many of the tastemakers we interacted with, to catch up with the West and move from the periphery to the center of global trends.

ONE

Poland and Its Food in History

TODAY, POLAND'S FOOD PRODUCTION is quite large, not only in comparison with its Central and Eastern European neighbors, but also relative to the European Union, which it joined in 2004. The largest market for food and beverages in Central and Eastern Europe, Poland is also one of the largest processed-food producers in the region; in fact, in 2021 the sector accounted for 5 percent of Poland's total GDP, with exports worth over $34 billion (Figurska, Peterson, and Galang 2023).

Although the total agricultural area decreased from 18.793 hectares in 1990 to 14.500 in 2021, and arable land from 14.388 hectares in 1990 to 11.078 in 2021 (FAO n.d.), the land used for food production is nearly half of the country's territory (Statistics Poland 2023). The rural population is still 39.9% of the total (FAO n.d.). Although for many of them agriculture and husbandry do not constitute their main source of income, these activities continue to play an important role, at least from a social and cultural perspective. The direct support from the EU Common Agricultural Policy (CAP) programs is similar to other Central and Eastern countries, but much lower compared to Italy or Greece. These funds play an important role for farmers: the share of direct payments in rural income is 29 percent (against an EU average of 22.3 percent), similar to Czechia and Hungary but lower than the Baltic countries (European Commission n.d.). In our ethnography, we observed plates acknowledging EU support on new buildings and infrastructure related to food production.

According to Statistics Poland (the Central Statistical Office), the number of agricultural holdings is decreasing, while their average size is increasing, pointing to a consolidation of fragmented land ownership in larger commercial enterprises. However, this phenomenon is not happening at the same rate in the whole country: while the southeast sees a prevalence of small holdings, the largest conglomerates are found in the in northwestern areas. In 2022, the share of the population occupied in agriculture ranged from 4.7 percent in Silesia to 30.1 percent in the region around Lublin (Statistics Poland 2023).

While agriculture contributed only 1.8 percent of the GDP in 2019, in that same year the value of the agricultural output was 26.358 million euro: 6.3 percent of total EU production. In particular, Poland ensured 9.7 percent of EU cereal production, 12.3 percent of root crops, 8.3 percent of fresh vegetables, 9.2 percent of milk, and a notable 19.5 percent of poultry meat (European Union 2020). In 2021 exports of agricultural products, primarily directly to the EU market, were close to 48 billion euros (Sas 2023).

Although the economic relevance of food cannot be overlooked, it is its cultural and social significance that has turned it into an arena in which political and national identities are negotiated among stakeholders with very different interpretations of the country's past and visions for its future. To examine the current transformations in contemporary Polish culinary culture, in this chapter we will briefly explore their historical roots and the role food played in shaping politics and society at different points in time. This excursus is particularly necessary as Poland's complex past is little known outside of the country. Its goal is to provide a better understanding of dynamics and events that otherwise may remain obscure to external observers. As we will discuss in chapter 5, the dimension of time, the diverging evaluation of historical periods, and their use in current cultural, social, and political negotiations contribute to the current revaluation of local, traditional, and artisanal food.

FROM THE ORIGINS TO THE PARTITION

Poland first appeared as an autonomous polity around the end of the first millennium AD. Poles often mention 966, the year when Prince Mieszko I converted to Christianity and established his dominion over the territories in modern-day western Poland, as the beginning of the Polish nation. Those lands, which are still called *Wielkopolska* ("Great Poland"), were inhabited by Slavic populations that were at times referred to as Polanie, probably from the word *pole* (clearing, plain, open flat terrain). From the late Middle Ages, the region functioned as a buffer borderland between Western Europe, the orthodox East, and the Eurasian world from which frequent waves of nomads originated. This position has contributed to Poles' interpretation of their country's historical role as the defender of Catholic and Western civilization.

Its territorial extension has changed over the centuries. Parts of today's Poland belonged to other polities and were not inhabited by Polish-speaking populations. From the early thirteenth century, for instance, at the invitation of a local prince the Teutonic Knights settled on the right bank of the Vistula river, later conquering Gdańsk in 1308 and establishing their headquarters in Malbork, near the Baltic Sea. The Polish monarchy stabilized itself in 1387 with the conversion of Jogaila of Lithuania to Catholicism and his coronation as Władysław I, the founder of the Jagellonian dynasty. The new nation, with the support of the Grand Duchy of Lithuania, the large and powerful polity to its east, was able to stop the expansion of the Teutonic Knights at Grunwald in 1410. These events would later be interpreted as harbingers of the long-standing tensions between Poles and Germans.

Lutheranism and the Reform were perceived as a German phenomenon, as the former spread mainly among German-speaking city dwellers, while Calvinism was mainly embraced among the nobility. However, Protestants in Poland did not suffer the same persecutions as in other Catholic countries. The tolerant attitude of the state reflected the established presence of various religions, including Eastern Orthodoxy, Islam (Tatars had settled in today's eastern Poland in the late fourteenth century), and Judaism (Bideleux and Jeffries 2007, 156). Starting in the thirteenth century, the monarchs of Poland relied on the Jews' commercial and professional skills to boost their kingdom's economy, welcoming those who fled persecutions in other parts of Europe to settle both in cities and in the countryside. Special statutes protected their rights to work, travel, and manage their internal affairs according to their religious regulations, including food production and slaughtering according to kashrut rules. Through hybridization and exchanges, the contribution of Jewish foodways to the cuisines of Poland cannot be understated.

The influence of the Catholic Church was nevertheless important, especially after the successful reaffirmation of Catholicism in the second half of the seventeenth century. The frequent and severe fasting customs that spread with it were so harsh that they attracted the attention of foreign travelers (Dumanowski 2021). The Church of Rome's centrality to local intellectual life explains the spiritual connection the educated elites felt with the West. From the late Middle Ages, the monasteries became centers for the diffusion of food production and culinary techniques, which the ecclesiastics learned during their pilgrimages or through exchanges with other religious communities. These influences determined the development of Polish wine, vinegar, aged cheese, and cold cuts, as well as the introduction of vegetables and fruit of southern origin; the aristocrats, who had access to sugar, were able to turn the latter at times into candied fruits, confitures, and gelées (Smołucha 2023, 62).

The connections with Italy, in particular, fostered the participation of Poles in the Renaissance during the fourteenth and fifteenth centuries. Nicolaus Copernicus, for instance, studied at the University of Padua. Princess Bona Sforza of Bari, who was married to King Zygmunt I, is often credited with the introduction of Italian courtly food customs in Poland (Smołucha 2023, 65–66). Similarities with the stories about Catherine de Medici and her influence on French cuisine are evident. Urban legends—frequently mentioned by our interlocutors—somehow connect Sforza with a mix of vegetables called *włoszczyzna,* from *Włochy,* the Polish word for Italy; widely available in grocery stores to make broth, it includes leeks, parsley root, celery, and carrots.

The scions of the Polish landowning nobility, although mostly living on their rural estates outside of major cities, studied Latin (the first university was founded in Kraków in 1364), read widely (books were printed from the late fifteenth century), traveled throughout Europe, and employed chefs who mastered both the local cuisine and foreign gastronomic practices, as cookbooks such as *Compendium Ferculorum* by Stanisław Czerniecki, first published in 1682, suggests (Czerniecki, Dumanowski, and Spychaj 2012).[1] However, not all nobles had access to the same financial means; in fact, many of them were far from wealthy. The vast majority of the population was illiterate and worked as peasants on the countryside estates of the nobility, often forced to live on the land they cultivated through different forms of serfdom, which intensified from the fifteenth century.

Unable to directly invest in international commerce due to their financial limitations, the noble landowners focused on the production of cereals, timber, and livestock to be exported to Western Europe, turning Poland into what Immanuel Wallerstein (1974) considered a semi-periphery in the emerging world economy of capitalism. Nevertheless, trade connections through ports such as Gdańsk, closely associated with the Hanseatic League cities, allowed for luxury goods, including spices, to circulate. The recipes from that period frequently appear to be richer in non-local flavors than contemporary ones, a fact that tastemakers often mention as a rationale for both experimentation and the rediscovery of the country's culinary past. By the late eighteenth century, the food culture of the nobility, resulting from a unique mixture of fascination with oriental spices, Catholic fasting, medieval cooking styles, and influences from European courts, was dominated by the tensions between the followers of the material culture connected with Western Enlightenment ideas and those who instead supported local customs.[2]

In 1569 Poland and Lithuania (at the time much larger than today's country by that name) had signed a union treaty that established the Polish-Lithuanian Commonwealth or the "Commonwealth of Two Nations" (*Rzeczpospolita Obojga Narodów*). The Commonwealth covered most of today's Poland, Ukraine, Belarus, Lithuania, Latvia, and even portions of Russia. It extended from the Baltic to the steppes of today's Eastern Ukraine, almost reaching the Black Sea. Despite the end of the Jagellonian dynasty in 1572, a destructive Swedish invasion between 1655 and 1660, constant strife with Russia, and a Cossack rebellion within its eastern territories, the Commonwealth survived until the end of the eighteenth century. Its shared monarch was elected by all nobles wishing to participate in what was known as the "free election" (*wolna elekcja*).

The Commonwealth had a parliament (*sejm*) controlled by a diverse nobility (*szlachta*) that ranged from very powerful magnates to impoverished nobles (Lukowski and Zawadzki 2019). The Sejm was able to check the king on matters such as taxes, international relations, and declarations of war. Moreover, every member of the Sejm had a power of veto (*liberum vetum*) on decisions and legislation approved by the majority, imposing the need for consensus; this institutional mechanism was often used as a political weapon not only by Polish domestic factions but also by foreign powers, which constantly tried to influence the internal decisions of the polity (Jędruch 1998).

The unique political structure of the Commonwealth became the object of interest for Western European intellectuals such as Daniel Defoe and Jean Jacques Rousseau (Defoe 1705; Rousseau 1985; Wolff 1994). Attempts to limit the instability embedded in the system led to the adoption of the Constitution of 1791, the second modern constitution in the world, after the one ratified in 1788 in the United States of America. The new legislation ended the *liberum veto* and asserted political equality between townspeople and nobility, while limiting the abuses of the nobles against the peasants.

Despite these reforms, the monarchy was not able to oppose the expansion of nearby empires. In three successive partitions between 1772 and 1795,

Russia, Prussia, and the Austrian Empire split the Polish territory among themselves, erasing it from the political map of Europe until its reestablishment in 1918. During the partition, Poland managed to maintain its cultural identity in terms of religion, literature, and above all language, despite attempts by the Prussian and Russian imperial authorities at limiting its usage.

While the areas of Poland under Vienna and, above all, Berlin experienced some technological modernization and industrialization, investments were less significant in the territory under the Czar, where the most important economic sector remained agriculture, with the exception of the city of Warsaw. The construction of railways by the Prussians integrated the western regions into the German market. To a lesser extent, Russia also built railways into the areas of eastern Poland under its control. It was there that pogroms took place in the 1880s, causing massive migrations of Jews toward other European countries and the Americas. When mechanisms for local autonomy were introduced in the Habsburg empire, Poles in Galicia could maintain a higher degree of political self-determination, with Kraków and Lviv as their main centers (Lukowski and Zawadzki 2019, 155–190). The difference in development among the regions of contemporary Poland which had been part of different state entities is still visible. The debates regarding the positive or negative legacies of the partition, along with the selective memory and oblivion associated with them, persist to this day (Zarycki 2012).

THE SECOND REPUBLIC AND WORLD WAR II

At the end of World War I, the 1918 Treaty of Versailles made it possible for nation states to emerge in Central and Eastern Europe on the ruins of the old imperial regimes. However, these new formations often fought with each other to determine their borders, generating diplomatic enmities that, in the case of Poland and Ukraine, lasted until after World War II when the Pax Sovietica was imposed on the region and all territorial disputes were forcibly solved. The international agreements, however, did not completely solve the issue in terms of popular sentiments. During the interwar period, the newly established Eastern European states struggled to build functioning political and institutional systems, from parliaments to postal services and educational systems. They also strove to construct coherent cultural identities, whether by creating national currencies, national visual styles, or cookbooks presuming the existence of "national cuisines," in the Polish case spanning locations as diverse as Lviv, Kraków, Warsaw, and Poznań. This was a time when cafés and restaurants thrived in large cities, a memory that our interlocutors often brought up to explain why the country's existence as an independent state is necessary for Polish cuisine to flourish.

Poland's independence was short-lived: in 1939 its invasion by Nazi Germany, which had formed an alliance with the Soviet Union, marked the beginning of World War II. Poland was supposed to provide the *lebensraum* that the Third Reich deemed necessary for its future. After the 1943 Warsaw Ghetto uprising, in the summer of 1944 the Polish Underground State launched what came to be known as the Warsaw Uprising (*powstanie warszawskie*), with the goal of freeing the country's capital and bringing it back under Polish control before the Soviet-backed Polish Committee of National Liberation occupied it (Białoszewski 2014; Richie 2013). However, the uprising failed and the Nazis razed the city to the ground.

At the Yalta conference of 1945, the Allies tacitly acknowledged Soviet interests over most of Central and Eastern Europe (Karski 2014). The Poles felt they had saved Europe from the Communist "hordes," and they expected recognition from the great powers. The decisions at Yalta increased a sense of betrayal and victimization that already been brewing since the nineteenth century among Poles who described their country as the "Christ of Nations" or the "Christ of Europe," a metaphor popularized by Polish Romantics and still circulating (Jakubowska 1990; Walicki 1978). Moreover, Poland had already functioned as a protective bulwark for the West: after its reunification, in the 1920 Battle of Warsaw the country had stopped the advance of troops from revolutionary Russia into Europe, and Western leaders had acknowledged its crucial role in international security (Zimmerman 2022, 5–6). For that reason, many Poles experienced their treatment after World War II as bad faith on the part of the Western world. The socialist government and the inclusion in the Warsaw Pact and the Soviet sphere of influence did not do much to assuage the fears that Poland was destined to eternally suffer from foreign enemies and their allies within the country.

SOCIALIST POLAND

After World War II, Poland obtained territories in the west and north that were previously part of the German Reich, including the cities of Wrocław, Szczecin, Olsztyn, and the former Free City of Danzig (Gdańsk). These were meant to balance the loss of its eastern territories, which became part of the Soviet republics of Lithuania, Belarus, and Ukraine. The territorial reshuffle was followed by huge resettlements, as the new socialist state moved workers around to respond to strategic and economic priorities. Poles from the lost eastern areas relocated to the recently acquired western areas, newly emptied of their German population. The result was a remarkable ethnic homogeneity, which some Poles consider a badge of pride and others a cause of political malaise.

The devastation of World War II and the subsequent reconstruction and industrialization turned food security and food production into central issues for the government of the new Polish People's Republic (*Polska Rzeczpospolita Ludowa*, or PRL), which found itself torn between the push toward the efforts aimed at establishing a socialist state and the immediate needs of the population (Burrell 2003). Efforts to modernize the food system and to ensure sufficient nutrition for the whole population after the war's destruction shaped the socialist state's priorities, which focused on industrializing agriculture and manufacturing to increase outputs. Plant varieties and animal breeds that did not perform well in the modernized system fell to the sidelines, and so did artisanal techniques that did not allow for speedy and abundant production. Local manufacture did not disappear after their nationalization: some cheese and cold-cut factories, for instance, were managed efficiently but did not produce enough to distribute all over the country. Mass production of food still maintained spaces for local specificities.

The central government aimed at taking control and coordinating economic activities, an almost impossible effort. The socialist project included a vision of top-down technological and social modernization, understood as industrialization, urbanization, social mobility, emancipation, lifestyle change, and the decreasing role of tradition (Zysiak 2017). The state authorities also intervened to modernize food distribution, as well as nutritional knowledge and culinary habits (Brzostek 2010; Czekalski 2011; Bachórz 2024; Węgiel 2024). These strategies turned out to be only partially successful, due to the constant gap between declared goals and the inefficiency of the state-regulated economy. The lack of raw materials or badly timed deliveries, mismanagement, and the need to respond to centralized plans that did not reflect the reality of the economic system constantly plagued production, despite workers' ingenuity and their often-unsanctioned initiatives to keep factories running (Dunn 2004). During the second half of the twentieth century, on the one hand availability of meat, fruit, fat, sugar, and processed dairy grew (Kopczyńska and Zielińska 2016; Stańczak-Wiślicz 2020; Straczuk 2016a). On the other hand, the state was not able to satisfy the Poles' consumer aspirations, including those newly awakened after World War II (Milewska 2022).

Poland's history of unrealized agricultural collectivization sets it apart from other Central and Eastern European countries under socialist regimes (Gorlach and Drąg 2021). In September 1946, an agrarian reform was launched to install displaced peasants on over a million farms. However, in 1948 Bolesław Bierut, a former official of Comintern, changed the government's rural agenda, putting in place efforts toward collectivization under the State Agricultural Farms system (Państwowe Gospodarstwo Rolne or PGR) (Jarosz 2014). This attempt was never fully accomplished (unlike in strongly collectivized states like Romania or Bulgaria), and crop production lagged. Scarcity, which soon became endemic, was particularly grievous to a population that was aware of the "*sklepy za żółtymi firankami*" (shops behind yellow curtains), secret places that sold hard-to-find foods and other consumer goods to operatives of the Ministry of Public Security, senior officials, and members of the political office of the Polish United Workers' Party (Polska Zjednoczona Partia Robotnicza or PZPR) (Milewska 2022).

In 1956, riots over "bread and freedom" (*chleba i wolności*) took place in Poznań, resulting in the death of dozens of workers. The events spurred the rise of Władysław Gomułka, who had been purged back in 1948, to the party secretariat. Taking advantage of the "thaw" after Stalin's death, in his position as First Secretary of the PZPR Gomułka managed to ensure greater autonomy from the Soviet patrons. As a gesture of goodwill toward the population, the "shops behind yellow curtains" were formally closed. However, the upper echelons of the party and government functionaries still maintained preferential access to rare or exotic products. Irregularities in the distribution system were also politicized in the "meat scandal" (*afera mięsna*) of the early 1960s (Jarosz 2019). A specially appointed party commission discovered that good-quality meat was being stolen, exchanged for monetary bribes, or replaced with worse cuts for the general public, while the best pieces were sold on the side to those with connections. Over four hundred people were arrested and tried in legal procedures, including the director of the City Meat Trade in Warsaw's Praga neighborhood, Stanisław Wawrzecki, who was sentenced to death and executed by hanging in prison in 1965. In 2004, when the socialist justice system became the object of criticism and reform, some of the trials were eventually declared illegal by the Polish Supreme Court.

During the Gomułka years, most of the agricultural land was gradually returned to private peasants. Collectivized management continued in large farms located in the western and northern areas that had previously belonged to Germany and had been turned into public property at the end of World War II (Nagengast 1982). While productivity in state farms did not improve, small peasants as a class continued to be considered a hindrance to the socialist future. In reality, their capacity for larger outputs was limited by almost nonexistent investment, high prices in inputs and machinery, and bureaucratic nightmares concerning land ownership rights. As a consequence, shortages and kinks in the distribution system often made shopping for groceries time-consuming and frustrating. Once again, demonstrations about rising prices erupted in December 1970, when the army opened fire and killed workers protesting in Gdańsk and Gdynia, leading to Gomułka's resignation.

Edward Gierek, who replaced Gomułka as PZPR first secretary in 1970, ushered in the era of "consumer socialism,"[3] a period of economic revitalization, industrial investment, and relative comfort fueled by money the state borrowed from the West (Blazyca 1980). Unlike citizens in other Warsaw Pact countries, Poles were allowed to own dollars, which often came in the form of remittances from migrant family members and friends. In 1972 the government launched the bank Pekao, where accounts in dollars and other foreign currencies could be opened and used to buy consumer goods in the bank stores. The following year, the stores became their own company, Pewex (short for *Przedsiębiorstwo Eksportu Wewnętrznego*, Internal Export Company), where hard-to-find items such as liquor, cigarettes, home appliances, and even cars could be purchased outside of the local currency system and without the need to stand in line. In the early 1970s the promised availability of sought-after products, including meat and ham, legitimized Gierek's reforms. At the same time, the government was constantly attempting to lower meat consumption through dietary advice and propaganda (Milewska 2022).

Rural populations that migrated to cities to be employed in new industrial enterprises often experienced a sense of nostalgia for the countryside. Those who remained in rural areas kept on sending food to recently urbanized relatives. This led to the emergence of an "old-style cooking" (*kuchnia staropolska*), an idealized version of simple but tasty and wholesome peasant food rather than a reflection of historical realities. *Kuchnia staropolska* became popular in the 1970s, as urban populations imagined a lifestyle projected into the past. This culinary fantasy constituted an expression of the very recent rise in the standards of living that tangibly translated into the (ultimately short-lived) availability of mass-produced chicken and pork meat (Kleśta-Nawrocka 2016). In reality, the "countryside" products found in stores were quite industrialized and homogeneous.

Although the central planners maintained food prices at relatively low levels in relation to salaries, by the mid-1970s the short-lived hopes of the urban population were disappointed by frequent shortages of goods. Facing their government's failures, Poles partially shifted to the techniques for food procurement that characterized all the socialist countries in the region (Burrell 2003; Caldwell, Dunn and Nestle 2009). Self-provisioning, foraging, making preserves, and fermenting vegetables allowed families to take advantage of what was temporarily available (depending on the season or some fluke in the distribution system) and store food for harder times. Those who had a *działka* (allotment garden) grew all sorts of vegetables and fruit for family consumption but also as a means of exchange for other goods. As the oil crisis and the following global recession made the service on foreign debt unmanageable, in 1976 Gierek decided to suddenly raise consumer prices. Riots exploded at the Ursus tractor factory in Warsaw and at the armaments works in Radom, causing the party to delay the food prices rise (Lepak 1989).

When the government tried again in 1980, it was the turn of the shipyard workers in Gdańsk to vent grievances (over unaffordable food, among other things). The protest eventually led to the formation of the independent workers union Solidarność and the proclamation of a strike. The twenty-one demands that its leaders wrote on plywood panels and hung at the entrance of the shipyard included: "9. Guaranteed automatic increases in pay on the basis of increases in prices and the decline in real income. 10. A full supply of food products for the domestic market, with exports limited to surpluses. 11. The introduction of food coupons for meat and meat products (until the market stabilizes)." The demands emerged from what can be defined as a socialist economy of scarcity. Workers with strong ties to the farmland from which their families came witnessed the incapacity of the socialist state to manage food production and distribution. The lack of food and the onerous efforts necessary to procure it contributed to the political delegitimization of the system. At the same time, the eleventh demand of the Gdańsk shipyard workers also suggests that food constituted a medium to negotiate social equity and solidarity: although the promise of the PZPR was the welfare of the whole working class, some had access to meat while some did not. Its presence in the demands underlines how meat had quickly become central to the Polish idea of good life (Mroczkowska 2019).

The outcome of the Gdańsk events was the martial law imposed on December 1981 by the first secretary of the Communist Party, General Wojciech Jaruzelski, and his Military Council of National Salvation (Wojskowa Rada Ocalenia Narodowego, WRON, or *wrona*, the crow, as it was often popularly referred to), with the support of the USSR. A few months later, in February 1982, food costs skyrocketed by 300 percent, and many products became unavailable. Extreme scarcity, long lines in front of stores, waiting lists and other acquisition strategies (Mazurek 2010), black markets, and illegal provisioning networks (Kochanowski 2010) became the norm for most Polish citizens, with the possible exception of the nomenklatura (Chase 1983). Poles still describe those times with sentences such as "there was only vinegar on the shelves." Informal economies emerged: people would come from the countryside to sell pigs to urban populations from the back of their small FIAT cars (as illustrated in Chris Niedenthal's famous photos). Having family members in the countryside meant securing access to sources of basic staples such as potatoes, root vegetables, eggs, or big jars (*słoiki*) of preserved or fermented foods.

POLAND AFTER 1989

The transformation that followed the first free elections on June 4, 1989, was touted as a model for other countries in the region, yet it created stark differences between the haves and the have-nots (Ghodsee and Orenstein 2021; Ost 2005). Those who reaped the benefits of the dismantling of the socialist safety network and took advantage of the rise of the service economy became the face of the new Poland: among these, the intelligentsia, those with connections, and risk-taking entrepreneurs with financial capital (Mark et al. 2019). The new postsocialist authorities made only limited efforts to protect the weakest segments of the population from the "shock therapy" introduced by Finance Minister Leszek Balcerowicz, which launched the privatizations of state enterprises (Dunn 2004) and was accompanied by wage reduction and high unemployment.

Jacek Kuroń, a leftist Solidarność politician, thought it was in the interest of the nation to join forces with Balcerowicz, the architect of the economic transformation (Dudek 2020). Joining the new government as the labor minister and taking it upon himself to try and ease the suffering of people, Kuroń established unemployment benefits while also organizing free distributions of split-pea soup. This soup, which came to be known as *kuroniówka* after him, became an iconic element of the period. Kuroń himself publicly served soup to the needy.[4] More recently, the term *kuroniówka* has been used in general for unemployment benefits from the government.

In the 1990s, the legacy of the socialist past lingered: food maintained its centrality in political discussions, albeit with different meanings. The need to clearly identify Polish products and to support them both domestically and internationally emerged from the very beginning of the postsocialist transformation. In 1991, the new government launched the Polish Promotion Program (Polski Program Promocyjny), a marketing initiative that established the logo *Teraz Polska* (Poland now), a Polish flag in which the lower red section is modified to evoke hills (Fundacja Polskiego Godła Promocyjnego n.d.). The use of the logo is awarded to the best products Poland can offer, determined through a yearly selection. As of 2024, thirty-four editions of the competition have been held: over 5,000 firms participated, among which over 750 obtained the logo.

Concerns about the status of Polish cuisine seem to have reached the highest political spheres. While pride in local gastronomy has become de rigueur among politicians of all affiliations, the more nationalist ones also make a point of displaying a certain amount of suspicion for foreign culinary traditions. Law and Justice (*Prawo i Sprawiedliwość*, *PiS*) conservative party leader Jarosław Kaczyński proudly informed the audience of a popular morning show of his eating habits, claiming that he only has soup for lunch. Appearing on *Pytanie na śniadanie* (Question for breakfast) on the state-controlled channel TVP2 in May 2019, Kaczyński declared: "I like *bigos* (hunter's stew), *placki ziemniaczane* (potato latkes), *pierogi ruskie* (cheese and potato pierogi), *schabowy* (breaded and fried pork chop) with cabbage, and *naleśniki* (pancakes). I like all grilled items, especially sausage." And he continued: "I have eaten very refined dishes in very good French restaurants in my life and I will be honest: I was not shocked by their [supposedly] extraordinary quality. I was told that they were extraordinary, but I couldn't feel it. In Poland there are many such things that are not at all worse than in very good French restaurants" (Kaczyński 2019; Salon24 2019). These statements reflect a broader narrative of anti-European, nativist populism: according to such understanding, Poles have been forced over and over to accept the superiority of the West, including its ideas and products; conservative politicians profess that it is time to end the mimicry, stand proud, and assert the value of the Polish ways (Krastev and Holmes 2020). To a certain extent, these undertones resonate also in more progressive circles, albeit with a stronger focus on overcoming the postcolonial inferiority complex than on denying the centrality of internationalization in Poland's modernization.

It is in such a context that foreign food became a flashpoint for heated but short-lived controversies. In June 2014, former Foreign Minister Radek Sikorski from the Civic Platform (Platforma Obywatelska) party was criticized, along with other high-ranking officials, for indulging in baby octopus, depicted as a foreign, decadent, and inherently corrupt food (even though at the time it was widely available and relatively affordable as a frozen item, thanks to the expansion of supermarket chains). Sikorski's menu choice was made public through a set of tapes recorded at the upscale restaurant Sowa i Przyjaciele, one of the favorites of the Warsaw political and financial elites (Cienski 2015). Sikorski and the other guests were heard lamenting the institutional weakness of the Polish state, criticizing US-Poland ties, and discussing the possibility that the Central Bank could support the government by easing monetary policy in case of an economic downturn before the elections, which were to take place in 2015. PiS ended up winning those elections, attacking the previous government as out of touch with the real Poland, which the consumption of octopus by its leaders supposedly demonstrated (Buckley 2014). In October 2016, out of resentment toward France for having disinvited Poland from an arms fair, the then deputy Defense Minister Bartosz Kownacki, also from PiS, portrayed the French as "people who learned to eat with a fork from us," once again aligning food with the ongoing right-wing discourse around who is "truly" civilized and stands for Western values (AP News 2016).

As new sources of prosperity emerge, the benefits from the economic transformations are not equally distributed among the different strata of the population (Brzezinski, Myck, and Najsztub 2021; Bukowski and Novokmet 2021; Tomescu-Dubrow et al. 2018). The current political debates about those who best took advantage of the fall of socialism and how the resulting power balance should be renegotiated are especially heated. The country is struggling with its identity; this is evident in the rise of nativist political movements (Davies 2001; Lukowski and Zawadzki 2019; Porter-Szücs 2014) and the debates about the nation and its culture, which can be easily leveraged to pander conservatism and xenophobia. After the 2015 elections, the populist PiS party enjoyed the majority in the Parliament, controlled the executive, tried to reshape the judiciary, and enjoyed a vast influence over the media and the public opinion (Bluhm and Varga 2019). PiS policies were culturally conservative and politically populist, buttressed by traditional forms of Catholicism and the institutional backing of the Catholic Church (Bill and Stanley 2020). At the same time, the party and its allies claimed to focus on providing economic support for those who suffered the brunt of the postsocialist transformation while urban elites thrived, especially the working and lower middle classes in rural locations and in the eastern regions of the country (Toplišek 2020). Incidentally, those are also areas where artisanal food traditions are still maintained, a repository of culinary wisdom that several of the tastemakers we interviewed consider still unrefined but worth exploring.

Despite far-reaching inequalities and internal conflicts, the current shifts in the culinary landscape are taking place in a rapidly transforming society that in terms of national GDP has experienced an economic boom that has lasted almost uninterruptedly for more than thirty years, rivaling the fast development of the Asian "tigers" in the 1980s (Gomułka 2016; Koryś 2018; Wudyka 2016). As of January 1, 2025, Poland's minimum wage rose to 30.50 zloty per hour before tax—equivalent to about $7.35, slightly over the US federal minimum wage of $7.25 an hour (Menendez-Roche 2025). Today the demographic structure of the country is in flux. As deindustrialization and urbanization continue and large urban centers are populated with service- and creative-sector workers (Galent and Kubicki 2012), new visions of the "good life" appear together with a rise in higher education, international travel, lifestyle media, and a boom in restaurants and cafés not seen since before World War II. For instance, Warsaw enjoys a reputation as the most vegan-friendly city east of Berlin, and features more international food events and festivals that we can count.

The culinary world is taking notice. In 2022 five Polish restaurants were included in the French ranking La Liste, among which Epoka in Warsaw was the highest placed (more about it in chapter 5); at the time of writing, the number of Polish restaurants in that list has risen to six. In 2023 chef Przemysław Klima obtained the first Polish two Michelin stars at Bottiglieria 1881 in Kraków, which is also home to several Bib Gourmands. At the time of writing, Muga in Poznań, Giewont in Kościelisko (a village around 85 km south of Kraków), Rozbrat 20 and Nuta in Warsaw, as well as Arco by Paco Perez in Gdańsk, all boast one Michelin star; sixteen restaurants are celebrated as Bib Gourmand, fifty-five received the "selected restaurant" distinction, and Eliksir in Gdańsk was awarded the first Green Star in Poland in recognition for its sustainable practices. Whatever one may think of the Michelin guide, in the Polish gastronomy scene it represents an important accolade in terms of international visibility.

To help the economy after the pandemic shock and improve citizens' standards of living, in 2022 the government launched Polski Ład (the Polish Deal): it included measures such as lower taxes, better healthcare services, more affordable housing, higher retirement pensions, and more jobs. At the time of writing, it is still unclear how effective the plan has been or how much of it was actually implemented. The opposition against PiS (the government until October 2023) critiqued the plan as just a publicity stunt that did not really change anything and did not reduce the clientelism and the advantages PiS politicians and PiS-led city and province councils enjoyed. From 2021 to spring 2024, double-digit inflation turned into an urgent issue; although it has since eased up, it had an obvious impact on citizens' personal finances and opportunities to secure loans to buy a home, as well as on entrepreneurs' ability to secure loans.

The government that emerged from the October 2023 elections—a coalition of center and center-left parties led by former president of the European Council Donald Tusk—is trying to alter juridical and administrative decisions by their predecessors that the more liberal and progressive voters perceive as a threat to Polish democracy. As we write, it is still hard to tell how the policies they are embracing will influence the future of Poland, in part because PiS continues to be a powerful political force. By undoing the reform of the Constitutional Court and other legal measures the PiS government had imposed, the new coalition has succeeded in defusing tensions with the European Union, which has freed huge solidarity funds that had been frozen because of the constitutional controversies the PiS government had been embroiled in. Many funds will be directed to agricultural development, but they may be less easy to access for small farmers, who frequently lack the bureaucratic savvy and the political connections on which larger rural enterprises rely. Tensions also simmer—and at times explode—between countryside and cities, between educated and less educated citizens, between have and have-nots, between conservatives and progressives, between chauvinistic nationalists and patriotic internationalists, and between those who still identify the soul of Poland with the Catholic Church and those who instead consider the Church one of the causes of its problems. Many among those who voted in the new coalition in 2023 express dissatisfaction with the new government's apparent lack of initiative on issues like abortion, same-sex marriage, and migration, reflecting its intent of securing the support of the more conservative sectors of Polish society.

The domestic debates we have just illustrated, however, cannot be separated from Poland's increasing visibility on the global scene. In the next chapter, we will explore the current culinary field in Poland and its transformations, often closely inspired by Western-inflected cosmopolitanism.

TWO

The Social Life of Polish Food

IT WAS A SUNNY, crisp day when we first visited the Mleczna Droga (Milky Way) dairy farm on the Celejowskie Hills in the Wąwolnica commune, not too far from the city of Lublin in Eastern Poland. The owners, Rafał Duszyński and Anna Łuczywek, were expecting a group of foreign journalists near an impressive spread of their products on a rustic wooden table. The small cabins on their property, surrounded by intensely green fruit trees and meadows dotted with grazing cows, have been transformed into agritourism spaces. It's hard to imagine a more idyllic farm. The owners were proud to let the visitors taste their products, from yogurts to their versions of local cheese, both fresh and aged, together with large, triumphant slices of locally produced Stilton.

Just like many of the tastemakers we met, Duszyński and Łuczywek are career-changers. In their previous professional lives as lawyers they traveled to England and fell in love with Stilton cheese, precipitating a major life change. Back in Poland, they quit their corporate jobs, bought a farm, and started producing yogurt and cheese, including their own version of Stilton. On their Facebook page they state: "We develop our farm towards a self-sufficient organism that harmoniously combines animal husbandry, land cultivation and food production.... We obtain milk from Jersey cows that graze on pastures in summer and stay in a free-stall barn in winter.... The entire production process takes place on our farm. All products are free of preservatives and artificial flavors." After the tasting, the visitors had the opportunity to tour the modern, clean, and well-organized production facilities, where they met one of the cheesemakers, a local woman who contributed her experience in the dairy industry and her skills to the farm. They were shown the production of yogurt and fresh cheese in the local style. The dairy's artisanal methods met new customers' demands, mixing old flavors and modern marketing with a personal touch. As the two entrepreneurs were starting out, back in 2012, urban consumers (including coauthor Halawa, based in Warsaw) would receive weekly emails from them with information on the changing seasons and amusing anecdotes about everyday life of the farm: "The cows also feel that the pasture season is approaching and went for a walk, which for us ended up in an unforeseen chase."

Such an approach is an example of the changes that in many cases have revamped the manufacturing and the sales of traditional Polish products. The owners of Mleczna Droga embody the culinary cosmopolitanism of many Polish tastemakers. They display an intense fascination with food-related material objects, ingredients, recipes, practices, and narratives from outside their country, together with varied degrees of association with and subordination to foreign or global or international standards of taste and value. While honing their ability to see Poland "from outside," tastemakers also show a growing interest in the revitalization and reinterpretation of their own local and traditional foods, as they have seen happen in other countries. Mleczna Droga's Stilton represents an outward-looking captivation with not only foreign products per se, but also worldliness and international expertise, implicitly appreciated as superior. Yet its celebration as a locally produced specialty also suggests an inward-looking attitude that reflects the enthusiasm among global foodies for domestic products with a clear provenance, manufactured artisanally from high-quality ingredients. Duszyński and Łuczywek—like many others we met in our fieldwork—create a hybrid: they communicate the values and priorities of both aspects of culinary cosmopolitanism in a language that appeals to both local Polish food enthusiasts and foreign audiences.

However, our tastemakers rarely employ the concept of cosmopolitanism, which can be translated in Polish as *kosmopolityzm,* to explicitly frame or describe their activities. More charged than *międzynarodowość* (internationality), a somewhat neutral and descriptive expression used for instance for international collaborations or conferences, during the socialist years authorities identified *kosmopolityzm*, a foreign loanword, with a deplorable, excessive interest in the West. In that, it was different from the government sanctioned *zagraniczność,* which involved foreign policy (*polityka zagraniczna*) or interactions with foreign visitors, selecting and curating Polishness for a Western gaze. Foreign goods, desired by those living behind the Iron Curtain, were also called *zagraniczne;* these were more coveted than Polish

40 · CHAPTER 2

commodities for export (*produkty eksportowe*), which were supposed to have better quality and more apparent cosmopolitan value.

Kosmopolityzm was also used to describe anti-patriotic attitudes, for instance in the context of debates about the role of Jewish intellectuals or the local clergy's connections with the Vatican. After the fall of the socialist regime, the term acquired more positive meanings, indicating an important driver in the postsocialist transformation processes. Today, while conveying praise in expressions such as "a cosmopolitan city," it can also carry negative connotations when weaponized in conservative and right-wing narratives to criticize elites and their perceived rejection of or embarrassment about Polish culture. In our research, however, we apply the term as an analytical tool, regardless of the local usage. Embracing these omnivorous forms of culinary cosmopolitanism, foodies from Warsaw or Poznań are likely to appreciate and be willing to pay a premium for the uniqueness, the sensory characteristics, and the stories behind traditional, artisanal, and rural products. As we witnessed at Mleczna Droga, only if the setting and the presentation conform to educated and upwardly mobiles foodies' expectations, do local, artisanal, and traditional foods—even when produced and consumed in the countryside—move into the cosmopolitan circulation of ideas, values, and preferences that resonate more easily in faraway cities and foreign locales than in nearby rural areas.

REDISCOVERING THE FAMILIAR

The inward-looking aspect of culinary cosmopolitanism is central to the process through which Polish tastemakers reassemble and redesign the local culinary landscape. In post-1989 Poland, rural life and lower social strata have been turned into objects of interest as "the internal Other" and a kind of local periphery for Polish elites in general and intellectuals in particular, often with negative connotations (Buchowski 2006). Those elites tend to communicate with their Western peers by distancing themselves from their fellow citizens. Thus the alien and intriguing Other is not necessarily beyond national borders but can also be found in familiar environments, from the domestic kitchen to the countryside, which tastemakers explore, seek to understand, and mine for resources. This peripheral Other is often framed as remote both in space and time. As with the nearby but prestigious New Nordic Cuisine, nature can also be treated as "the most exotic unexplored context, highlighting further the reterritorialization of global cosmopolitan consumption, where food trends can only be consumed authentically in their context of origin" (Emontspoola and Georgi 2017, 306).

Such attitudes have emerged as part of what Naccarato and LeBesco (2012) have defined as "culinary capital": the food-related narratives and practices that confer status and power on those who are knowledgeable about them. The concept, which builds on the French sociologist Pierre Bourdieu's (1984, 1993) analysis of cultural capital, indicates the symbolic, material, and embodied resources that the participants in a culinary field define, accumulate, and activate to competitively secure their positions in terms of prestige and authority. Since Poland's culinary field is still in a formative phase, its dynamics and the strategies employed by the tastemakers that strive to establish its legitimacy and autonomy are easier to assess.

In today's Poland food connoisseurship, based on expertise in recognizing and defining sensory elements and on access to information and knowledge, has gained significance as a legitimate manifestation of cultural capital, often developed in connection with foreign values and practices. This is in keeping with trends among cosmopolitan foodies around the world (Caldwell 2014; Strong 2011). As we will further discuss in chapter 6, even when concentrating on the familiar, Polish food connoisseurship tends to express itself through specialized language and categories of taste that circulate globally. The latter may include a certain disdain for local and traditional foods—from *schabowy* (fried pork chop) to *smalec* (rendered pork fat)—that are still produced, prepared, and consumed according to older paradigms and may carry connotations of ignorance and backwardness.

Inward-looking aspects of cosmopolitanism are not uniformly embraced. In our focus groups and interviews with consumers outside of the food cognoscenti in the culinary field, we noticed little interest in concepts such as *local* or *artisanal*. These dimensions remain at the margins of the worldviews of non-foodies. Interestingly, thanks to the various meanings attributed to it, the idea of tradition appears to have more traction, as we will discuss in chapter 5. However, the working-class Poles we interacted with in our research frequently reveal a not-always-explicit desire to distance themselves from the rural world and manual occupations which they and their family may have left only relatively recently. Even when they do not separate themselves from their immediate environment, they do not consume local food as purposely and reflexively as those who identify themselves as food enthusiasts belonging to the upwardly mobile middle classes.

Polish cosmopolitan foodies reconsider domestic nature and history by comparing their heritage with the information they encounter on Instagram or foreign blogs and magazines. They frequently adhere to a prevalent global visual regime that influences not only what food should look like but also how it is produced, presented, and represented around the world (Contois and Kish 2022). Reaffirming existing hierarchies (Peterson and Kern 1996), those who feel confident in their social status display consumption habits that range from the high- to the low-brow. They feel secure enough to enjoy foods that until recently carried negative connotations of backwardness and uncouthness, such as above mentioned *schabowy, smalec* or offal (*podroby*) (Ferrant 2018). Those specialties are reinterpreted, made attractive in terms of cultural capital and expertise, and experienced in appropriate environments and among peers who share the same approaches to food and its sociocultural relevance.

Chefs like Michał Kuter at A Nóż Widelec (A knife fork, but also a pun on *a nuż*, "what if") in Poznań, Marcin Popielarz at Biały Królik (White rabbit) in Gdynia, as well as Łukasz Cichy at Gavi Restaurant and Mateusz Suliga at Artesse in Kraków, just to name a few, made a name for themselves by presenting refined ("elevated," in cosmopolitan foodie lingo) versions of traditional dishes, selecting high-quality local ingredients and applying refined culinary techniques. In fine dining, instead of full plates chefs show great care for presentation, the tableware itself often comes from designers or artists, and each course contributes to well-thought-out and varied tasting menus, frequently with recommended wine (or vodka) pairings. A new batch of restaurants, such as Oma, The Eatery, and Źródło in Warsaw, Monka in Toruń, and Masło Maślane in Gdańsk, opt instead for a more accessible and affordable revaluation of traditional dishes that is nevertheless still made appealing though a variety of strategies that include design choices, nostalgia, and at times even some well-meaning irony.

POLAND AS A CASE STUDY

The dynamics shaping the culinary field intersect with the shifts in class structures and aspirations taking place in Poland since the 1990s. The post-socialist transformation was significant from the perspective of both the change in the economic status of Polish residents, as well as in the cultural dimensions of social structures. The new market economy—instead of political power—became a dominant factor in shaping society, resulting in the appearance of the unemployed as a novel category, as well as poverty. New occupations also emerged, such as managers and specialists in finance, marketing, and public relations. Other existing professional categories (nomenklatura, industrial workers, bureaucrats, peasants) saw their standards of life, numbers, social status, and role diminish or in certain cases disappear (Janicka and Słomczyński 2014; Słomczyński, Tomescu-Dubrow, and Dubrow 2018). Polish society also experienced an educational boom, with easier access to universities. Some argue that these processes have led to a greater social mobility. Others point instead to the still limited flexibility of social structures and the growing income gap within the population (Bukowski, Sawulski, and Brzeziński 2024; Domański 1998, 2002; Janicka and Słomczyński 2014).

At the same time, the rising middle class became the object of intense scrutiny in public discourse as an unprecedented yet desirable social formation. Confirming that Poland was back on a "normal" (that is, Western and capitalist) development pattern, the middle class also became a normative ideal with positive ideological connotations (Domański 2012; Lepczyński 2021; Mokrzycki 2002; Świrek 2023). Initially, it was associated with the emerging private entrepreneurship and, later, also with professional expertise—a knowledge class rooted in the intelligentsia. Although largely defined as an economic category, using income and wealth as criteria (Kukołowicz 2019), perhaps the most important characteristics of the middle class, besides type of employment and social status, turned out to be lifestyle, ambitions, and worldviews, including political perspectives (Bachórz et al. 2016; Domański 2002; Gdula and Sadura 2012; Horolets 2013; Lepczyński 2021). Soon, the lifestyle of the middle class, or the "middle classes" in the plural, was recognized as a crucial source of inspiration, although still limited in terms of numbers.

However, while assuming the distinctive role of cultural choices, including food, we do not follow Bourdieu (1984) in identifying regular correspondences between specific individual dispositions and particular positions in society that establish predictable relationships between class and consumption patterns. Partly due to the ethnographic rather than quantitative nature of our research, it is difficult to identify correlations between social stratification and the various approaches we observed among urban, upwardly mobile, and educated actors in the culinary field. Through our focus on the culinary field's actors, we prefer to draw attention to the practices and attitudes of the intense identity work that anthropologist Deborah James (2014) has described as "middle classing;" the aspiration to the characteristics and standards of living that are locally attributed to domestic and international middle classes, regardless of the actual social and economic status of the individuals or the groups under examination. Looking at class formation through this dynamic approach allows for a more flexible examination of issues of status and social stratification in societies undergoing rapid and sustained transformations, such as Poland. To reflect the fluidity of the changes we examine, we treat class as relational and emerging (Gdula and Sadura 2012). We are not "studying up" (Nader 1972; Orstrander 1993): as the tastemakers we observe rarely belong to the moneyed elites of Poland, they are in general not so different from us in terms of worldviews, aspirations, and lifestyles. We are in fact "studying sideways" (Hannerz 2006; Ortner 2016).

As already mentioned, the discourses and practices that surround local, traditional, and artisanal food are not unique to Poland. Among urban, educated culinary enthusiasts around the world, it has become fashionable and attractive to eat products like *prosciutto di San Daniele* in Italy, homemade *mochi* in Japan, and artisanal cheese in the US (Ayora-Diaz 2021; Finnis 2012). This phenomenon has been described as "gastronomization" (Poulain 2011) or "gourmetization" (Harris and Phillips 2021) of rural and working-class cuisines, a process through which foods are not only elevated domestically but made available for international commercialization. We argue that such shifts in the global culinary landscape are most clearly analyzed in all their complexities—including the contested hierarchies of taste that support them and the cultural negotiations around them—in the relative semi-peripheries of the phenomenon, like Brazil, India, China, and the countries of Central and Eastern Europe. In these areas, the culinary fields are still in their formative state and their internal mechanics have not stabilized yet. Italy, France, Japan, or the United States function instead as the locus of elaboration of hegemonic standards and values that may be embraced, opposed, or adapted to local contexts in other parts of the world. Having observed these trends develop and become mainstream in Italy in the 1990s and in the US in the 2000s, we believe that the Polish case, more recent and still in its initial phase, can provide a useful lens to examine the globalization of cosmopolitan culture and the dynamics shaping center-periphery relations while assessing the responses and, sometimes, the resistance the local context may generate. As we will discuss in the next chapter, the formation of an autonomous culinary field and the associated processes of gastronomization taking place in Poland are frequently linked to the exposure of local taste-makers to cosmopolitan trends, social and physical mobility (at times in the form of temporary or permanent migration), and familiarity with foreign customs and locations.

We argue that in Central and Eastern Europe, as well as in other low- and mid-income countries, food is entangled in the intense identity work involved in "middle classing," in which growing segments of the population engage, often encouraged by state and market actors (James 2019). As Polish stand-ards of living continue to rise, although hampered by high inflation rates from late 2021 to early 2024, "living well" and "eating well" become a con-scious project to achieve respectability and cultural citizenship amid social adjustments.

COSMOPOLITAN FOODIES

The inward-looking aspects of culinary cosmopolitanism have developed next to more established outward-looking attitudes that hinge on showing off one's knowledge and access to foreign (*zagraniczne*) foods. Polish taste-makers and the foodies that share their enthusiasm and attitudes can both be enamored of ramen or kimchi, and excited about local liquors, homemade jams, and smoked sturgeon. Both passions are framed and experienced in ways that resonate with their aspirations toward global foodie-ism. Food scholars in Poland and elsewhere have described these attitudes as omnivorism: the desire to be open to a variety of ingredients, products, and culinary worlds, both national and international, as an expression of adven-turousness, access to a wide range of experience, and cultural refinement (Domański et al. 2015a). Such omnivorism presents itself as one of the salient traits of culinary cosmopolitanism, often meant to embody ideals of democ-racy and inclusiveness while actually providing tools to claim distinction (Pellerano and Riegel 2017; Richard and Kern 1996).

Until recently, upwardly mobile, educated, mostly urban Poles embraced foreign foods as their preferred expression of openness to the world and marker of class distinction (Domański 2017). Such outward-looking interest was a central characteristic of consumer culture in Poland during the social-ist decades, as foreign products were hard to procure and for that reason constituted tangible tokens of power. Exotic fare maintained its attractive-ness during the postsocialist transformation, when access to international goods became an expression of catching up with the rest of the Western world, even if in many instances these opportunities were limited to the most affluent sectors of society. Status and premium prices were attached to products that allowed individuals to symbolically leave Poland (usually for some imagined vacation destination) or at least to adopt styles and flavors from abroad.

As international tourism, migration, and educational exchanges became increasingly available (although far from common), so did the knowledge and enjoyment of dishes from around the world. For example, in Warsaw, the Vietnamese community—a legacy of the circuits of migration between the former brotherhood of socialist countries that intensified after 1989—successfully promoted its cuisine in affordable establishments around the city. Georgian restaurants (and later bakeries) became ubiquitous in large and mid-sized cities, giving the Caucasian cuisine a visibility that is rare elsewhere. The chain *Kuchnie Świata* (Cuisines of the world), selling foreign ingredients and products, popped up in shopping malls, while large urban supermarkets started adding exotic food aisles. These phenomena have been examined by Polish scholars in terms of social distinction, intergenerational mobility, and highbrow-lowbrow tensions (Domański and Karpiński 2018; Domański et al. 2015b).

While many Polish tastemakers, along with increasingly large segments of consumers, are embracing and rediscovering local and traditional cuisine, the most visible facet of culinary omnivorism continues to look abroad, as seen in recent trends such as the success of high-end American-style steak houses and cocktail bars. The willingness—at times the desire—to explore and adopt food and foodways from other countries still constitutes an important response to the transnationalization of supply networks (Cappeliez and Johnston 2013; Zhang and Hanks 2018).

While the availability and affordability of food from abroad has certainly played a role in such internationalization of local foodways, not all Poles have cultural and financial access to the same material and intangible foreign imports. The Polish situation seems to resonate with anthropologist Ulf Hannerz's (1990) observation that cosmopolitanism appears to be closely connected to unequal access to transnational cultures and local expressions of cultural diversity. The operative word here is "unequal." While forms of omnivorism have become available to growing segments of the Polish population, consumers' level of education, financial means, and social connections are far from uniform. Competence and mastery of food-related topics often present themselves in opposition to what experts in the culinary field perceive as dilettantism. The practices of Polish food enthusiasts and aspiring cosmopolitan foodies are increasingly recognizable to their peers abroad, from dining in a high-end restaurant to sipping a 17-*złoty* flat white coffee (a little over US $4) in a carefully designed bohemian café, or shopping at an organic farm right outside a large city. Such attitudes are "based on the resource-endowment of persons" and show "a strong link to the traditional highbrow model of distinctive consumption" (Rössel and Schroedter 2015, 93). In Poland as in other low- and mid-income countries, self-aware forms of highbrow cosmopolitanism are transmitted from parents to children as aspirational forms of cultural and social capital that take advantage of processes of globalization (Weenink 2008).

Such internal dynamics cannot be separated from Poles' exposure to the broader world and their position in it. What counts as worthy of social and cultural distinction at the international level is closely connected with the power relations that have shaped globalization since the age of imperialism. Sociologist Craig Calhoun (2002, 873–74) has described cosmopolitanism as "a discourse centered in a Western view of the world ... a 'Third Way' between rampant corporate globalization and reactionary traditionalism or nationalism" that reflects "an elite perspective on the world" but nevertheless is meant to provide a moral compass in globalized liberal democracy. In other words, what is valuable is not determined in the peripheries of the world but rather at its political and financial centers: cosmopolitanism can be interpreted as an alternative framework that perpetuates and conceals global inequalities. While it can be argued that Polish tastemakers may contribute to global culinary cosmopolitanism with their focus on local techniques such as fermentation and smoking or traditional practices like foraging, these elements acquire greater prestige—among Polish food enthusiasts as well—if they are acknowledged or praised by foreign experts.

Outward-looking expressions of cosmopolitanism can also be observed beyond the upper classes. Outside of the consumption of fine-dining mainstays like risotto or lobster, the desire to enjoy foreign food has also circulated to less affluent consumers, who now have access to previously exotic products such as mangoes, avocados, and shrimp through nation-wide retail chains with strong international connections. Affordable fare like hamburgers, pizza, and kebab are among the most popular items in Poland. In 2016, kebab was the first choice for 45 percent of people when asked about dining-out preferences; in 2017, although it fell to 40 percent, it remained popular, still placing before pizza and "Polish food" (Nowak 2020). However, according to a study by the magazine *Polityka* and the marketing company Kantar, one in three Poles in their thirties and younger, when asked what they would like to eat for their next dinner, indicated *schabowy*, fried pork chop with cabbage. This would be twice the number of those who mentioned kebab (17 percent) and sushi (12 percent), with pizza trailing behind (Bunda 2022). Sushi especially reflects these changes: in less than twenty years, it has shifted from an exclusive and expensive specialty to be consumed in selected restaurants to a quick snack that can be bought in roadside kiosks and at train stations or ordered online.

Access to these foods allows Poles to finally claim their imagined "rightful place" in the West after having been "kidnapped" on the wrong side of the Iron Curtain (Kundera 1984; Mark et al. 2019). These shifts draw attention to those aspects of cosmopolitanism that sociologist Ulrich Beck (2002, 28) has interpreted a process of "globalization from within the national societies" that generates "banal cosmopolitanism, in which everyday nationalism is circumvented and undermined and we experience ourselves integrated into global processes and phenomena." Through the consumption of takeaway sushi and kebab, or the domestic preparation of Italian-style pasta, Poles from all walks of life can include elements of cosmopolitanism in everyday experience.

ALTERNATIVE NETWORKS OF FOOD CIRCULATION

The borrowing and adaptation of ideas and approaches from abroad is not limited to commercial commodities and enterprises. Practices that are meant to oppose the prevailing consumer culture and the industrialized and unjust food system that supports it, such as the anarchist movement Food Not Bombs and food banks, are partly inspired by templates borrowed and adapted from the West as well (Gracjasz and Grasseni 2020). While they follow very different principles and strategies to provide free food, both initiatives draw inspiration from foreign models.

Alternative food networks such as community-supported agriculture, food cooperatives, and neighbors' associations that focus on access to organic and healthy products have also emerged. Such networks are active and resilient in other areas of Central and Eastern Europe, providing spaces for female entrepreneurship, supporting local biodiversity, sustainability and generating forms of food sovereignty (Blumberg and Mincyte 2020; Blumberg 2022; Smith and Jehlička 2007; Mincyte 2011). They have proven crucial in ensuring food security after Russia's attack on Ukraine, which has profoundly affected the regional food systems (Jastrzębiec-Witowska 2023; Kovács et al. 2022). However, in Poland they seem to focus mainly on consumers' experiences, their preferences in terms of food quality, and individualistic motivations of well-being and health.

Far-reaching social transformations, changes in the relationships between rural and urban cultures, or issues of food sovereignty appear to be less central to these initiatives (Goszczyński et al. 2019). Preoccupations with the environment and long-term sustainability also emerge as relatively secondary when compared to individualistic motivations (Bilewicz and Śpiewak 2015, 2018). The actors involved are not necessarily socially conscious "transition activists," committed to new models of life and the economy (Escobar 2018). As organic, high-quality products tend to be expensive, participants in food cooperatives and farmers' market shoppers are very often relatively privileged individuals who are more concerned with being part of social networks embracing cosmopolitan trends than with critique and resistance (Kopczyńska 2017).

The emergence of new models for alternative food networks does not diminish the centrality of pre-existing approaches to food procurement that developed locally as a reaction to the inefficiencies of the food system under the socialist regime. Such modalities, often practiced among rural populations and less affluent urban dwellers, are visible in larger scale events such as markets, festivals, and fairs, still thriving outside the dynamics that Goszczyński and Śpiewak (2024) have defined as "gastrogentrification." More or less legally, with or without the necessary permits, Polish farmers sell their goods in neighborhood and city markets that, with their matter-of-fact approach, low prices, and utilitarian interactions, still maintain traits that clearly differentiate them from more upscale farmers' markets or market halls.

Although they may not offer heirloom varieties or unique artisanal items, these markets and the nearby streets make good quality, hand-made foods available, from breads to *kapusta kiszona* (fermented cabbage) and *ogórki kiszone* (fermented cucumbers). These goods may be sold out of plastic drums, car trunks, or baskets placed on the pavement. They are presented in forms that do not necessarily reflect affluent consumers' aspirations for refinement and distinction. The ladies who make *twaróg*—soft fresh cheese—in their home kitchens and sell it on sidewalks are strictly speaking artisans, but not the kind that foodies tend to appreciate. For the tastemakers these foods are invisible until they "discover" the maker and translate her product and her story into "a find," both quaint and exciting.

Działki (or *ogrody działkowe*), little allotment gardens in the cities or in their immediate vicinities run by the local branches of a national association (Polski Związek Działkowców) according to specific regulations, have survived the postsocialist transformation both in Poland (Netczuk 2016; Pawlikowska-Piechotka 2010) and in other Central and Eastern European countries (Gibas and Boumová 2020; Szumilas 2014). During the socialist years, vegetables and fruit were grown in these tiny plots, providing a connection with old customs and activities to new urban dwellers who had recently left the countryside to take jobs in the industrial or service sectors. *Działki* used to provide a welcome addition to many urban Poles' diets during the scarcity that intermittently plagued them during socialism. Today, older Poles still produce food in them, not just for sustenance but also as a form of physical activity (Rowiński, Dąbrowski, and Kostka 2015), pleasure, and sociability (Szczurek and Zych 2012; Błaszczak and Cebula 2016). Harder and harder to come by, *działki* are increasingly a mark of prestige and social connection, regardless of their ecological function. Garden associations make sure the occupants comply with regulations (for instance, they should not be run as businesses). Because of their history and their contemporary usage, *działki* cannot be considered equivalent to urban farms in Western cities, which are frequently experienced as an expression of alternative food networks (Gracjasz 2024). The new lessees sometimes prefer to use *działki* as a place for calm and relaxation, rather than to garden or grow produce (Maćkiewicz et al. 2021).

The circulation of foods processed at home and sent as gifts, usually from relatives living in the countryside to urban newcomers (Mroczkowska 2018) and from older to younger generations (Bachórz 2018a), is a long-standing phenomenon as well. As it appeared clearly in our focus groups and interviews, grandmothers (*babcie*) loom large in Poles' imagination and in the reality of their kitchens; they constitute a source of comfort food like jams, cured meats, fermented vegetables, or home-brewed liquors, often packed in glass jars (*słoiki*). As central as these networks are to the everyday life of most Poles, the products at their core are often the object of profound ambivalence and class tensions (Lewicki and Drozdowska 2017). Emotionally rich, they are connected to a rural world that urban Poles tend to consider bogged down in the past and forgotten by modernity and progress. However, *słoiki*— just like allotment gardens—are enjoying a certain renaissance, as more and more food enthusiasts engage in jam making, pickling, and fermentation. This phenomenon has been observed across the world and grew precipitously during the COVID-19 lockdowns, when many families used cooking as a way to entertain themselves and create shared moments of pleasure (Giesbers 2021; Lagrue 2021).

It may be surprising to some Poles that their socialist and postsocialist survival practices—such as food preservation, foraging, *działki*, and even the old-style, unfashionable urban farmers' markets—which they could find boring, backward, or even slightly shameful, show similarities to activities that are globally regarded as important in terms of food security and socio-cultural sustainability (Bachórz 2018b) or even "hot" from an aesthetic and cultural point of view. Constantly negotiating their status with changing consumers' preferences, these informal practices may have their legality questioned within the newly introduced EU regulatory frameworks (Mroczkowska 2019). However, they are thriving in postsocialist countries, often reproduced through existing infrastructures and material facilities (Blumberg and Mincyte 2019). Smith and Jehlička (2007) analyze these habits as an Eastern European—and as such, marginalized and scarcely acknowledged—approach to resilience that deserves to be highlighted and appreciated. The authors suggest the use of the term "quiet sustainability" in relation to everyday food practices that are widespread, inclusive, unforced, and noncommercial, while at the same time having positive environmental effects. Accordingly they should be included in policy-making (Smith and Jehlička 2013).

The new attention paid to local, artisanal, and traditional food also differs from previous modes of appreciation that resulted in the hearty fare found in *karczmy,* the roadside restaurants whose architecture and interior design are supposed to evoke old-timey inns and a mythical rural tradition (Baranowski 1979). *Karczmy* eateries are connected with the *zajazdy,* the roadside diners that the government started building in the 1970s while attempting to create a network of expressways. They were part of a project of socialist consumerism and auto-mobility, in which car owners could eat while traveling. To this day, the *karczma* style is inspired by what architects conceive as old rustic constructions, with a prevalence of wood, large common spaces, and soaring ceilings. Decorations consist of folk sculptures, paintings, and supposedly artisanal objects like doilies and embroidered tablecloths. The menus tend to offer surprisingly large and affordably priced portions of familiar dishes like soups, pierogi, and kiełbasa sausage that are also common in domestic festive consumption, with some additions or tweaks inspired by the local gastronomy in the *karczma*'s whereabouts. Although *karczma* dishes are often presented as rooted in peasant and folk culture, in reality they are closer to what the upper classes used to consume and to the construct of *kuchnia staropolska* ("old-style cuisine") we described in chapter 1.

FOOD AND CULTURE WARS

As the culinary field develops within the global foodie culture, the appreciation of Polish food (or lack thereof) is often experienced as a reflection of the international status of the nation, revealing a worldview where the sense of being a periphery of the West and, as a consequence, of modernity, is still prevalent. For instance, many consumers suspect that Western European companies dump products of lesser quality into Eastern European markets, even if the brands are nominally the same (Matijevic and Boni 2019). Their "Western" cachet is used to drive up product prices despite their inferior quality. In other words, many Poles are convinced that a yogurt sold in Poland under the same brand marketed in other European countries may not be as good. This perception of a dual standard threatens the confidence of Eastern European consumers toward the benefits of the free circulation of goods.

In order to combat this belief, the EU authorities commissioned a study of seventy-one products across nineteen countries that was presented in June 2019. It demonstrated that citizens in eastern EU member states are not being sold products of inferior quality (Teffer 2019). However, the study admitted that at times products with different compositions were sold under the same brand, although not along a West vs. East divide. Due to this revelation, the results did not pacify Polish audiences. The website Polityka.pl, in an article titled "The Double Quality of Products in the Union Is a Fact," argued: "There were plenty of products that were sold in identical form throughout the EU (e.g. Pringles chips). However, the differences and geographical key give food for thought. The double quality of products usually means that the goods are of better quality in the north and west of the Union, and worse in the south and east. As a rule, also, probably by accident, the best version of the product was available in the country of origin of the manufacturer" (Szyszko 2019).

Therefore, it is not without reason that in September 2023, a month before the national elections that would mark the end of the PiS party political rule, one of the points in the ruling party's election program referred to what was called *lokalna półka* (local shelf). The government promised to impose an obligation on supermarket chains that at least two-thirds of the fruit, vegetables, dairy, meat products, and bread on sale come from local suppliers. The proposal was presented at a very general level and—although it was generally warmly welcomed by farmers—critics indicated its shortcomings: not only the potential non-compliance with EU regulations, but also the difficulties related to the seasonality and regionality of production, lack of a definition of "locality," and the possible opposition on the part of consumers. Most shoppers, despite their attachment to "Polishness," are in fact guided by price in their choices (Kowalczyk 2023). Despite numerous reservations and legal doubts, not many in the political scene criticized the idea of favoring local Polish products. Representatives of opposition parties pointed out that they had submitted similar proposals before (Jaźwiński and Kunert 2023). A certain consensus seems to exist across the political spectrum regarding Polish origins as an important feature of food products.

The entanglements between food and politics are not a new phenomenon. As we discussed in the previous chapter, food has been the metaphor, the cause, or the catalyst for political action. However, these dynamics have become more apparent both because of the value that food has acquired in terms of cultural capital among urban, upwardly mobile educated Poles, and its increased visibility in civic debates, partly due to its pervasiveness in social media. In April 2019 bananas became the object of political theater, when the 1973 video installation *"Sztuka konsumpcyjna"* (Consumer art) by the recently deceased artist Natalia LL, depicting a naked woman suggestively eating a banana, was removed from the National Museum in Warsaw because of its possibly offensive content (Robinson 2019).

The installation, however, was not a gratuitous provocation, but rather a piece of social commentary: in socialist Poland, imported bananas represented an unaffordable, exotic product, emblematic of elite consumption in a supposedly classless society. Although Natalia LL's piece has been remembered almost mostly for the iconic bananas, the series also presented models eating sausages, bread sticks, jelly, and pudding, providing a commentary on consumer culture in late socialist Poland (Cseh-Varga and Czirak 2018). As soon as the news of the removal of Natalia LL's art piece circulated, many social media users, especially women, started posting pictures of themselves eating bananas. On April 29, during a demonstration in front of the National Museum, participants publicly ate bananas as a form of protest against censorship (Keep Freedom Unlocked 2019). Following the event, which attracted international attention and embarrassed the cultural authorities of Poland, the museum director announced that the work would be reinstated until the beginning of scheduled renovations, slated to occur the following May.

In October 2020, while Poland was struggling with the first wave of COVID-19, huge demonstrations took place to condemn a decision by the Constitutional Tribunal aimed at restricting women's reproductive rights to the point of virtually banning any form of legal abortion. Citizens of many different backgrounds expressed their outrage, ignoring declarations from members of the government that minimized the impact of the decision, which enjoyed the support of right-wing nationalists, conservative pundits, and the Catholic Church. The protesters showed up with signs and posters, held high and visible so that they could be photographed and circulated through traditional media and the internet.

Jokes and wordplay against PiS politicians, considered the originators of the Constitutional Tribunal's decision, made frequent references to food. A sign with the image of food TV personality and culinary entrepreneur Magda Gessler read: "Today we will be stewing a duck," using the assonance between Kaczyński and *kaczka* (duck) and turning the strong man of Polish politics into a fowl, ready to be plucked and cooked by a brash and powerful woman. Unappetizing food generated all sorts of whimsical gags against the PiS party and its leaders: "Better cottage cheese with raisins than PiS," "You are worse than watered-down Aperol," "Jarek [Kaczyński's first name] smells like cheese Cheetos," "PiS is worse than licorice jelly beans," and so on. A meme circulated on social media, based on a picture found in the streets of the city of Gdynia. In it, a woman in plain house clothes sits at a table, peeling potatoes. The caption reads: "Since I am so stupid and irresponsible that I cannot make decisions about my own uterus, why is nobody afraid to eat what I cook?" The supposedly natural connection that, according to conservative points of view, exists between women and food was turned into a call for political resistance.

FOOD AND INTERNATIONAL CONFLICTS

Food as a hot political topic—both metaphorically and literally—becomes much more urgent when it comes to actual international confrontations. In 2014, when Russia occupied Crimea in Ukraine, the EU imposed economic sanctions on Russia, and in retaliation Russia limited imports of several EU products. Apples from Poland fell under the restricted categories. As Russia was a major importer of Polish apples, the policy had immediate repercussions for farmers in many areas of the country. In reaction to the Russian move, a Facebook campaign was launched that prompted Poles to "eat apples to spite Putin" (*jedz jabłka na złość Putinowi*). The initiative found a wide following in the country. The hashtag *#jedzjabłka* (#eatapples) on Instagram and Twitter feeds accompanied pictures of people picking apples, biting into them, or using them to cook (Oltermann 2014). Farmers had to come up with new uses for the fruit to make up for the lost sales to Russia; some of them turned to cider as a value-added product and increased its production—both industrial and artisanal.[1] Under the circumstance of the trade war with Russia, eating apples—both in reality and in media representations—was framed as a form of patriotism that all citizens could express, bringing ideological issues to a more tangible level.

After the full-scale Russian attack on Ukraine in February 2022, food gained even more importance. Anti-Russian sentiments were high in Poland, bringing government and opposition together when it comes to "Putin's war." Especially in the months immediately following the attack, Poles faced the arrival of over five million displaced Ukrainians, mostly women and children (men were not allowed to leave the country and were expected to join the army). Individual citizens, businesses, associations of volunteers, religious groups, NGOs, and local administrations at the city and province level generously mobilized to provide food to the displaced. Many Poles took in refugees who were waiting to get back to their homes in Ukraine or moving on to other destinations, often in Western Europe. In June 2022, Ukrainians organized a March of Gratitude in Warsaw.

However, over time the emergency of feeding growing numbers of people strained individuals and communities, due in part to the lack of sufficient support from the national government, which basked in international praise without doing much in terms of funding or operational logistics on the ground. The state has allowed Ukrainian refugees to obtain a Polish ID number (known as *PESEL*), which is necessary to be hired and to have access to healthcare services. Children have been integrated with more or less success into Polish schools. From a cultural point of view, many Poles are discovering or rediscovering the similarities between their culinary traditions and Ukraine's, their shared past (although marred by tensions and wars), and their common heritage. At the time of writing, however, war fatigue has become a widespread phenomenon; a poll carried out in November 2024 by the Polish state research agency CBOS found that 55 percent of Poles wished for the end of the conflict, even if that meant that Ukraine would cede part of its territory to Russia (Ptak 2024).

Despite the temporary rapprochement, the war also caused Polish-Ukrainian tensions around food. Right after the Russian attack on Ukraine, Poland eased its customs regulations to allow Ukrainian wheat to flow through its borders toward the rest of the world. However, it turned out that Ukrainian wheat (which does not have to meet EU requirements and is cheaper than the Polish one) was not just transiting through the country, but was partly distributed and competed with Polish agricultural production, causing domestic speculation and fraud. The crisis led to the resignation of the Minister of Agriculture, as well as to the imposition of an illegal (from the EU point of view) ban on the import of Ukrainian grain and other types of food. The European Commission approved a temporary embargo on import of wheat, corn, rapeseed, and sunflower seeds to Bulgaria, Hungary, Romania, Slovakia, and Poland (money.pl 2023). In the spring of 2024, the protest of Polish farmers merged with a larger movement that saw farmers in many other countries opposing Brussels bureaucracies and in particular the EU Green Deal plan, meant to enhance the overall environmental sustainability of the European food system and its resilience against climate change (Koper and Blenkinsop 2024).

OF MEAT AND HUNTING

Besides these political flashpoints, specific aspects of food customs, such as meat-eating, have become arenas for cultural and political debates. As we discussed in chapter 1, meat has become an essential element of the ideal Polish cuisine, even if not always understood in accordance with historical facts. Well into the twentieth century, meat and other costly ingredients were not frequently available in farming communities or were not consumed because of religious restrictions such as fasting (Urbański 2016). Its prestige is still high, both as a part of everyday meals and as a celebratory food. Almost as a reaction to its scarcity for prolonged periods under the social regime, meat consumption rose precipitously from the early 1990s to the late 2010s, although in recent years it has been plateauing. Many cannot imagine special occasions without a meat dish. Among rural dwellers and working-class Poles, meat is still considered the centerpiece of the meal, especially on

Sundays and holidays. Even today, it is experiencing a certain resurgence among the youth, in the form of the *schabowy* fried pork chop (Bunda 2022). However, there is a growing awareness, by and large among the upwardly mobile urban milieus, that too much meat may not be healthy, especially when fried or stewed in the traditional way, with generous amounts of fat. This perception was evident not only in our interviews with tastemakers but also in our conversations with consumers and in focus groups.

Flexitarians and individuals trying to eat less meat are becoming more numerous (Bunda 2022). Although there is no conclusive data, vegetarians and vegans are more visible than before, at least judging by the numbers of cafés and restaurants catering to them—although mostly in urban centers (Kopczyńska 2021). According to Happy Cow, a leading vegan restaurant guide, in 2019 Warsaw was in the top ten among the most vegan-friendly cities in the world (Tilles 2019). New vegetarian and vegan cookbooks have gained popularity, some of them focusing also on plant-based versions of Polish cuisine. Among these are books written by Marta Dymek (2020), Michał Korkosz (2020b, 2023b), Paweł Ochman (2020), and other popular social media content creators.

In the countryside and among the urban working classes, many scoff at these new trends, often considered as an effect of dangerous foreign influences on Polish society. In a 2016 interview with the German magazine *Bild,* then–Foreign Affairs Minister Witold Waszczykowski declared that "the world according to the Marxist pattern had to automatically develop in only one direction—a new mixture of cultures and races, a world of cyclists and vegetarians who use only renewable energy sources and fight all manifestations of religion. It has little to do with traditional Polish values" (PAP 2016). By conflating various categories perceived as outsiders to what he assumed is mainstream Polish culture, the minister was suggesting that not eating meat is as foreign to Polish identity as cyclists, atheists, and Marxists.

While in July 2019 the Polish edition of *Newsweek* drew attention to the excessive consumption of meat in the country (Omachel 2019), the October 2019 issue of the conservative magazine *Do Rzeczy* featured an article titled "Who wants to ban us from eating meat?" (*Kto chce nam zakazać jedzenia mięsa?*) describing the meat reduction trend as "leftist madness" (DoRzeczy. pl 2019). Once again, the changes in dietary preferences were blamed on nefarious international pressures, reinforcing the perception that Poland is besieged by secularism coming from abroad—and in particular from the EU, which the elites are accused of willingly embracing. In fact, the cover of the

March-April 2018 issue of the Christian ultraconservative magazine *Polonia Christiana* carried the cover title "Bug on the plate: a culinary revolution" (*Robak na talerzu: kuchenna rewolucja*) and included articles decrying EU's alleged attempts at forcing Poles to eat insects (*Polonia Christiana* 2018).

The topic emerged again in public debate in the months prior to the October 2023 parliamentary elections (Dąbrowska 2023). In February 2023 a report C40 Cities published four years earlier was re-released to the public. C40 Cities is a global network of nearly 100 mayors of cities around the world that are united in coping with the climate crisis. Warsaw, whose mayor at the time of writing is the liberal politician Rafał Trzaskowski, has belonged to it since 2007. Along with the reduction of travel and material consumption, the report recommended eating less meat and dairy products. After the topic was brought back to the limelight, right-wing politicians not only accused their opponents to lobby for the reduction of meat consumption, but also published photos of themselves with meat dishes, including those served in expensive restaurants, regardless of the inflation taking its toll on Poles (Pikuła 2023). Jarosław Kaczyński, the leader of the PiS party, then in power, declared: "We reject the projects endorsed by the mayor of Warsaw, Rafał Trzaskowski, which assume bizarre restrictions on, for example, the consumption of meat and dairy products. I want to emphasize this strongly: we stand for freedom, we do not want artificial restrictions in the name of some ideologies. Poles will never hear from us that they have to limit eating meat or drinking milk, that they are obliged to change their car to an electric one or to wear two shirts or dresses" (Gruszczyński and Wojtczuk 2023).

The clashes between different visions about what Poland is and should be are also evident in the heated controversies that emerged when in June 2019 the government suggested including beavers and bison among the species that could be legally hunted. The proposal stimulated reflections on the role of these animals in Polish culinary customs from the past (Niedźwiecki 2019). Some adventurous chefs who had been working on seventeenth- and eighteenth-century recipes added them to menus for special occasions. Famed food expert Robert Makłowicz publicly expressed his bafflement at considering beavers as food, stating that he had never eaten anything so hideous in his life (Kawczyńska 2019). Historians noted that up to the nineteenth century beavers were considered fish, and as such could be included in fast-day menus and in Christmas Eve dishes (Modelski 2015). While observing that beavers' testicles were considered an aphrodisiac, food historian Jarosław

Dumanowski from the Nicolaus Copernicus University in Toruń also pointed out that the meat was almost exclusively consumed by the aristocracy, the landed gentry, and the Catholic Church's top hierarchy, who owned much of the Polish land, including villages and forests. Nevertheless, illegal poaching by commoners was widespread (Rogacin 2019).

Animal activists and environmentalists decried the inclusion of beavers and bison to the species that can be legally hunted as an attack on Poland's natural environment, an accusation that had already been directed at PiS when in 2017 it allowed large-scale logging activities in the Białowieża Forest, the last stretch of primeval forest left in Europe. Protected by UNESCO's Man and the Biosphere Programme, the forest is home to the European bison, which is in danger of extinction but is showing signs of resilience (Żuk and Żuk 2021; Hackett 2023). Although the government justified this logging as a last-resort intervention to limit the damage caused by the bark beetle, the decision was condemned internationally and prompted a court order by the European Court of Justice to halt the activities (Easton 2018). Nevertheless, the felling of trees in the Białowieża Forest continued (Reuters 2021). However, the new government in power since the end of 2023 has been reflecting on the protection of forests (Mikos 2024).

The controversy about beavers emerges from larger, long-term debates about hunting, which is relatively widely practiced in Poland. The activity is not without its critics. These include the Nobel Laureate Olga Tokarczuk, author of the 2009 anti-hunting novel *Prowadź swój pług przez kości umarłych* (Drive your plow over the bones of your dead), which in 2017 renowned filmmaker Agnieszka Holland turned into the movie *Pokot* (Spoor). Nevertheless, venison and other kinds of game are not a rarity on Polish tables. At the 2017 Flavor Festival in Gruczno, we spoke with Piotr Beszterda, a specialist for game and hunting in the local division of the National Forests government office, which controls large swaths of the country's forests. He was at the festival to present products such as smoked, cured fat of wild boar and deer ham, which are being sold to raise funds for the activities of the National Forests office. Beszterda explained that hunting clubs pay the public institution for the rights to a certain area for a given length of time, with permission to shoot a specific number and species of animals as a form of population control. What they hunt belongs to the hunting clubs and is often distributed as gifts to family and friends; only rarely is it sold. Nevertheless, many citizens still perceive hunting as a heavily classed political issue, as the activity was connected in the past with nobility and land ownership. It also intersects with different perceptions about wildlife (Rancew-Sikora 2009) and underlines the vast chasm between rural and urban culture.

ONE OR SEVERAL POLISH CUISINES?

The apprehension caused by debates about what constitutes "real" Polish food and customs is amplified by the historical presence of various national communities within the territory that now constitutes Poland: Germans, Ukrainians, and Lithuanians, just to mention a few (Snyder 2003). Ethnic and regional groups such as Kashubians and Silesians are perceived as a part of the Polish nation, although different from the majority. Moreover, some culinary traditions, while felt as quintessentially Polish, are similar to those in other countries: the *kotlet schabowy* extolled by Kaczyński in his interview on the morning show could be traced to Munich, Vienna, or Milan.

The legacy of Poland's intricate past is also made evident by the existence of different religious communities, such as Protestants, Jews, and Tatar Muslims, besides the majority Catholics. The actual numbers of practicing Catholics are a constant object of controversy, as many baptized Poles do not consider themselves Catholic, even when they do not go through the administrative process of apostasy that canon law requires for one to be officially separated from the Church of Rome. Coming to terms with the past is not a straightforward process: culinary traditions from religious and ethnic minorities—including previously persecuted ones—are now increasingly appreciated, played up, and commodified. It is enough to take a stroll in the Kazimierz neighborhood in Kraków to see the extent to which Jewish food has been turned into a tourist attraction, often with little or no connection to the surviving Jewish community (for more about Jewish culinary culture see chapter 6).

In their desire to highlight and support local, artisanal, and traditional food productions, liberal tastemakers find themselves negotiating with conservative forces about what "Polish" means and what its value is, both domestically and internationally. Moreover, political outlooks vary noticeably among tastemakers, on a spectrum ranging from progressive to conservative. In their embrace of and active participation in the efforts to define Polishness, they constantly face the risk of establishing it as an exclusionary cultural category rather than an open one that is able to fully take into account the inherent complexity and fluidity of food history, the contributions of different local communities and non-Polish ethnicities to Polish food, as well as its constant entanglement with nearby countries and populations.

When invited to give talks or to participate in panels in Poland, coauthor Fabio Parasecoli often asked the provocative question: "Should we be talking about Polish food or food in Poland?" (Warszawski Festiwal Kulinarny 2017). The goal was to stimulate the audiences to self-reflect on the motivations and the modalities of their search for shared elements, qualities, and an intrinsic coherence that would mark some food as recognizably Polish, expressing a well-defined, essential national culinary identity. In fact, it is often difficult to identify practices that all Poles could appreciate as uniquely theirs, especially when they share many characteristics with their Ukrainian, Belarusian, and Lithuanian neighbors who, at different points in time, participated in the same cultural spaces, if not the same polity.

The national character of Polish food came to the forefront in 2018 on the one hundredth anniversary of Poland's reunification as an independent nation-state after World War I. To celebrate the event, Makro (2018), the most important wholesale distributor of food products for the restaurant industry, published a volume in Polish and English with the title *One Hundred Recipes for One Hundred Years of Independence (1918–2018)*. The book, meant to celebrate the "culinary unification of Poland," was part of a larger educational initiative: "Polish culinary treasures, yesterday and today." The book is composed of historical recipes, interpreted by contemporary chefs and commented upon by the already-mentioned Professor Jarosław Dumanowski. The content is organized in three main large sections according to the areas from which the recipes originated: the territories controlled by Russian, Prussian, and Austrian-Hungarian empires after the eighteenth-century partitions (see chapter 1). There are also smaller sections dedicated to Jewish cuisine (which seems to be playing a mere supporting role, rather than being fully integrated in the history of Polish culture), military cuisine, and breakfast. (The latter may feel a bit out of place, but there were not many historical breakfast recipes to complete a book that had to please contemporary readers.)

These editorial decisions are a rhetorical strategy meant to depict the nation as forged from the confluence of three different empires, each with their own impact on food culture in the prewar period. At the same time, other axes of differentiation were marginalized. In the introduction of the anniversary book, signed by the "MAKRO Polska Team," we read: "We immediately associate celebrating with a feast and food-sharing; however, one hundred years ago the Poles had no time for that, as they faced poverty and hunger, with struggles for borders being in progress. . . . We want to tell you about the long and winding road that led from the Partitions of Poland, through the declaration of independence, to the reconstruction of community—through the prism of culinary art. This is due to the fact that the history of food is not just an anecdotal tale about cuisine: it's a question of survival and identity" (Makro 2018, 9). The connection between past struggles for food, cultural heritage, nation's survival, and the political identity of contemporary Poland is front and center in this initiative.

Partly to mark the hundredth anniversary of national independence, partly to take advantage of the growing interest in food, and partly to promote products from Poland, in 2018 the Ministry of Agriculture and Rural Development launched the project of the Canon of Polish Cuisine. The goal of the Canon, as stated in the Ministry's website, was to answer the question: "What is Polish cuisine?" (Ministerstwo Rolnictwa i Rozwoju Wsi 2019). The conservative government's desire to anchor any discussions about the nature and development of Polish cuisine in history was evident. After a few informal conversations with invited experts, a first list of recipes was officially presented on August 29, 2019, at the Museum of King Jan III's Palace in Wilanów, in Warsaw. For the occasion, Professor Dumanowski discussed dishes that were interpreted by chefs from the museum, working under the direction of chef Maciej Nowicki.

The list was organized in four sections: appetizers, soups, main courses, and dessert, following the structure of the menu in many Polish restaurants. It illustrated classics that are common all around Poland, from *kaszanka* (blood sausage) and meat tartar to *rosół* soup (meat broth with vegetables and noodles, often served on Sundays), pierogi, and carp, including its "Jewish" version. It also included regional specialties that enjoy national visibility, such as goose and goose-neck recipes, the savory potato casserole *babka ziemniaczana,* and the duck-blood soup *czernina.* The focus was clearly on dishes and not so much on ingredients, techniques, cultural practices, or stories. The reactions to the launch of the Canon were quite positive among food professionals, including those who did not subscribe to PiS's political vision for Poland; they were overall excited about the fact that the government was finally taking food culture seriously, beyond yields, rural development, and economic output. The Ministry then opened ongoing consultations, in order to further develop the project.

The initiative was under the Ministry of Agriculture and Rural Development, rather than the Ministry of Culture, showing how for the

Polish government food was still mainly an issue of production, economics, and availability. The Ministry later transferred the project to the newly formed Narodowy Instytut Dziedzictwa (National institute of cultural heritage), which, in the words of the then Deputy Prime Minister Beata Szydło, has the purpose of "nurturing rural traditions and culture—everything that is part of a tremendous heritage and contributes to our national culture" (*Kancelaria Prezesa Rady Ministrów* 2019).[2] Heritage-making became an increasingly important element in the political agenda of the PiS-led government, which claimed to be the interpreter and the defender of Polish culture and traditions against any internal or external threat. However, the reference to a canon pointed to a political desire for cuisine to capture and stabilize something essential and unchanging about the Polish character and identity. This gesture was at odds with the current debates, especially in UNESCO, about the construction and preservation of heritage as immaterial culture, that tend to be more flexible and inclusive.

The positive attitude of the gastronomy sector toward the initiative was quite different from the critiques that many expressed about another campaign by the Ministry, Poznaj Dobrą Żywność (Get to know fine foods), launched in 2000 and meant to highlight the best of food production in Poland. The idea was to create a mark that identifies high-quality Polish products for national and international markets. The specialists charged with judging the items were not experts in food marketing, food culture, or consumers' preferences, but rather food scientists, economists, and lawyers. As a result, despite the presence of some artisanal and semi-artisanal products, the overall focus turned to industrial food, definitely "good" from the food safety point of view, but did not engage with the sensory qualities of the products or whether they fell under what most Poles and Polish tastemakers considered legitimate traditions and customs.

When in 2018 Poland participated in the Fancy Food Show at the Jacob Javits Center in New York City, one of the largest food fairs in the world, its pavilion included hamburger sauces, industrially produced mozzarella, and microwavable dinners. In the introduction to the catalog, then-Minister Jan Krzysztof Ardanowski stated: "The PiS Agricultural Program, which I had the opportunity to create, included preferences for the development of high-quality food production in Poland—organic, traditional, regional—produced in small family farms, using rich culinary traditions and generational experience for attractive, tasty and healthy products" (Ministerstwo Rolnictwa i Rozwoju Wsi 2018, 3). The desire to attribute the program to PiS was glaring, as the party is particularly strong in rural areas and aimed to reinforce the image of a robust internationally prestigious Poland. However, the propaganda element ended up backfiring. The backlash on social media was immediate and merciless, describing the New York debacle as "sad" and "comical." Some commentaries showed clear political overtones connecting the failed effort of bureaucrats to PiS's overall foreign affairs strategy and its general incapacity to project any cultural soft power in the West. Buyers in New York City most likely had no idea of these political dynamics within Poland.

The hundredth anniversary of Polish independence was not the only historical event that became a battlefield in the food culture wars. In 2019, to celebrate the thirtieth anniversary of the first free elections on June 4th, 1989, journalist Aneta Kołaszewska launched the idea of organizing dinners across the country under the name of *menu wolności,* or "menu of freedom" (Menu Wolności n.d.) The website included clear references to the negotiations between Solidarność and the socialist regime: "The round table is a symbol of a time of democratic change. It served the government and Solidarność side not only to make decisions and arrangements regarding the fate of the state, but also simply to eat. The two-month meeting was attended by several hundred people who ate together at tables arranged in the lobby of the Governor's Palace (today the Presidential Palace) served by the best waiters from the Orbis restaurant in Wilanów.[3] Archival footage shows that during the dinner at the end of the Round Table, guests ate 'chicken jelly, tomato soup with rice, pork escalope and a donut for dessert.' It is this menu—captured in the historical moment—that can become the starting point for anyone wanting to celebrate the thirtieth anniversary of free elections" (Menu Wolności 2019).

The political landscape is constantly shifting because of the internal tensions within government coalitions, between the government and the opposition, and between the government and the European Union. In this chapter, we explored the relevance of food in Polish culture and society, which in turn provides the framework for the current negotiations about the past, the present, and the future of the country and the ongoing revaluation of local, artisanal, and traditional food. It is against this background that tastemakers strive to introduce changes in Polish gastronomy and culinary culture. In the next chapter we will meet many of them to better understand their experiences and aspirations.

THREE

People

"TEN YEARS AGO, it was us—the chefs—who changed [our own] consciousness so that we knew what we wanted to cook. It took us these ten years to make the [restaurant] guest conscious and that is the most important thing. There is nothing more pleasant than to cook for a conscious guest who appreciates searching for the product, looking for the technique, how we cook and the whole project, the idea of the restaurant." We heard this reflection from Paweł Stawicki, at the time the chef at the Mercato restaurant in the city of Gdańsk. It is a straightforward declaration of the project of the culinary renewal of Poland.

This project is uncoordinated, does not have a formal manifesto, and is still in the making; however, these words suggest that at least some tastemakers see the processes taking place in the Polish culinary field as leading to a much-needed transformation. Tastemakers see themselves as central actors in these changes. In Stawicki's statement, we can also trace a didactic approach according to which tastemakers are working to turn local audiences into knowledgeable and mature consumers. The chef's words convey agency and self-confidence, voicing the desire to remodel not only Polish food but also its creators and recipients. His statement can be also read as an expression of the urge to establish a network of people who understand the emerging culinary codes with their underlying values and preferences. This chapter calls attention to the tastemakers who may be considered initiators, contributors, and champions in the redesign of Polish "good food," although at times they may not self-identify as such or may not even be fully aware of the role that they play in the shifts taking place in the Polish culinary landscape. We shed light on how they are claiming legitimacy and autonomy for the field in which they operate, while establishing forms of cultural capital and authority that allow them to position themselves within it. In the process, they are defining new categories of prestige and status that create tensions with those who maintain other ideas about what the field should be, what should count as skills, and what formation is necessary to properly belong to the field.

In order to better understand their backgrounds, their motivations, and their aspirations, we examine the tastemakers' personal and professional trajectories, as well as their interpretations of them. In this chapter we are especially interested in why and under what circumstances tastemakers became interested in food. We explore the role of the childhood memories and family homes of the chapter's protagonists, who often state that these experiences may have shaped their professional paths. We look at the foods they yearn to revisit and those they prefer to leave behind. The tastemakers' reflections on the influence of the historical and political contexts in which they grew up and began their careers in the culinary field are also explored. We discuss whether, from their point of view, their decisions were shaped more by domestic Polish and Eastern European habits, tastes, and values, or by ideas, practices, and objects adopted from abroad. We also try to address how these tastemakers position themselves in a society where the traditional intelligentsia strives for centrality but is often politically overshadowed by populism. Last, we investigate how educated tastemakers balance their social aspirations with work that often involves physical labor and artisanal craft.

The tastemakers who are the protagonists of this chapter fall under several professional categories: artisans, chefs, entrepreneurs, media and communication professionals, writers, experts, events and festival organizers, and cultural impresarios, to name a few. Because of this variety, we take into consideration diverse types of engagement in food culture and different ways to understand Polish cuisine and the culinary field. Some of these individuals are mentioned by name while others remain anonymous, but all contribute to the vibrant food scene that we have introduced in the previous chapters.[1]

Sometimes the boundaries between the different professions the tastemakers choose and the projects they undertake are blurred. Actors within the culinary field, especially in its more upscale and globalized echelons, are engaged in expanding their opportunities across multiple positions and roles across industries or segments of the food sector, at times operating in more than one endeavor (Hollows 2022; Matta 2019). As a high-status food culture is a relatively novel phenomenon in Poland, where formal culinary education used to command low prestige, many tastemakers are self-taught and come to gastronomy as career-changers: individuals who have become chefs or food

PEOPLE · 67

producers, not to mention journalists or event organizers, may still be active in other professional fields.

Our goal is not to present all the actors we met during our research but to make sense of the overall emergence of new tastemakers as a social and cultural category, focusing on their stories to identify the core elements and the building blocks of the current transformations in the Polish food scene. Their life stories were usually not the main topics of our conversations. In fact, dishes, products, and their profession were far more central in our interviews, together with their opinions and ideas. When we highlight biographical moments (origins, childhood memories, formal and informal education, foreign influences), we do it because they are the ones the interviewees themselves define as important.

The professional paths of tastemakers may be seen both as a reason for and a result of the dynamics shaping the transformation of the culinary field and of Poland as a whole. Their biographies were "lived" during intense social, cultural and political macro-events that still influence the present day: some of our interviewees' life decisions—including those regarding their education and their professional choices—partly resulted from structural or political circumstances. Yet, the inverse is also true: macro transformations emerged from myriad bottom-up decisions—from travels to midcareer changes— made by individuals who wanted to take advantage of the new possibilities and improve their personal situation. Tastemakers adapted to shifting criteria in defining success and determining value that were the result of the interaction between macro-phenomena and micro-choices.

Within the transformations of Polish society, the rise of new entrepreneurial elites who make food their main concern and the evolution of consumers' preferences and priorities are intertwined with old but still important concerns and worldviews. Just like a significant part of the Polish new middle class, some of the tastemakers and their audiences in Polish society have roots in the intelligentsia (Domański 2012). Most of all, their undertakings are at least partly based on the intelligentsia's ideas about their educational mission and their presumed social status as leaders, their appreciation for the social networks that they build and leverage as sources of social capital, and their openness to the Western world (Zarycki 2009, 2019; Zarycki, Smoczyński, and Warczok 2017). For these tastemakers, preparing and selling food is not just manual toil; they perceive it as knowledge, art, a creative activity, and sometimes a didactic endeavor. Many of them also display their privileged background by speaking to us about their experiences abroad, often in English.

68 · CHAPTER 3

PERSONAL GEOGRAPHIES

As the material we gathered is of a qualitative nature, it is difficult to provide statistical data about "who comes from where" or "who lives where" and to draw a quantitative map of the Polish food boom. We reflect, however, on the impact of spatial categories on the tastemakers' individual biographies, which in turn influences how people imagine and design the food scene. As we traveled around Poland, we interviewed and interacted with tastemakers in localities that may be different from the places where they were born and grew up. Whole generations of Poles are influenced by the fact that they or their parents moved to the cities during the massive urbanization that took place not only during socialism, but also in the years following the end of the regime.

Tastemakers' trajectories point to polycentric geographies that transcend the existing center-periphery divide and the way locations and spatial scales are valued. They live and work not only in the capital Warsaw and a few large cities such as Kraków or Wrocław, but also in smaller towns and even in the countryside. The distinctions that emerge from the tastemakers' provenance and their current locations reminds us that Polish regional diversity, despite the more or less explicit attempts at homogenization during the socialist years, has profound historical foundations. For instance, Agnieszka Wilbrandt, head chef of the Oranżeria restaurant in the Wzgórza Dylewskie Dr. Irena Eris Spa, serves variations of food from the surrounding Warmia region, an area that belonged to East Prussia and was part of the German cultural sphere before World War II. The chef was born and raised there, and her menu, as she declared in our interview, is strongly connected to home food: "It was mainly fish; lake fish, not from the sea. It was ducks, chickens, but not the kind of chickens we have now, it's not that kind of chicken.... The real kind. So, poultry, pork, veal, that's what I brought from home."

Some tastemakers feel such a strong connection with their place of provenance that they decide to return after prolonged stints elsewhere, describing the decision to settle down in the periphery as a positive and self-fulfilling escape from the hustle and bustle of the big city. Chef Marcin Pławecki, whom we met in his restaurant Gęś w dymie (Goose in smoke) in Laskowa, a village located nearby Kraków, and later at Figatella restaurant in the castle of Nowy Wiśnicz, both in the Małopolska region, explained to us that, although he was born in Kraków, he is not planning to go back and practice his craft in the city. His argument concerns the category of "slow life" outside large urban centers, and his choice embodies a reversal of the center-periphery relationship: "They [the customers] come to us, so we do not need to move." Tastemakers assign value to personal experiences of spatial mobility, turning small localities into sites for successful professional lives and destinations for tourists and foodies.

Although we find tastemakers with backgrounds connected to different Polish regions and residing in localities of various sizes, the whole process of reinterpretation of Polish cuisine should be understood as elite-driven and associated with urban social circles. Regardless of their actual locations or the dynamics of their migration and return, tastemakers around Poland are connected through networks of acquaintances and relationships. Those who identify with these communities of ideas and ambitions—as geographically dispersed as they may be—share similar points of reference, often mentioning the same books or people as inspirations. This is also the reason why, despite the growing visibility of the culinary scenes in other major cities, the foodie revolution may still be revolving around Warsaw, the capital, as its core and starting point. A new appreciation of regional specificities is taking place, as has also been observed elsewhere in the world (Appadurai 1988): tastemakers in the center, including those who have moved from the peripheries, are starting to look outwards.

At the same time, some tastemakers reveal a certain ambivalence about their places of origin and the culinary traditions with which they grew up. Personal histories might be interpreted as connections with uncomfortable or backward geographical or class environments. However, we observed that over time these histories also become assets in their professional ascent, justifying claims of authenticity and expertise. Arek Andrzejewski, a Warsaw-based artisan baker, told us: "My knowledge is not only from the Warsaw area. I am not from Warsaw. I grew up in the Lublin region. That is in the east of Poland. But I was born by the sea, in an area that used to be German and after the war was incorporated into Poland." Once he decided to embrace the rural breadmaking practices that he had at first shunned, his past experiences away from the big city contributed to establish his standards for flavor, texture, and quality. It is not rare that, in tastemakers' youth, attempts at upward mobility and social promotion engendered a temporary disdain for home-made food.

Andrzejewski reminisced: "For a long time, in my family bread was baked in the countryside, in such an old wooden house, and there was a bread oven in this old wooden house. This is about one hundred kilometers south of Warsaw.... It was my aunt and grandmother who lived there. Very poor land, rye was grown—they didn't grow wheat there, because the soil was poor. And once a week, on Saturday, bread was baked. Bread was baked on Saturday for the whole week. The bread was good to eat for the next five, six, or seven days and beyond. But I was young and stupid. I didn't appreciate this bread. When I came to Warsaw I ate very badly. My consciousness was like that: big city, new opportunities." For some of the tastemakers, entering the culinary field is seen as a return to their places of origins or to family and collective traditions. Several admitted to us that they often began to understand the relevance of these social and cultural resources only after years of rejecting them. In their narratives, such a lack of interest in traditional food is variously connected with growing pains, with their enchantment with foreign novelties that became available in Poland after 1989, or with experiences gained during periods of temporary emigration abroad.

FAMILY TIES

While early in their careers some tastemakers rejected homemade food or Polish food in general, today their memory of rural dietary traditions is a recurring topic. In their stories, children were often involved in the preparation of food at home, while parents were burdened with managing daily life. Tastemakers may consider home kitchens, childhood flavors, and domestic food labor as important factors in their current life decisions and professional trajectories. For instance, Agnieszka Wilbrandt recalls that, having been raised in a Polish family with a large farm, she was engaged in food work since early childhood: "I come from a family where we did a lot of cooking. I had only brothers, I was the only girl at home, so I needed to help my parents—my mum—at home. We had a big farm, so mum had a lot of responsibilities. So, it kind of all fell on me." Even those who cannot claim rural roots or childhoods spent in the countryside make frequent reference to their grandmothers' simple but tasty food, the normality of preparing food at home, and the habit of being dependent on one's own handwork.

In some cases, the home kitchen serves as a direct, though selective, inspiration and a source of recipes for future gastronomic enterprise. Justyna Słupska Kartaczowska, chef at the now closed Jadka restaurant in Wrocław, told us: "I have green tomatoes now, I will be making a salad. But that's only because I have such a mega-fondness for the green tomato salad that my grandmother used to make in jars. Just that taste in the winter, when she would open that jar: there were potatoes, I don't know, *kotlet mielony* (ground meat cutlets). And there were these green tomatoes, and it was such a taste of summer. It was sour, sweet. Just think, this is a salad from a jar. It's not a lettuce vinaigrette." Słupska Kartaczowska turned those embodied memories into refined and creative interpretations of Polish dishes, transformed by her deep knowledge of and admiration for French haute cuisine techniques. (She was one of the few chefs we met who preferred speaking French instead of English).

At times, tastemakers may even refer to the family or collective memories passed down from the times before socialism as a source of skills and authenticity. Marcin Pławecki connects his opening of the goose-focused restaurant Gęś w dymie to the experience and the knowledge acquired from his family's farmhouse where they raised poultry. Attributing the loss of the memory of eating goose to the socialist period, he goes far back in time to his grandparents' generation. This connection became the core concept for Pławecki's first restaurant. Although located in the countryside, it enjoyed the patronage of customers from nearby Kraków, who were intrigued by his impeccable interpretation of a fowl whose culinary use they felt had almost disappeared in their part of the country.

Through the lens of contemporary nostalgia, tastemakers turn homemade food memories into a justification for their discriminating taste ("I know how real food tastes"), their ability to understand the nature of ingredients and produce, and their knowledge of basic culinary techniques. Chef Tomasz Łagowski at the Belvedere restaurant in Warsaw recounts: "I was born in Poland, so I know the taste of all Polish food from my grandma, from my mother. Because they cook, they prepare traditional Polish cuisine, so I know the flavor, the taste, and how to make borscht, how to make *żurek* fermented rye soup, and how to bake. Also pork, duck, goose and stuff like that. And also how to make good dumplings—[I learned that] from my mother and grandfather."

Shared interpretations of the Polish past generate collective patterns that make the tastemakers' narratives about themselves and their families sound quite similar. The origins of their personal interest in food production are embedded in family histories which, in turn, are part of national vicissitudes: twentieth-century modernization, spatial and social mobility after World War II, massive demographic movements from the countryside to the cities, and the evolution of urban-rural links. Nowadays, many adult Poles— including the tastemakers we met—reinterpret these at times unwelcome collective experiences as informal education and opportunities for socialization. They tend to subscribe to the widespread narrative that their shared past, marked by the tribulations of socialism, left them with basic food-related knowledge and skills, deriving from their enduring connections to their families' survival strategies and the countryside.

This attitude is not exclusive to Poland. Monica Stroe (2018), for instance, describes the retraditionalization of middle-class consumption in contemporary Romania after a period of fascination with modernity associated with the West; she shows how making preserves and self-provisioning, rooted in a culture of scarcity, gained market recognition for its "artisan feel." Many of our interviewees expressed the opinion that the mere fact of being born in such a cultural and historical context (mature or late socialism in Poland), provides a certain embodied competency regarding taste and culinary techniques, almost predestining them, in one way or another, to cook, produce, or write about food.

Tastemakers are able to turn experiences that many Poles are familiar with into discursive resources, claims to authenticity, and standards of expertise that justify their current positions within the culinary field. The framing of well-known and widespread products and dishes as valuable and attractive demands a certain capacity for producing and leveraging cultural capital. "Eastern," "rural," "provincial," "backward," and "necessity-based" practices that many tastemakers have personally experienced have the potential to be reinterpreted as resources in designing the future of Polish culinary culture. This process, however, is clearly selective and unfolds through modalities that are influenced by social status, education levels, and political outlooks.

EDUCATION

Despite the widespread belief among tastemakers that they have "soaked up" food skills and knowledge since childhood, the transition from domestic food work to an occupation in the culinary field is by no means simple. It requires a combination of different formal and informal educational paths. Some Polish tastemakers have emerged from the pool of formally educated professional chefs, who mostly received their training in high schools, as until recently there were no university-level culinary courses.[2] Others, however, have entered the field with different educational backgrounds, frequently through midcareer transitions. Such differences are part of the

PEOPLE • 73

ongoing negotiations among tastemakers with different backgrounds about their own legitimacy and authority, as well as about how the field itself should develop.

The partial discontinuity resulting from the political transformations of the 1990s and the relative novelty of the sector, which is widely still considered "in the making," create dynamic pathways and a diverse landscape. Skepticism about culinary education is common in Poland. Critiques are often linked to a general disparagement of the state of Polish gastronomy during the socialist period and its aftermath, when professional culinary education continued to be limited to technical high schools (*szkoła zawodowa* or *technikum*). For example, chef Marcin Pławecki, who has a formal culinary education, when asked if he uses his knowledge from school, replied: "I've learned enough to turn on the tap and pour water into the pot [laughs]. Or to switch on the burner." In his interpretation, the sources of his professional knowledge are—in line with what we already discussed—his recollections from the home kitchen (and the mother who ruled it) and his work in a French restaurant in London.

Many chefs and tastemakers expressed the opinion that there was a period when finding skilled Polish chefs was challenging. They think the change happened rapidly as Poles began traveling, gaining experience in Western countries and then returning to share their knowledge with others. According to them, it was only by opening up to foreign practices and standards that the field was transformed and a new generation of Polish chefs started to emerge in the early 2000s. Chef Grzegorz Gręda at Romantyczna restaurant in the Wzgórza Dylewskie Dr. Irena Eris Spa pointed out that today's professional culinary schools—even if better equipped and employing good instructors—have limited financial resources and therefore teach simple and inexpensive dishes, those that are sufficient to pass the final exams. There is not much room for exercising the culinary imagination in this system because of economic and formal constraints. In this case, it is internships and subsequent employments in restaurants that determine career dynamics, rather than school training.

However, some of the protagonists of today's culinary revolution notice that they did in fact benefit from the knowledge offered by public culinary high schools. Some of those who were educated in them remember the experience fondly, observing that doors opened to them because of that training.[3] Chef Tomasz Welter (Coach of the Polish Military Chefs' National Team at the Culinary World Cup Luxembourg 2018 and bronze medal winner at the

Culinary Olympics Erfurt 2012) emphasizes the importance of formal culinary education. In his opinion, the fact that he entered the field in the 1980s allowed him to be trained by the chefs "from the prewar school" and, thanks to that style of teaching, he was able to learn how to do everything from scratch, supplementing school learning with extensive hands-on experience. Chefs that share a public-school background gravitate to traditional associations such as the Klub szefów kuchni (Club of the chefs de cuisine) or participate in international competitions like Bocuse d'Or. The up-and-coming chefs who did not receive formal culinary training tend not to favor these activities, often discarding them as an old way of approaching the profession.

There are also tastemakers who expressed the opinion that a lack of institutional culinary education among food workers cannot be easily remediated. From the early 2000s, private culinary institutions opened to make up for this gap. Swiss chef Kurt Scheller launched a famous school which brought techniques and approaches from Europe that most local chefs had not been exposed to yet. Many of our tastemakers mention him as an important point of reference in their culinary careers. In the face of an educational gap, some express interest in creating a new professional schooling system in close cooperation with experienced practitioners. Tomasz Łagowski from Belvedere restaurant in Warsaw has contributed to the establishment of the Akademia Mistrzów Smaku (Masters of taste academy), a twelve-month, free-of-charge cooking academy for students aged sixteen to eighteen from professional public high schools, to be attended—after recruitment on a competitive basis—in addition to their regular classes. Continuing education is also offered to chefs at the Akademia Inspiracji established by Makro, the largest food distributor to restaurants and food businesses: five-day courses on specific topics and a variety of shorter classes are made available to Makro's professional clients from all over the country.

NEW PATHS TO THE KITCHEN

While many chefs perceive the lack of institutional culinary schooling in Poland as negative, some tastemakers assert that the shortcomings of culinary education paradoxically made the food scene emerging at the turn of the 1990s and 2000s more flexible and open to absorbing individuals with diverse backgrounds. This, they imply, had positive consequences for food in Poland. Chef Agata Wojda, now at Ferment Bistro in Warsaw, was trained as a musicologist. She recalls the beginning of her involvement in the food industry in the early 2000s: "It was also a cool time, an interesting time in the sense that there were people like me in gastronomy: non-professionals, not [formally] educated people, not those who went to schools. We know our schools are not the best, I mean the education system is terrible. But nevertheless, people who went to [culinary] school naturally went to work in restaurants then and the appearance of a person like me, who had no education, was a novelty, in my opinion." Maybe precisely because of her unorthodox trajectory and her artistic, creative approach, she became one of the first chefs to offer an innovative interpretation of Polish cuisine when she worked at the Opasły Tom restaurant in Warsaw.

In order to fully understand the phenomenon of the influx of new people into the profession, it is necessary to consider the new educational and class trajectories in postsocialist Poland. In the 1990s, access to university education, no longer just for a narrow segment of the population, became an obvious step for upwardly mobile youth, who were able to live out the academic dreams of previous generations. In that period, those educated in both public and private institutions were largely drawn to career paths that were deemed suitable for the emerging middle classes (Duczmal 2006; Gulczyńska and Jastrząb-Mrozicka 1994; Parker 2003). Work in the food sector was not among those trajectories.

Many of the career-changers we spoke with told us that while they were considering their future, their parents suggested they choose respectable fields of study that would open doors to "better" professional opportunities. Chef Bogdan Gałązka from Stolica Café in Warsaw explained to us that he did not choose culinary education after finishing primary school because his parents convinced him of the bad prospects linked to that profession: "It was the time when being a chef was nothing special. Okay, so right now a chef is like a fashionable person or a celebrity. Twenty-five years ago, it was like: 'If you don't have any talent, you can be a chef'." So he studied as an electrician, then trained as a nurse, joined the navy for a couple of years, enrolled in a Jesuit university studying theology and psychology, and finally moved on to human resources management. After some time in that sector he was inspired to pursue his passion for cooking by Kurt Scheller, who at the time was among the first celebrity chefs in Poland. He started taking classes with Scheller in Warsaw, then moved to New York City, where he interned for Daniel Boulud for a few weeks, to study and get some experiences. It was only after his return to Poland that he opened the now closed Gothic

Restaurant in the Malbork castle in northern Poland, which put him on the culinary map.

To explain his unique path to culinary fame, former host of *Top Chef Poland* Grzegorz Łapanowski points to the lack of institutional opportunities for culinary training within the country during his formative years. He recounted: "So I did study political science in Szczecin and then in Warsaw, and sociology, but from the very beginning, I mean, from being like maybe fifteen, sixteen years old, I thought that cooking was something cool, you know, and I would like... that's something what interested me, I wanted to do a culinary university, cooking school, but there was none so...." Watching Robert Makłowicz, one of the first TV food experts, he realized that there were undiscovered arenas for gastronomy in Poland that he wanted to explore. After working on the culinary segment of a TV morning show, he also started taking classes with chef Kurt Scheller, launching his culinary career.

Class differences, although rarely directly mentioned in our interviews, manifest themselves as a result of the new professional paths available in the culinary field. In some cases, different worlds could collide. The influx of highly educated individuals, who saw food work as a creative and knowledge-intensive endeavor, was a novelty for the Polish food world, where most used to come up from the ranks of the culinary professions. Chef Agata Wojda recalls her first job interview in a restaurant: "I went to a job interview. It made me wonder if I knew what I was doing and that I would have to work with people who had a different education than me, who were, let's say, simple, because somehow they were not educated. Will I be able to cope? Will it not be a big problem for me? These were people who had different ideas, reacted differently. I think that the set of people who worked [in the sector] slowly changed. There were people who had a little better education or were a little bit, I don't want to say intelligent, because that's not the point.... They wanted something more, they didn't just want to come to work, they were interested in what we were going to do and how we were going to build it all, and that's it, so I stayed." Like Wojda, many of the tastemakers with whom we spoke felt more at ease in the world of gastronomy when they found "like-minded" people also entering the same field. We read this affinity as heavily influenced by class awareness.

The current changes in Polish cuisine are strongly rooted in writing and speaking about food rather than in just cooking as a manual activity. From the start, this field showed a strong familiarity with textuality and storytelling, establishing a self-perpetuating mechanism in which individuals with an intellectual background were attracted to what they felt increasingly was a cultural industry rather than just physical labor. Some of the tastemakers may turn food into a domain for creative endeavors meant to facilitate broader reflections about Polish culture, as is the case for the Food Think Tank in Wrocław, a collective that includes chef and food entrepreneur Michał Czekajło and culinary school graduate Tomasz Hartman. Their activities range from events, installations, and performances, to educational initiatives, fanzines, and filmmaking. In the recently launched Restauracja FTT restaurant, located in the Nobel Prize in Literature winner Olga Tokarczuk's Foundation, they explore the connections between food and literary culture.

This intellectual aspect is indeed visible in many of our tastemakers' stories; this is not only true for those who primarily write about food, but also for chefs, many of whom are comfortable around media or write about food. Chef Bogdan Gałązka, for example, wrote his doctoral dissertation in food history on nineteenth-century chef and cookbook author Jan Szyttler while running his restaurant business. TV host and food journalist Łukasz Modelski has a background in medieval art. He started focusing on culinary topics after spending the beginning of his career writing about lifestyle. He recalls that in the early interviews he conducted while working for travel and women's magazines, food was mostly about lifestyle and as such had to be luxurious. His radio broadcast, his books on culinary culture, and his TV shows on historical cuisine are the result of a long accumulation of cultural capital and knowledge. Magdalena Tomaszewska-Bolałek studied Japanese culture and language before becoming a food culture expert and heading the first post-graduate food studies program at the SWPS University in Warsaw.

CAREER-CHANGERS

The previous examples suggest that, for many tastemakers, stepping into the budding food scene meant leaving successful careers that were totally unrelated to food, including white-collar jobs. Although diverse in backgrounds and experiences, they show similarities in terms of intentions, aspirations, and paths. The unstructured and vibrant entry of these individuals into the Polish culinary field has taken place in an atmosphere of novelty and enthusiasm. They sometimes mention personal rather than economic reasons to explain why they chose to work in food: health and well-being, family, or just pure passion. The Folwark Wąsowo farm, which produces artisanal preserves made from organic vegetables and fruit, was launched as a response to owners Piotr and Magda Wieła's concerns about health and nutrition. Similarly, the founders of the *kiszonki* (pickled vegetables) Zakwasownia company in Gdańsk declare that it was their focus on personal health that led them to start producing beetroot fermented drinks for their own consumption, and only later did this passion grow into a formal business. Others turned passions pursued in their leisure time into more structured, professional engagements in the culinary field.

What follows is a quick panoramic view of the variety of professional backgrounds among career-changers. As dizzying as it may feel to the reader, it gives a good sense of the protagonists of the current food scene in Poland. Adam Łukawski, an entrepreneur in the printing industry, donated his private collection of old vodka bottle labels to launch the Muzeum Wódki in Warsaw. Tomasz Czudowski, founder of the Muzealna Restaurant in the National Museum and co-owner of AleWino in Warsaw, one of the first wine bars in Poland, told us he had always been into wine and food (as a foodie), vaguely fantasizing about becoming a chef. An IT and media entrepreneur working for YouTube, Czudowski slowly shifted his career toward gastronomy and the hospitality business.

Małgorzata Minta, a successful food writer and blogger, used to be a science journalist, while Kati Płachecka, a restaurant social media and PR specialist in Kraków, studied pedagogy and used to work in a kindergarten. Food writer and author Magdalena Kasprzyk-Chevriaux was a lawyer, similarly to the owners of the Mleczna Droga dairy farm, whom we mentioned in the introduction. Chef Tomasz Łagowski outlined his career trajectory from gardening design to cooking in a food truck all the way to the prestigious Belvedere restaurant in Warsaw. Interestingly, in our interview he underlined the parallels between garden design and restaurant work. He argues that they are both based on similar design processes: they demand imagining shapes and colors, planning, and understanding links between plants and season. Before opening her first food establishment, Justyna Kosmala, cofounder of the Charlotte Menora café in Warsaw, had embarked on a diplomatic career, and her sister and collaborator Basia Kłosińska studied political science. The two have launched several businesses, including the bar Wozownia and the very successful Italian restaurant Lupo. Also on their team are Basia's husband, the political marketing expert Filip Katner, and

Justyna's husband Tomasz, an expert in natural wines who studied economics at University College Dublin. Paweł Błażewicz from the Kormoran brewery in the town of Olsztyn switched from being a historian to a beer maker. Artur Kinasz, one of the founders of the Targ Pietruszkowy farmers' market in Kraków, has a career as a genealogist.

These career-changers represent a small but well-oiled community, often inspiring each other in their efforts. As they all followed unusual paths to their current culinary undertakings, they understand that they all are bound to face challenges but that by sticking together they are likely to have better outcomes. While they are engaged in positioning themselves within the culinary world and conflicting interests may impact their decisions, they are also aware that only through collaboration can they build up the emerging field as a whole. They often team up in business endeavors, initiatives, and events, creating a powerful echo chamber that resonates in the media, as many of them are experts in communication. Moreover, they share ideas, priorities, and practices, frequently in connection with the global foodie culture. They have a collective vision for what Polish food should be in the future and this in turn strengthens their resolve.

In her previous research, coauthor Agata Bachórz (2023) observed how career changes from middle-class, white-collar jobs to professional food work have contributed to the growing appeal of the food sector in comparison with seemingly stable and more prestigious professions. Career-changers' decisions follow different motivations, frequently connected, on the one hand, with the idea of a stress-free good lifestyle and counter-hegemonic career patterns and, on the other hand, with neoliberal flexibility and resourcefulness. Career-changers often embody the hybrid nature of professional food work, mixing manual and intellectual dimensions.

Some of the emerging dynamics have to do with global shifts in the cultural economy: many occupations previously discredited as working-class manual jobs are now considered legitimate outlets for creativity, also gaining social prestige in countries that Poland still values as models (Fine 1996; Ocejo 2017; Matta 2019). When recounting their professional path, career-changers also point to a set of motivations related to the transformation of the work ethics and conditions in the contemporary world. Manual jobs seem less alienating to them and provide opportunities to be more in touch with the results of one's own work. Occupations in the food sector are seen as a response to the bureaucratization, standardization, and excessive focus on efficiency experienced in other sectors (de Solier 2013; Furrow 2016).

Midcareer entries into the culinary field are an attempt to seek agency, influence one's surroundings, and establish direct contacts with other people, using food as a means of communication and energy exchange. Clients and customers come, eat, and when they return empty plates are happy: those working directly with the public often enjoy quick and satisfactory rewards (Bachórz 2023).

A BRAND-NEW PROFESSION: WINEMAKERS

The receptiveness of the emerging food scene to new voices is particularly evident in the case of winemaking, which has been taken up in recent years by people with a wide variety of backgrounds, life experiences, and educational paths. As we discuss further in chapter 6, until recently there was simply no commercial winemaking in Poland, apart from the historical vineyards in the so-called *Ziemie Odzyskane* (the "recovered territories" from Germany), which have been operating continuously except for a break during the socialist years. Marcin Niemiec from Winnica Amonit, a winery located in Jura Krakowska near Kraków, is a lawyer by trade and a career-changer himself. He explained to us that the winemaking community is diverse because "people did not assume they were going to be winemakers, but somehow it happened. . . . There was the internet, internet forums, discussions, and then, just by chance, at a wine event I met a man who had a vineyard a few kilometers away, and then another one." The centrality of networking and collaborating that we noticed among tastemakers is even more crucial in the development of the burgeoning wine industry, in which almost everybody is a newcomer.

When we met Niemiec and his wife Joanna Spałek-Niemiec, a landscape architect, they were exploring ways to entice tourists from the city to rediscover the rural traditions of Poland in their "authentic" and "natural" form. They were planning to make cheese and build a bread oven and a smokehouse, both new activities to them. They are fully aware that they are not the originators of these traditions: "It's never a story like you find in France, because it can't be from grandpa, great-grandfather [who had passed the tradition from generation to generation]. We just start somewhere and learn from scratch. . . . We laugh that we will be in these photos of the vineyard, the founders: our grandchildren will hang us on the wall. We will be the first generation." Because they do not have networks built into their families, they feel that the community of new winemakers is central to their operation. In

2016 Niemiec started the association of the winemakers of Jura Krakowska (Stowarzyszenie Winiarzy Jury Krakowskiej), of which he was still the president when we met.

The owners of Winnica Amonit are native Europeans; they came of age after Poland's accession to the EU. It is easy to notice generational differences between winemakers; the opportunity to cross borders at any time is still a big deal for the older ones. Wojtek Bosak, a well-respected wine expert, took us to a producers' meeting at Robert Zięba's Winnica Kresy winery, one hour north of Kraków. The meeting took place outdoors, in a large shed that seemed to be part of the production structure. A screen and projector were placed in front of a U-shaped table, around which the participants—mostly men from neighboring villages—sat. From the conversation, their class background seemed to vary from well-off rural to urban middle class; they were educated and well-traveled. As they spoke, it became clear that they had not known each other until they started making wine. This is a practice-focused community that emerged to learn together and support each other in a new venture.[4] When they gather, they exchange experiences and tips about vine growing, technology, and marketing.

During the meeting, Bosak offered "additional training" (*doszkalanie*, also meaning "continuing education"); the topic was traditional winemaking techniques, which in his opinion result in wines that are quite different from the *nowoczesne wina* (new-style wines) everybody knows from restaurants and stores. He explained it is not only a matter of techniques, which in the past were transmitted orally: traditional winemaking is based on a different philosophy that is against monoculture and supports agrobiodiversity. Bosak advises and consults on production, marketing, design, and enotourism. He has played an important role in the development of Polish wine in general, and especially in the Małopolska area around Kraków. One of the pioneers in the industry, he planted his first vineyard in 1996 and received formal wine training only later. He started writing professionally about wine in 2002 for *Magazyn Wino*, a magazine launched by wine expert Wojciech Gogoliński; he now has his own web page, winologia.pl. He also teaches wine-related courses in Kraków, Warsaw, and at the Podkarpacka Akademia Wina (Subcarpathian academy of wine), established in 2014 with the support of the Galicja Vitis foundation to offer year-long courses.

The shared experience of "starting from scratch," as well as the lack of winemaking traditions and intergenerational transfer of knowledge and resources, all explain why the recruitment process into the profession is based on self-education and may even appear random. In the future, the professionalization of Polish winemaking is expected to advance, incorporating individuals with formal education into the industry while at the moment there are few of them.

Interactions with the international winemaking scene are also relevant. When Srebrna Góra vineyard cofounder Mirosław Jaxa Kwiatkowski and his business partner Mikołaj Tyc were looking for a potential location for a vineyard, they prepared a map of the Małopolska region on which they highlighted areas suitable for viticulture, at least according to the international knowledge represented, among others, by specialists from Germany. They then arranged a second map, on which they identified historical Polish vineyards. They started to look for a location in the areas where the two maps overlapped. They later succeeded in gaining access to foreign partners and launched international business collaborations with experienced winemakers from Austria and Germany whom they met while working in those countries. They also secured technical support from Germany-based academic specialists on wine production and bought vines from them.

KNOWLEDGE AND CULINARY CAPITAL FROM ABROAD

The Srebrna Góra vineyard cofounders' work process is the perfect metaphor to illustrate how foreign experiences and knowledge interact with local skills and know-how in generating the changes we have been tracking. While the elements that we have so far identified in the biographies of our tastemakers point to domestic dynamics, their professional trajectories are also influenced and inspired by the international circulation of ideas, practices, and materials in cosmopolitan foodie culture. The protagonists of the Polish culinary field are often inspired by trends from Western Europe and the United States, at times already perceived as passé by innovators in those countries. As we already noticed, some Polish tastemakers explicitly acknowledge their attempts to "keep up," "catch up," and join worldwide developments, while appreciating that the lag between the rise of international trends and their adoption in Poland is becoming increasingly shorter.

Some tastemakers have been embedded from birth in cosmopolitan networks. TV food celebrity Magda Gessler, a daughter of diplomats, grew up in Cuba and studied in Spain, acquiring a certain foreign flair. Food author and expert Tessa Capponi Borawska, member of a noble Florentine family and married to a Pole, contributed to the reemergence of those who "remember" and "know" quality and style on the cultural stage. Flavia Borawska, her daughter and a well-respected chef in her own right, is able to move between Italian and Polish cultures: she headed the Opasły Tom restaurant in Warsaw while writing two books about Italian cuisine with food writer and blogger Małgosia Minta. Food journalist Paweł Bravo spoke Italian at home, as his father is Italian. He started his career as a book translator while also trying his hand at film distribution and marketing research. While his father was quite uninterested in cuisine, his knowledge of Italian culture allowed him to collaborate with two young Italians who organized cooking events in Warsaw during which they read Dante. With them, he wrote a cookbook and opened the Italian restaurant Culi-in-Aria ("culinary," but also a pun in Italian—"asses in the air"). He later became a food columnist for the prestigious Kraków-based weekly magazine *Tygodnik Powszechny*.

Acquiring experience abroad became much easier after the 1989 political earthquake and especially after the country's accession to the European Union in 2004. Poland has been a country of emigration since the nineteenth century, primarily to North and South America as well as to Western European countries. During the Cold War Poland was a "country with no exit" (Stola 2010), in which migratory processes were severely curtailed. The collapse of the socialist regime served as a catalyst that altered migration patterns, making government acts—including issuing or retaining passports—a less significant factor in influencing mobility (Iglicka 2000). During the postsocialist transformation, the demographic and social characteristics of migrants evolved and permanent relocation decisions have begun to give way to more diverse trajectories, including temporary and return migration. The economic crisis and high unemployment Poland faced at the turn of the twenty-first century prompted many Poles to seek opportunities abroad, where more jobs and higher wages were available.

It was not until 2004 that a sea change in Polish migration history occurred. In that year Poland joined the European Union (followed in 2007 by accession to the Schengen Area, the European zone of free movement of people and goods). As EU citizens, Poles were finally able to reside and make a living in other countries of the Union without a visa, with the UK as the single most popular destination (Grabowska-Lusińska and Okólski 2009). From that time on, migration from Poland to EU countries has increased and the diversity of destinations expanded to include Belgium, Ireland, the

Netherlands, Norway, and Iceland (Burrell 2016; White 2015). Some migrants traveled from country to country, eventually settling abroad (Bivand Erdal and Lewicki 2015). While intra-EU migration is now slightly less intense than twenty years ago, transnational networks have become a permanent characteristic of Polish society (Bivand Erdal and Lewicki 2015; White 2015), and for the first time in history more people now come into Poland than leave it (Okólski 2021).

Our interviewees' experiences reflect these demographic and sociocultural trends. For example, Winnica Amonit's owner Marcin Niemiec told us that the decision to open up a vineyard was influenced by the inclusion of Poland in the EU: "It seems to me that Poland's accession to the EU has given a lot here. It has triggered such a sense of belonging to this West that we also want to have what was previously unavailable to us."

INTERNATIONAL EXPERIENCES

Our interviewees with professional experience abroad did not always plan on working in the gastronomy sector in other countries; in fact, there were some who stumbled into it as a way to support themselves while abroad, taking menial jobs for which an extensive knowledge of the local language was not essential. The sector offered ample employment opportunities and did not always require previous experience or education. Only later did some individuals who discovered their interest in food and wine while abroad return to Poland to build their own future in the culinary field while contributing to its reconstruction.

Working and getting professionally trained in other countries resulted in a transfer of skills and knowledge "imported" from the West. Mirosław Jaxa Kwiatkowski, one of the Srebrna Góra vineyard owners, recalled he used to hire cooks from abroad when he was running an Italian restaurant in Kraków in the 1990s: "There was a time when it was very difficult to find good Polish cooks. Polish cooks tended to be the generation taught according to the old school." He further clarified that it was not until the turn of the twenty-first century that the first Polish chefs "of a new generation" appeared: "And then it went very quickly, because indeed Poles started to travel and gain experience in the West; this group came back, started to teach their peers." Nevertheless, tastemakers may express a certain ambivalence about practicing one's craft abroad, where they were made to feel less accomplished than locals. Some came back to Poland because they desired to achieve a more prominent position, higher prestige, and greater financial success than they could aspire to elsewhere.

Other tastemakers refer also to leisure and business travel along with short- or long-term employment when illustrating their professional trajectories and, implicitly, their international culinary capital. Although borders began to formally open after 1989 (Horolets 2013, 75–80), to this day international travel experiences constitute an important element in middle-classing dynamics (Bachórz et al. 2016). To some extent, when Polish tastemakers tell stories about leisure travel abroad, they indicate their elevated class positions.

Kresy vineyard's owner Robert Zięba says his interest in wines and food was "inspired by travels" to Italy and Croatia. Similarly, restaurant entrepreneur Justyna Kosmala recalls that she was influenced by foreign culinary customs she experienced as a student; she had an especially strong admiration for French food culture. The idea for her first business, the bakery and bistro Charlotte in Warsaw, came from the atmosphere she had enjoyed in French and Californian cafés, together with her interest in Polish breadmaking traditions. Restaurateur Tomasz Czudowski told us: "We got to this because of travel. That's just the truth. We saw this in the world. Food [in Poland] was not going in this direction, you know. When you would go to the UK or the States or, you know, even France, people were taking big pride in their local cuisine, only they were redoing it. . . . Use local ingredients, use local inspiration. But do it in a very novel way. It doesn't have to be heavy. It doesn't have to be exactly the same that it was originally. . . . So that inspiration came mostly from travel because you couldn't see it in Poland, right?"

Although today Polish tastemakers can easily travel to learn or improve particular skills, spatial mobility is not the only way to get inspiration from foreign phenomena and trends. Media also plays a central role. Images and other visual material that do not need translation, such as videos on TikTok or YouTube, as well as the ever-improving translation features on many popular social networks, make trends and cultural phenomena accessible to those who are not fluent in foreign languages. Similarly to Joanna Jakubiuk, whom we met in the introduction, chef Grzegorz Gręda from Romantyczna restaurant admits he was trained in Poland only. He is not directly connected to the international networks of practice that allow many of his peers to stay abreast of the newest innovations, although he is immersed in the global culinary media circuit via both social media and traditional media and books.

However, his lack of experience with labor migration is rather an exception. He confirmed that he often needs to explain his choice to work only in Poland: "After all, there was a time in Poland when you couldn't make a name for yourself at all because you hadn't been to England. You hadn't worked in England. And I often get this question: where did you learn your profession? Where did you work abroad? I say, nowhere, I'm Polish! So that's it."

Polish tastemakers do not simply "copy-paste" what they learn from foreign sources. Their professional strategies are deeply influenced by their own environment. They may borrow ideas from abroad (like celebrating a country's diverse regional traditions) while adapting them to the local context. The interaction between two types of resources—the global circulation of knowledge and internal dynamics with deep historical roots—causes cosmopolitan abstract ideas to become concrete through a complex process of translation into Polish culture. As the culinary field grows and matures in Poland, its protagonists may feel more entitled to deviate from their international inspirations. Winnica Amonit's owner Marcin Niemiec explained to us that what he and other Polish winemakers try to do is to develop their own methods and flavors through experimentation, enhanced by knowledge gained from abroad: "That's what's nice about Polish winemaking: that there is no such thing as repetitiveness, that it's not the same all the time, but every year you can try something new from every winemaker, and that's also the reason why the offer expands with something new all the time. We have such unpredictability that we can surprise people with something and we have the possibility to do it. No one is forbidding us from doing it, as in the appellations: that we have to collect so much and do it in such a way."

Polish tastemakers now feel that their cuisine is on its way to get on a par with other European ones, which will allow them to shake off any sense of backwardness and inferiority. "We drive, we watch, we sneak peek. We come to the conclusion that we are not at all very inferior. Europe—really? And it gives a lot, getting rid of complexes," Winnica Kresy's owner Robert Zięba told us. Noticing growing similarities between Poland and western Europe in food quality and prestige, rather than just differences, turns out to be a liberating experience that disrupts any center-periphery logic and the cultural hierarchies that inform it. In the next chapter we will look more closely at how the cultural and social dynamics that we have outlined in the career paths of Polish tastemakers interact with geography to create a new sense of place and locality.

PEOPLE · 87

FOUR

Place

IT IS A SUNNY and warm late summer day in Warsaw. Bees are lazily buzzing around their wooden hives, half asleep after the smoke that beekeeper and entrepreneur Kamil Baj administered to them before allowing us to get closer. We are all wrapped up in appropriate gear, including net hats; Kamil, on the other hand, is only wearing black jeans, a black T-shirt, and white sneakers. He uncovers a hive and pulls up a frame still covered in bees, explaining what taking care of colonies and producing honey in an urban area entails. In fact, the hives we are observing are located among the trees of Fort Mokotów, set apart from the buildings that were previously part of the fortification surrounding the city, recently repurposed as commercial spaces occupied by offices, startups, a cooking school, and a wine bar. It is the perfect location for the hives managed by Pszczelarium, a company that since 2015 has produced, packaged, and marketed honey in the middle of Warsaw. The name of the business combines the Polish word for bee, *pszczoła,* with the Latin word *cellarium,* which indicated the underground storerooms in medieval monasteries.

The headquarters of Pszczelarium that we visited were also home to modern machinery for honey processing: the company does not refuse innovation in the name of tradition, but tries to straddle the two. Similarly to the farmers in alternative food networks surveyed by Wojciech Goszczyński (2023), they perform rather than reproduce rural practices without giving up on modern production processes. Pszczelarium takes a systemic approach to its mission, creating educational and volunteer programs and organizing workshops. It manages to present a contemporary, hip image, with plenty of references to the priorities and preferences of its mostly urban, relatively affluent customer base, while maintaining the cultural value of semi-artisanal honey production. Graphic design is central to the brand identity: their logo shows a hexagon above two hives in the shapes of partial hexagons. The low, round honey pots, with black lids and bright yellow labels written in black font, are packaged in cardboard cubes made of light brown recycled paper.

The hives Pszczelarium gets its honey from are spread all over the city. They produce different varieties that are named after the neighborhood in which the hives are located: a multiflower spring honey from Żoliborz, a chestnut and hawthorn honey from Wilanów, a linden and meadow honey from the central Śródmieście, and so on. There are also the more generic labels "Warsaw" and "Mazovia," the region in which the capital is located. For those, honey is collected from different areas in and around the city. Locality emerges as a flexible category that can span from a neighborhood to a whole region: what counts is that consumers know where their honey comes from, establishing cognitive and emotional connections with specific locations. The idea that honey reflects the place where the bees live is central to Pszczelarium's business model, harking back to preindustrial manufacturing processes.

Honey making in general is ubiquitous in Poland, with thousands of producers, mostly in the countryside, ranging from domestic beekeeping, meant for the consumption by family, friends, and neighbors, to artisanal enterprises and industrialized mass production. What Pszczelarium offers is the taste of urban places, interpreted through an otherwise rural activity, purified from negative connotations of alienation, pollution, and lack of connection with nature. As they state on their website, "We give bees new places to live in the city," (Pszczelarium n.d.) highlighting their role in protecting the environment and establishing favorable living conditions for the insects so they can pollinate surrounding plants. The city government is sensitive to the issue: many flower beds are planted with wildflowers, which contribute to the atmosphere of city streets from spring to fall while supporting the pollinator population. A law was introduced in the early 2010s that legalized honey production in the city, an activity that many private citizens had already been conducting in their *działki* allotments.

Pszczelarium, however, offers a refined experience to its customers. By emphasizing the local nature of the product, the company implicitly argues that urban settings allow for the development of culinary identities. It highlights the specificities of city neighborhoods while building on practices and design strategies that appeal to the preferences of well-off urbanites in Warsaw and elsewhere. The company's approach has been quite successful:

its example has been followed in other large urban centers all over the country.

The connection between food and place is not experienced in the same way all over Poland. It varies depending on context, scale, and the identities of the stakeholders involved. The Festiwal Kuchni Kujawskiej, the food festival that takes place every year in Lubraniec, in the northwestern Kujawsko-Pomorskie province, presents a different take on what the local may mean in more rural environments. Lubraniec is a small town of about three thousand inhabitants in a relatively affluent territory that belonged to Prussia for part of its history. The festival, which takes place in late summer, has become a showcase for products and culinary traditions from the area, like smoked trout, pork sausages, and *smalec* (ground cured pork fat to be spread on bread). Some brands build on local products and practices while embracing cosmopolitan trends, such as local chef Piotrek Celtycki's "deviled" fermented herring (a spicy take on a classic preparation) and smoked salts from the company Zwędzone Naturze.

Next to commercial enterprises, in our visit to the festival we observed that numerous women's associations[1] had booths where they proudly presented their interpretations of the "old-fashioned" local specialty *czernina,* a soup with duck blood, which was also the theme of a competition whose winner was determined by a panel composed of local, national, and international judges (including coauthor Fabio Parasecoli). The competitors presented the soup together with cornucopias of local specialties: duck and goose smoked breasts, stuffed breasts, *pasztet* (paté), *barszcz,* smoked fresh cheese, as well as home-baked breads and desserts. The apparent goal was to stun with abundance, variety, and cooking skills. Each booth was beautifully decorated with traditional tableware, wood slats, baskets, handmade doilies, ears of wheat, colorful flowers, and vegetables. Many of the women also wore traditional costumes in bright red, blue, and white. They proudly presented their dishes to the judges, explaining what they had prepared and looking for the seal of approval of national and international experts, who are supposedly well versed in what counts as good quality and what does not. The winners were eventually announced on a large, well-lit stage, where the best producers also got prizes.

The event, a heartfelt celebration of what is practiced and experienced as local cuisine, was no simple countryside get-together. It attracted great numbers of visitors, mostly from the region; inevitably, politicians made appearances to connect with their constituency, and some of them gave speeches

90 · CHAPTER 4

from the stage. The open field where the event took place was right outside town. On the road to get there, trucks sold all sorts of industrial desserts, snacks, and drinks that did not reflect the more artisanal fare offered on the event grounds. Musical acts provided entertainment during the daytime. When it got dark there was an enthusiastically received performance of disco polo, a local adaptation of 1980s European disco pop, on the main stage. What is on display here is a festive sense of locality and regional identity rooted in rural customs—or rather, the current interpretation of what those could have been—made accessible to people of all walks of life and socioeconomic background.

A more upscale food festival, promoted as a "picnic," took place at the Warsaw horse track Służewiec in the summer of 2022 as part of the program Poznaj Dobrą Żywność (Get to know good food). This initiative, as we discussed in chapter 2, is meant to highlight the best of food production in Poland by creating a recognizable mark for national and international markets. The setup was, on the surface, not too different from the one in Lubraniec: booths selling products ranging from the artisanal to the industrial, tastings, culinary demonstrations by well-known chefs, product competitions, and a stage for official speeches and awards. However, there were many more booths than in Lubraniec; some of them were quite large, elaborate, and well designed, representing whole provinces or nation-wide businesses. A map of the event, in both Polish and Ukrainian, welcomed visitors at the entrance. Entertainment for the visitors was provided as well, including games and activities for children, while the VIPs could enjoy a well-appointed buffet in an elegant building beside the tracks.

Unlike in Lubraniec, where everything was about the foodways of the area, the focus of the culinary festival in Warsaw ranged from local and regional productions (from Podlasie, Lubelskie, Mazowia) to those of national associations.[2] A more flexible sense of place was conveyed at different scales, with "Polishness" clearly encompassing all other dimensions. The intention was arguably to offer a mosaic of Poland as a whole, with its great diversity of local culinary identities all contributing to the national cuisine as "general Polishness." Because of this, products were frequently described with less location-specific adjectives, such as *domowe* (from the domestic space), *wiejskie* (from the village, the countryside), and *swojskie* (from home). Such place-based descriptions overlapped with others such as *naturalne* (natural) and *tradycyjne* (traditional).

PLACEMAKING

Pszczelarium, the Lubraniec festival, and the Poznaj Dobrą Żywność "picnic" in Warsaw offer examples of the current placemaking processes taking place around food, and how varied they are in terms of scale, ranging from the local—the city (*miasto*) and the municipality (*gmina*, more relevant in rural areas)—to the administrative province (*województwo*), the region, the nation and, increasingly, the EU. Placemaking also reveals the centrality of socioeconomic status and education, interwoven with tensions between urban and rural environments. New understandings of culinary geography seem to vary depending on social and cultural environments. The stakeholders in the Polish culinary field seem keen on performing what Karl Polanyi (1957) theorized as "embeddedness:" the rootedness in cultural, social, and political institutions and networks that constitute a local community beyond economy-based market mechanisms. Such endeavors seemingly aim at offering experiences of lived authenticity, frequently connected with local economies, which consumers can access through food and which tastemakers incorporate in their activities and communications strategies. However, these performances could also be interpreted as marketing gimmicks on the part of private enterprises, producers' associations, and authorities at various levels of public administration.

In this chapter, we examine how food and drink generate and shape understandings of place, reflecting diversity in goals, priorities, and worldviews. Such a reimagined sense of locality is in a complicated relationship with ideas about nature, origins, and the history of the country. The emphasis on place, genuineness, and authenticity can also be interpreted as a reaction to the onslaught of industrial and mass-produced goods that started during the socialist regime and has intensified during the postsocialist transformations, following Poland's integration into the EU and in the global economy.

Similarly to other postsocialist societies (Stroe 2018), in Poland the growing availability and affordability of both foreign and domestic items is generally celebrated as an expression of economic success that contrasts with the hardships and food insecurity of the past. Nevertheless, consumers express anxieties about the provenance of food, as well as a desire for a greater connection with familiar places and well-defined cultural identities. Marketers have taken notice. In an advertising campaign that Lidl, one of the largest discount store chains in Europe, launched in summer 2018, well-dressed and handsome farmers, identified by name and place of production, posed with fresh, local ingredients. The posters, pasted all over the country, carried the slogan "*tylko z polskich pól*" (only from Polish fields). In these ads, an international retail corporation appealed to Polishness by referencing not only Polish produce, but also the specific places in which it finds its literal roots. Such communication strategies suggest that marketers now consider the Polish origin of products—especially fresh ones—as a concern or at least an aspirational motivation for shoppers (with price remaining a central factor). In the fall of 2022, TV celebrity chef Tomasz Jakubiak participated in the advertising campaign "*Najświeższe lokalności*" (the freshest locales) for the supermarket chain Lewiatan. The TV commercials, shot in the style of news segments, highlighted how the chain's 3,200 stores are always looking for local producers in their areas.

Attentiveness about the nation tends to be expressed in broad strokes, tinged with emotions and nostalgia rather than political terminology. This sentiment is not totally new, as already in the 1990s the Polishness of products was at times praised in opposition to new Western imports, especially in government initiatives; the establishment of the *Teraz Polska* label back in 1991, discussed in the introduction, suggests as much.

Today the private sector on the one hand embraces a flat, undifferentiated Polishness; on the other hand, it shows growing interest in internal distinctions and regionality, which have the potential to increase the value of and the preference for Polish food. Regional cuisines, like Silesian or Kashubian, are now visible in discount supermarket chains.[3] Makro, the largest wholesale distributor for restaurants, is also promoting products whose regional identity is easy to pinpoint; they do so by positioning regional products in the roughly 2,500 corner stores of their franchise Odido ("from and to" in Polish) and with the initiative Polskie Skarby Kulinarne (Polish culinary treasures), an educational program for chefs that is also connected with the Makro Akademia Inspiracji, the professional learning center that Makro has opened in the outskirts of Warsaw.

These companies contribute to shaping a popular image of Polish national and regional food that partly overlaps but at times clashes with the approaches embraced and promoted by the tastemakers we observed. The latter try to reconstitute good food in ways that either oppose or question the industrial mode of production, by reconnecting it with locality through ideas of authenticity, place, embeddedness, terroir, and community. As large food corporations also adopt some of the same categories and integrate them in their marketing strategies, tastemakers often react by creating niche products and culinary experiences that allow for distinction through knowledge-intensive consumption.

While showcasing the specificities of Poland and its historical evolution, the emerging valuation of food based on its connection with locality also reflects transnational trends of cosmopolitanism and connoisseurship, which Polish tastemakers absorb to varying degrees through travel and media, as discussed in chapter 3. To different extents, most stakeholders in the Polish culinary landscape are projecting and betting on interest in local and regional foods, even if the sense of place they strive for and the valuation processes they engage in may vary. But such interest in place and its articulations still appears marginal among consumers with more limited financial means.

To get a better sense of these dynamics, we examined this issue in our focus groups. Among low-income individuals with high school or lower educational levels, locality was conflated with proximity: the Chinese restaurant around the corner is local because it is close and convenient. Among participants with higher incomes, higher levels of education, as well as greater interest in the culinary discourse offered by the media, locality was more explicitly understood in terms of food value. While they were not always correct, participants tried to pin certain well-known ingredients and dishes to specific areas in Polish culinary geography. As we illustrate in this chapter, discourses and practices about place and locality are clearly articulated in fine dining, winemaking, and gourmet food production. Still accessible to limited segments of the Polish population, these sectors enjoy prestige and influence among the actors who are involved in emerging dynamics of valuation. They also contribute to shaping the connection between food and locality that is reaching the wider public through media and public discourse.

NATION AND NATURE

Among the geographical horizons that tastemakers invoke in rearticulating their sense of place, the nation often appears as the most obvious and widely understood, although frequently through the lens of political discourse. However, far from being transparent, it increasingly implies interpretations that need to be observed and unpacked, especially in terms of latent nationalism. Even among the tastemakers that most explicitly embrace progressive perspectives, the national dimension—with its cultural and ideological aspects—takes priority over more local or regional frameworks. We noticed a lack of critical reflection on the very idea of national cuisine. The concept that food can and should be defined through the category of the nation is taken for granted. Accepted as transparent and positively valued, the exclusionary potential of these approaches is not taken into consideration. As we pointed out in chapter 1, the acute awareness that Poland as a state was erased or made irrelevant at different times in history generates an urgency in asserting its centrality, even when that implies subordinating local, ethnic, and religious identities at various scales, or willfully ignoring and reinterpreting episodes in which Poland may have played the role of the occupier or oppressor. That said, spatial interpretations of the nation can be fuzzy, based on personal experiences, and deeply inflected with temporality. Moreover, these spatial identities tend to be heavily influenced by various readings of the idea and the experience of nature.

We continue our exploration of how this shifting sense of place affects the Polish culinary landscape in the Warsaw restaurant Atelier Amaro, which received Poland's first Michelin star.[4] Wojciech Modest Amaro is a bona fide celebrity, known among the elites since his early days at the private Business Center Club in Warsaw and among the general public from local productions of *Top Chef* and *Hell's Kitchen*. He has played a leading role in reinventing national gastronomy by focusing on Poland and its ingredients. His restaurant reflected the cosmopolitan visual style shared by celebrity chefs and their clients both locally and internationally.

Chef Amaro welcomed us with an amuse-bouche arranged to look like a tiny garden patch, with intensely green and hyper-designed bites sprouting out of black earth made of pumpernickel. A Zen-garden take on a Polish rural plot, its minimalism immediately communicated an elevation of the ordinary, with the flavor of common vegetables distilled, intensified, and showcased. We tasted the dish in a room with floor-to-ceiling windows overlooking a park, while our table was set with porcelain, stone, and wood. Both the dishes and the interior design were tangible expressions of how materiality and the emotional responses it generates can be activated in reimagining the space and place of Polish food (more about that in chapter 6).

Like many of the interlocutors we met in the previous chapter, Amaro gained his culinary expertise by apprenticing and working abroad after Poland joined the EU in 2004. After our meal, he reminisced that when high-profile foreign chefs asked him to "cook something Polish," he would go blank, feeling confused and embarrassed about the few stereotypical and bland dishes running through his head. He felt that nothing in the culinary

PLACE · 95

heritage of his country was worthy of European fine dining. As we mentioned in the introduction, such a sense of cultural inferiority of Polish cuisine, along with the narrative of the need to "create" or "regain" a sense of national self-worth, is a recurring theme in our interactions with tastemakers.

One day, while working at El Bulli in Catalonia under Ferran Adrià, the global celebrity chef of modernist cuisine fame, Amaro reframed the issue of perceived inadequacy and began talking instead about the wonders of Polish ingredients that Adrià had never heard of, like bison grass blade (*Hierochloe odorata*). "I realized I had ingredients but I didn't have the symphony," he told us, adopting a high-brow metaphor. For Amaro, Polish culinary traditions were dispersed elements, or notes, not yet arranged in any sophisticated, artistic, or culturally consecrated form. He was missing a Polish ensemble with a specific, recognizable identity. Designing new compositions by using well-selected meats, vegetables, fungi, and herbs while elevating them through skilled and highly technological transformations, would become Amaro's project, all the way to his Michelin star.

It was not easy to turn traditional Polish elements into what the chef and his peers, especially abroad, understood as cosmopolitan fine dining. Before opening his restaurant, he traveled around Poland for a year in search of suppliers offering local and artisanal ingredients, all while collaborating with them to improve the quality of their production and educating them about what counts as valuable and important in international gastronomy. He also embarked on foraging expeditions to acquaint himself with wild plant varieties that - he claimed - most Poles had forgotten about. Like other Polish tastemakers, he appreciated the work of Danish and other Scandinavian chefs and producers in the New Nordic Cuisine; the movement has spurred the growth of interest in extremely local products, rooted in a geographical environment that Poles considered similar to theirs in terms of climate and the limits on what can grow at all times of the year. In his exploration, Amaro came to see marginal areas and nature outside of urbanized landscapes as almost frozen in time and outside history, ready to be brought back into a reimagined Polish national space, embracing widespread notions of the countryside as "idyllic" (Goszczyński 2023).

Self-orientalizing narratives (Buchowski 2006) of urban elites' discovery of their own country recur in our research, suggesting that the countryside and its nature are expected to provide the raw material for new projects and experiences that will then be developed in the cities. These dynamics echo the ethnographic explorations by nineteenth-century Polish ethnologists who sought to study localities and traditions as part of a nation-building effort. They also resonate with the use of traditional arts, crafts, and design—from furniture to fonts—in the post–World War I Republic of Poland, whose intelligentsia aimed to express independence and reunification in a distinctly "Polish style" (Szydłowska 2018).

LOOKING FOR A POLISH TERROIR

Over time, under the influence of both the ideas and the practices of the New Nordic Cuisine and its chief proponent René Redzepi, Amaro developed forms of culinary creation that integrate what he calls "the spirit of place" (Amaro 2014), an approach that echoes the French concept of terroir (Trubek 2009). In 2012, during the Cook It Raw event (*Kuchnia* 2012), which we mentioned in the introduction as an important turning point in transforming Polish cuisine, Amaro was able to show top chefs from Europe around the Suwałki region, framed as "pristine and undiscovered," spending time with them in nature, local fairs, and villages, while discussing the properties of mushrooms, plants, and herbs foraged with the guests during the workshops. Rivers, forests, and prairies turn into tangible expressions of a natural environment that is experienced as almost primordial, despite the changes imposed on it by modernization and the needs of agriculture.

Besides exploring Poland's nature, Amaro is also trying to restore its lost biodiversity by growing disappearing crops on farmland he has bought, in a new culinary project called Farmdining, where he cooks with the produce he grows. In this process, he joins a worldwide network of activists, chefs, and consumers who are intent on rediscovering extremely local food through interpretative and generative interventions on nature and taste (Ulloa 2018). At times, these projects include reshaping landscapes, designing new productive geographies, and implementing long-term economic investment, as we will discuss in chapter 6. Overall, Amaro's frame of reference in placemaking does not reflect specific locations or regions. The wilderness of the Polish nature and the backwardness of the Polish countryside become a national *terroir* that constitutes an untapped reservoir of value within the global circulation of cosmopolitan values and practices, as reflected in the New Nordic Cuisine and foodies' rediscovery of the local.

During our ethnographic fieldwork we have participated in events and forums on such topics, including a conference in Warsaw in May 2018 in which international guests discussed with Polish professionals how to reframe flavors and food practices in terms of terroir. Titled "Terroir Warsaw," the small event counted around one hundred participants. Panels and talks were held in English, which points to an audience comfortable operating in an international environment. In the conversations, terroir was discussed together with heritage, tradition, history, authenticity, and identity. It was also examined in the frame of culinary diplomacy and the need for a "Polish brand," meant to overcome borders and give global visibility to Poland's culinary landscape.

In this approach to Polish *terroir,* however, local ingredients represent a regional diversity that is produced in elaborated, elevated versions. The focus on high-quality local ingredients, rather than dishes, and the need to support producers and distribution networks, pointed once again to the perception of nature and the rural world as an untouched repository of authenticity that experts can activate to raise the profile of national cuisine. Traditional dishes such as *schabowy, bigos, pierogi,* or *kiełbasa* were brought up with irony, if at all. Instead, in order to reflect *terroir,* valuable Polish ingredients (both wild and cultivated) were highlighted in the work of creative, innovative chefs (many of whom were in attendance).

Nevertheless, this heavily classed approach relies on those who ensure the survival of knowledge relating to nature, wild foods, and local ingredients. These include farmers and ordinary Poles who grow produce in their gardens, backyards, or *działki,* or forage in the woods for mushrooms, berries, and all sorts of edible plants. The tastemakers attending the terroir conference clearly saw a role for themselves in adding value to these elements, almost presented as diamonds in the rough that needed the touch of experts' hands to come to light.

Foraging, a widespread and primarily necessity-based practice among Poles and one that Amaro pointed out as crucial in his development as a chef, plays a central role in defining the relationship between nature and locality in the Polish terroir. One of the people from whom Amaro learned to forage, and a well-respected authority on the topic, is Łukasz Łuczaj, whose book *Dzika kuchnia* (2018) comes with the chef's blurb. Łuczaj is a university professor who publishes internationally on ethnobotany, a discipline that examines how people in a particular culture or region make use of plants, including native ones, and how they organize their knowledge about them. Łuczaj has collaborated with many Polish fine dining chefs, drawing attention to herbs and plants that have been disregarded or fallen out of fashion, while integrating them into his own culinary practices. He also promotes the replacement of manicured lawns with natural meadows. Łuczaj has studied wild plants in sites ranging from Poland to Laos and South America. In his academic publications, he also works with historical records of ethnologists describing customs, beliefs, and lay practices around species of plants and fungi (see e.g. Łuczaj and Nieroda 2011; Łuczaj 2021).

He is able to swiftly shift from biology and culture of wild edible plants and fungi in traditional settings to imagining new cuisines in the twenty-first century, discussing René Redzepi's New Nordic Cuisine and analyzing the wild plant taxa foraged for his Copenhagen restaurant Noma (Łuczaj et al. 2012). A long-haired, charismatic presence, and the author of a book praising sex in the forest (Łuczaj 2020), Łuczaj feels more at home around his cabin than at faculty meetings. An ethnobotanist "gone native," he used to host a TV show in which he cooked lunch from foraged ingredients. He blogs and runs an English language YouTube channel called *The Wild Food* where he explains how to use wild and domesticated plants for cooking and other uses (for instance, moss to insulate log cabins) (Łuczaj n.d.).

Coauthor Mateusz Halawa drove to the village of Rzepnik in the Subcarpathia region to participate in a foraging workshop that Łuczaj organized in a stretch of forest he owns. He spent two days camping, cooking, and talking with fifteen other people, a lively mix of well-educated survivalists, gardeners, and preppers. They followed Łuczaj, a Laotian bamboo basket on his back, into the forest. What is characteristic for him is to speak from and for traditional beliefs, discussing his own uses of herbs and plants for naturopathic medicine, while also applying scientific methodologies to examine such beliefs. He is one to push his own body to its limits, exciting or soothing it with plants and roots, taking risks to taste and experiment on plants, and often going beyond the reasoning of Western science to reconnect with folk traditions and points of view. In the workshops he leads in his forest, the bodies of participants, the landscape, together with local, ethnological, and taxonomic knowledge, become sites for designer experimentations with what Poland might taste like. Łuczaj's forest, like Amaro's kitchen, is an important site in which the work of materially remaking the Polish "taste of place" happens.

IN SEARCH OF REGIONAL FOOD

Despite the frequent references to local plant varieties, animal breeds, ingredients, techniques, and dishes, it's worth noticing that ideas about locality tend to extend to the whole of Poland as a nation rather than specific regions. This is not a contemporary phenomenon: during the years of the socialist regime cuisine became more uniform due to food production and distribution structures, economic necessities, and the state's political imperatives. The books on cuisine and nutrition published under the socialist regime often presented Poland as a unit almost without internal differences. Regions were mostly ignored or incorporated into general "Polishness," either because they could constitute a hindrance to national unity, or because contemporary historical events had forced many Poles to migrate, uprooting them from their original communities, their traditional customs, and their culinary habits.

Recently, there has been a shift in attention toward regionality. Cookbooks are now available that focus on specific areas ranging from smaller localities to provinces. For instance, chef Krzysztof Leśniewski's *Kuchnia Pałucka* (2016) focuses on a territory within the Kujawsko-Pomorskie province, not far from Lubraniec. According to the back cover, the author "leafed through dozens of old cookbooks and interviewed housewives from the region," and perfected the recipes by practicing them in regional events, thus—we can assume—incorporating the feedback of the community. Dishes include fish *barszcz*; *ruks pałucki,* a rustic soup or potatoes and groats; *szagówki,* potato dumplings cut in rhomboidal shapes; *gomółki,* flattened balls of cheese, onion, and cumin; and *drożdżok z rabarbarym,* a rhubarb crumble. These names of the dishes are unknown to most of the inhabitants of Poland.

Other books centered on the idea of regionality include Hanna Szymanderska's *Kuchnia polska: Potrawy regionalne* (Polish cuisine: Regional dishes, 2013), with recipes explicitly presented as Kashubian, Silesian, and Kuyavian, and Paweł Ochman's vegan book *Roślinna kuchnia regionalna* (Plant-based regional cuisine, 2020), which argues that Polish local cuisines were mainly based on plants. Artur Wasilewski (n.d.) wrote the richly illustrated cookbook *Kulinaria żuławskie,* where he reconstructs—in cooperation with Marek Optiz, a restaurateur whom we will meet in the next chapter—dishes characteristic of the Vistula's delta between Gdańsk, Elbląg, and Malbork. The area was inhabited by Poles only after World War II, when attempts were made to erase the earlier traditions of the people living there. Wasilewski tries to build a narrative about the cuisine of the region, taking into account both rural and urban traditions in different periods. His patchwork reconstruction is based on historical books, vague memories, and their contemporary interpretations. He proposes preparing dishes such as Mennonite sausage, Gdańsk-style herring, boiled crayfish, or swede goulash.

To better understand how tastemakers and foodies negotiate new perceptions and expectations regarding the regional cuisines of Poland, we met with chef Robert Trzópek, who has turned regionality into the core concept of his acclaimed Warsaw restaurant Bez Gwiazdek. The name means "without stars," a jab at restaurant guides and the institutions that support them. He came up with the idea of menus built from traditional Polish dishes province by province by adapting the interest he saw abroad in regional cuisines to Poland's specificities. Every month, the restaurant tasting menu features a different area and its specialties; at the time of our visit, customers could choose among three menus with an increasing number of courses and proportionally higher prices. The restaurant makes a point of having a Polish wine list from all areas of the country; it is a logical addition to the regional theme.

To accommodate regulars and returning customers, the chef also created a "best of" menu with the dishes that have had the greatest success among his customers. Trzópek has an immaculate culinary pedigree, which allows him to command respect among his peers: he has worked at Le Manoir aux Quat' Saisons in Oxford, Noma in Copenhagen, El Bulli in Spain, and Tamka 43 in Warsaw (Kasprzyk-Chevriaux 2015). He translates these prestigious professional experiences into a unique style that features contemporary techniques, a minimalist approach to plating influenced by the New Nordic Cuisine, and a true interest in the bounty of the traditional local cuisines of Poland.

Trzópek started thinking about regional traditions when he was still working in England, but the idea came to fruition in 2016. At that time, it was still uncharted territory, so he decided to look at the list of traditional products (*lista produktów tradycyjnych*) published online by the Ministry of Agriculture and Rural Development, which is organized around the sixteen provinces of Poland (Ministerstwo Rolnictwa i Rozwoju Wsi n.d.). As in other EU countries, the Ministry lists regional specialties in production categories (meat, dairy, vegetables, etc.) with the addition of ready meals and dishes (*gotowe dania i potrawy*); it is under the latter category that traditional recipes, techniques, and practices can be found. Trzópek is well aware that administrative structures such as provinces do not necessarily present recognizable culinary specificities: some of them have little to no identity. At the same time, a "culinary region" may extend over parts of several provinces.

The first region that the chef featured was Mazovia, the province of Warsaw; the second was Pomerania (Pomorskie), his home region. In our conversation, he indicated Świętokrzyskie as the most difficult area for him, because he could not "find much to choose from." Trzópek is transparent about the fact that he got inspiration from the administrative list. He does research in person and through friends, applying his creativity to the material at hand. He also considers the seasonal availability of local ingredients. The chef admits that he does not have extensive historical or anthropological knowledge of all regions, and as a result his work centers mostly on ingredients.

When we talked to the chef, he had already completed the first cycle of the sixteen provinces, and was well into the second. Based on his past experience, he was able to choose the appropriate month for each region based on the dishes he wanted to highlight. Fish from the coastal Baltic areas is best in May and June; it makes sense to feature Małopolska—the province where Kraków is located—in September and October because that is when he feels that the *powidła* smoked plum jam, *oscypek* cheese, and other products from the area are in season. During our visit, the menu of the month focused on Upper Silesia, a region that many Poles understand as having its own culinary traditions, some of which are quite recognizable around the whole country. It was the second time that Upper Silesia was featured, and Trzópek had been so happy with the dishes in the first cycle that he did not make changes. For example, the first appetizer was *modra kapusta*: purple cabbage stewed with onions, sugar, and vinegar, at times with bacon and apples. In Trzópek's interpretation, sugar was replaced by raisins and whole mustard seeds added a little spiciness. The dessert, *czarna hałda* ("black heap"—coal heaps are an element of the mining landscape of Silesia) was an interpretative divertissement: a vanilla mousse with currant and sorrel, dusted with a black coffee powder.

The success of Trzópek's Silesian menu is not unexpected. In fact Upper Silesia, together with Kaszuby in Pomerania, and the eastern region of Podlasie, close to the border with Lithuania and Belarus, are often imagined as relatively self-contained cultural areas, with their own habits (together with their own language, in the case of Silesia and Kaszuby) and unique food cultures.

REGIONAL CULINARY IDENTITIES

Most Poles would agree that the Podlasie culinary identity is particularly strong, as chef Joanna Jakubiuk, a native from the area whom we encountered in the introduction, is happy to remind anybody. During our visit to Białystok, the main urban center in the area, the efforts of local businesses to bank on the local food culture was evident, especially in the city center.

Restaurant after restaurant advertised "Podlasie cuisine" and its specialties. For lunch, the Gospoda Podlaska (Podlasie inn) restaurant offered a *deska rozmaitości podlaskich* (Podlasie medley) for, supposedly, two or three people, which included three kinds of pierogi (with cabbage and mushroom, with meat, and *ruskie* with potatoes and onions), *kartacze* (huge meat-filled dumplings), *babka ziemniaczana* (a savory baked casserole also popular in Belarus, made of grated raw potatoes mixed with cracklings from freshly pork fat or melted bacon and spices), *kaszanka* (a dark sausage made of groats, blood and offal such as liver, lungs, and tongue), and fermented cucumbers. The large wooden platter that landed on our table could have easily fed four or five people, confirming to tourists the famous heartiness and abundant portions that typify Podlasie's cuisine.

The bustling Browar Stary Rynek brewery, right on the main square of Białystok, features traditional dishes, such as pork cheeks, ham hocks and game pierogi, next to burgers, gyoza, and carpaccio. A different approach to regional cuisine is featured at the upscale Cristal Restaurant inside the Best Western Hotel, where chef Łukasz Rakowski proposes a modern take on local dishes that also carries the imprimatur of Slow Food, the international association whose declared goal is "good, clean, and fair" food and which works on the protection and support of disappearing ingredients, dishes, and traditions. In the summer of 2022, for instance, the menu included *biały chłodnik podlaski,* a local white soup with pickled eggs, porcini mushrooms, and sour cream, dumplings with venison and bison grass (the same that is used for the famous *żubrówka* vodka), and Lithuanian-style dumplings stuffed with beef and mustard.

To better understand Podlasie food, we met local food expert Andrzej Fiedoruk,[5] who invited us to dinner at his place to taste what he presented as authentic versions of dishes that now are being commodified in restaurants and cafés both within the region and elsewhere within Poland. For instance, the *babka ziemniaczana* he served us had whole sausages in them, because, as he explained, it was a celebrative version of the dish. Fiedoruk argues that potatoes arrived to Podlasie not from the Western areas that were part of Prussia, like Poznań, but from today's Lithuania; from there, where potatoes were common, many workers had migrated to nearby Podlasie in search of jobs. However, he pushed back against the interpretation of Podlasie food as an expression of an encompassing "borderland (*kresowa*) cuisine" that would extend from Lithuania to the Black Sea. According to him, there are too many environmental, cultural, and religious specificities in this part of the

PLACE · 103

world to justify such an encompassing category.[6] (For more about borderlands, see the next chapter).

Fiedoruk thinks that regional food now tends to be for rich people, who can afford higher prices and patronize the food festivals celebrated all over the country. Nevertheless, he has contributed to the "culinary path of the old Białystok" (*kulinarny szlak dawnego Białegostoku*), a tourist aid meant to guide (possible affluent) visitors to explore the culinary past of the city; many of the locations are new establishments that have added recognizable Podlasie dishes to their menus. The flier available to tourists actually points to the interwar period as the time when a national Polish cuisine emerged from the fusion of Old Polish cuisine (*kuchnia staropolska,* whose contemporary incarnation we illustrated in chapter 1) and "the flavors of individual partitions." However, since "not a single stone is left of the former Białystok restaurants" after the destructions of World War II, the initiative's intention is "to save dishes and products from those times, collect them together and invite tourists and residents of Białystok for a tasty trip along the trail of flavors that have not been forgotten at all." The text tightly connects a sense of place with history; however, as few tangible remnants still exist of the past bakeries, cafés, and restaurants in which local cuisine thrived, the only choice is to focus on flavors and dishes, or at least their current interpretations.

The tension between popular versions of regional traditions and more upscale ones, where the intervention of tastemakers is more visible, is a common phenomenon in Poland. Storytelling is central and artisans may use personal narratives to make customers feel they are connecting with something alive and valuable. Many entrepreneurs in the gastronomy field appear to have adopted this strategy, including Dr. Irena Eris, the founder of a cosmetics empire in Poland which is now expanding abroad.

Eris's spas focus on high-end dermatological treatments. As good nutrition plays an important role in maintaining good, healthy skin, her resorts have introduced menus that are designed to support guests' overall well-being. Fresh ingredients reflect close connections with nearby producers and the gastronomic traditions from the areas in which the spas are located. Chefs and managers collaborate with Slow Food Poland to identify local producers who can provide high-quality specialties, which the chefs use creatively, taking inspiration from tradition but exploring it in original and intriguing directions. The restaurants at the spa resort at Wzgórza Dylewskie, as well as those at the Krynica Zdroj location in Małopolska, host dinners as part of the Tasty Stories event series (Eris n.d.). This initiative, launched in

2017, introduces guests—both local foodies and visitors from other parts of Poland—to local producers (referred to as "heroes") and to regional gastronomy through specially designed tasting menus. Although the dinners are meant to be informal and fun, the preparation and the service are extremely well curated. The events are then documented in videos, pictures, and interviews, to be shared and generate buzz, especially in preparation for new editions.

When we visited the Restauracja Romantyczna, at the Dr. Irena Eris Spa resort in Wzgórza Dylewskie in the Warmia area, not far from the spectacular Masurian lakes, chef Grzegorz Gręda, whom we introduced in chapter 1, was presenting a tasting menu that was unexpectedly daring. For instance, in his deconstructed *golonka* (pig trotters) he transformed a heavy, working-class dish into something that suited the fine dining establishment. Jovial and enthusiastic, Gręda conveys familiarity with local products and practices that allow him to comfortably play with them in creative modes that many in the region would probably perceive as excessive or iconoclastic. The roots of his inspiration go deeper than current folk traditions: the chef articulated to us the need to (re)construct the cuisine of the area, which before the war belonged to East Prussia and was part of the German cultural sphere (as in in the case of Żuławy area, whose gastronomy is reconstructed and reimagined by the above mentioned Wasilewski and Opitz). As such it shows specificities that may distinguish it from other Polish regions. In the absence of generational continuity, when it comes to cooking, Gręda mused, "It rather turns out that this memory is not in people, but in places. . . . In ponds and fish. And in the woods, right?" However, he does not turn to nature per se, but to how people have interacted with it to bring back products that had almost disappeared.

THE POLITICS OF THE LOCAL

These attempts at creating a sense of place are developing within an administrative framework that is not only determined at the national level but at the international. EU laws and regulations, ranging from food safety to quality standards, also shape food in Poland. The legal system now includes geographical indications, an EU scheme launched in 1992 and revised in 2006. Geographical Indications are a kind of intellectual property that protects the name of a product (and the quality it signals) by connecting it with specific places, geography, and climate, as well as the practices and traditions of local communities (Parasecoli 2017). Champagne, Prosciutto di Parma, and Feta are protected by this kind of mark, which includes two main categories: the Protected Designation of Origin (PDO) and the Protected Geographical Indication (PGI).

A PDO indicates that the qualities and other characteristics that make a product unique are essentially or exclusively connected to its place of origin; for that reason, the regulation requires that all stages of production and transformation must be carried out in the designated geographical area. A PGI is less strict; it allows the reputation and traditional fame associated with the place of origin of the product to play some role while at least one phase in the production and transformation process must be carried out in the area mentioned in the name. Besides PDOs and PGIs, the Traditional Specialty Guaranteed (TSG) label, a category added in 2006, does not refer to specific areas of origin, but protects traditional composition and production methods.

Because Poland is an EU member, its food producers have the opportunity to apply for these designations. At the time of writing, the country lists ten PDOs, twenty-nine PGIs, and ten TSGs. Although the Polish government, through the Ministry of Agriculture and Rural Development, has been trying to promote this form of intellectual property, so far the results have been modest, especially compared to other EU countries such as France, Italy, or Spain. The uptake of this practice is more in line with other Central and Eastern European countries, where it has achieved varying levels of success. In Latvia and Estonia, for instance, Geograpical Indications in the EU systems were at first perceived as a substitute for lacking national quality schemes (Bardone and Spalvēna 2019). Research has shown that fruit spirits from Central and Eastern Europe, despite being covered by a geographical indication, were not as competitive as Western European spirits (Török and Jámbor 2013). In Poland, the PDO mark covers famous products like the *oscypek,* a smoked sheep cheese from the Tatra mountains, and less famous ones like the *redykołka,* cheese from the southern region of Podhale, together with honeys, freshwater fish, cured meats, fruits, vegetables, breads, and sweets. PGIs include baked goods as *rogal świętomarciński* (a pastry from Poznań we will mention in the next chapter) and *cebularz lubelski,* a round flatbread with onions from the area of Lublin, which was among the first products to receive a geographical indication.

The owners of Piekarnia Zubrzycki, one of the bakeries that produces the *cebularz lubelski* and among the founders of the association that obtained the geographical indication, express a profound pride in having brought back a piece of local history. When we visited the bakery, the wife of the owner, Mariola, showed us the black robe and the insignia worn by the local baker association members. They are kept together with an old handwritten recipe notebook and a prewar baking manual as proof of the family's historical connection with *cebularz*. The tradition almost completely disappeared during the Nazi and Soviet occupations when the local Jewish community, which originated and manufactured the specialty, was annihilated. After the war, a handful of non-Jewish bakers, including the Zubrzyckis, continued to offer the *cebularz*, despite the socialist standardization and industrialization of baked goods production. This revival is now in its third generation. We heard similar stories about many of the products that have obtained PDOs and PGIs in Poland.

Not many of the almost forgotten specialties that have been brought back into production boast Geograpical Indications whose potential tends to be underutilized (Ciarko, Poszwa, and Caner Timur 2022). In our conversations, administrators and producers mentioned various reasons for the limited interest in this EU form of intellectual property, despite an emerging interest among consumers (Oleksiuk and Werenowska 2018). The administrative process is quite complex, lengthy, and expensive, especially compared to other available schemes: many farmers in Poland feel daunted by the process and display skepticism toward authorities at all levels. The bureaucratic inefficiency and the corruption that marked the socialist decades still fuels a certain distrust toward the government and public institutions, including labels and certification (Goszczyński et al. 2019). Moreover, many producers doubt that their goods will ever have to defend themselves from imitations on the international market, which is one of the main reasons for applying for a geographical indication. The notoriety and consumption of these specialties tend to remain local or regional at best, which appeals to tourists looking for the taste of the places they visit but not so invested in the value of Geographical Indications. Many operators also admit they are hesitant to collaborate, as each individual producer fears being taken advantage of by competitors or suspects that some will be reaping the benefits of the shared efforts without investing much.

Besides its participation in the EU scheme, the Ministry of Agriculture and Rural Development has established the list of traditional products (*lista produktów tradycyjnych*) that chef Robert Trzópek uses as the starting point for his regional menus. Managed by provinces, the list was inspired by similar initiatives in other EU countries. Products that are considered unique and interesting can be added to this list; while not providing any protection from the intellectual property point of view, it can function as a "kindergarten for the registration at the European level," as the head of the Quality Schemes and Programs Division in the Ministry, Magdalena Głodek, explained to us.

As this chapter has shown, culinary placemaking works at all levels, from the extremely local to the national. The sociocultural aspects of local practices and traditions may be used for the commercialization of specific products and considered as a potential tool for economic development, especially in rural contexts. Tastemakers frequently find themselves involved in these processes, at times initiating them, at times participating more or less enthusiastically, depending on how much they align with their priorities and goals. They seem overall supportive of attempts at placemaking, partly because of their own involvement in local food scenes, partly as a reflection of the growing interest in local food at the global level, which they embrace as members of transnational foodie communities. However, place is not the only aspect in the rediscovery and revelation of regional products: as we saw in this chapter, in some situations place cannot be separated from the dimension of time. In the next chapter we will show how tradition, history, and the past have emerged as central categories in redesigning the future of Polish food.

FIVE

Time

GLASS CASE AFTER GLASS CASE, the history of Polish vodka unfolds in front of us. It is almost information overload: so many amazing objects, in such limited space. Adam Łukawski, the co-owner, is proud of the collection he has been putting together for years with the collaboration of Piotr Popiński, the food impresario and founder of the cocktail bar Roots and the restaurant Elixir, which together boast a formidable collection of vodkas to be paired with creative interpretations of Polish classic recipes. The Muzeum Wódki (Vodka museum) is located right behind the restaurant, a short walk from the National Theater in Warsaw. It consists of a few small rooms on the ground floor with hundreds of artifacts that illustrate the development of vodka in Poland from the seventeenth century on. We admire crystal travel drinking sets, metal flasks, wooden transportation sets, and also a funny but disturbing bottle in the shape of a Prussian helmet, with the plug shaped as the characteristic metal spike. Łukawski's background is in printing, so there are plenty of printed objects, from promotional material to label sketches; these ephemera record the history of product and graphic design in the country.

The objects come from regions that during Poland's long history have been part of its ever-shifting territorial composition. Poland's borders have shifted following clashes between its efforts toward self-determination and decisions made by more powerful neighbors: the Prussian, Russian and Austro-Hungarian Habsburg empires first and the Soviet Union later (see chapter 1). The story of the I.A. Baczewski distillery, from which artifacts are to be found in the museum, is illustrative of such geopolitics. This distillery was founded in 1782 in the city of Lwów, at the time Lemberg in the Habsburg province of Galicia. Lemberg was incorporated into the newly formed Polish republic in 1923 after a bitter war between Poles and Ukrainians. Now it is known as Lviv, and is part of Ukraine.

The Baczewski brand is still very much alive, and it's possible to taste their products at the eponymous restaurant in Warsaw, now labeled and promoted as Ukrainian. While the names on the menu, the dishes, and the drinks showcase Western Ukrainian gastronomy, which is centered in Lviv, the flavors and techniques underscore its undeniable cultural and historical connections with Poland. The Muzeum Wódki collection, full of reminders of the complicated past of the country, also includes bottles from the Jakób Haberfeld distillery in the town of Oświęcim, near Kraków. Founded in 1804 by one of the most prominent local Jewish families, this distillery sat not far from where the Nazis would later establish the Auschwitz and Birkenau camps, in which numerous members of Poland's Jewish community lost their lives. Several bottles carry recognizable Jewish symbols, names, and inscriptions, at times in Hebrew script, indicating how before World War II the community was large enough to support its own businesses (see chapter 6).

A bottle from the Brenntwein firm (founded in 1598) comes to the museum from nineteenth-century Gdańsk, at the time part of the Prussian Empire. Gdańsk was later declared a Free City under the protection of the League of Nations after the 1919 Treaty of Versailles, but was invaded by Nazi troops in 1939, and finally assigned to Poland in 1945. The pieces in the glass cases in the collection, each embodying this intricate history, are too precious or fragile to be touched in any kind of interactive experience, but near the exit there is a space to taste and buy some contemporary vodkas. This is not surprising in a museum closely associated with a vodka-centered business. The degustation allows visitors to enjoy the product that they just learned about and engage with new categories of taste and appreciation for an everyday (and at times frowned upon) drink. The museum turns vodka into a valuable cultural expression.

That is also the case in the other vodka museum in Warsaw, the Muzeum Polskiej Wódki (Polish vodka museum), located in the former Koneser vodka distillation plant, a red-brick nineteenth-century neo-Gothic building that was recently refurbished into a business center. Although its location is directly connected with vodka history, this museum is closely tied to the contemporary spirit industry and is more commercially oriented. The institution is supported by the Stowarzyszenie Polska Wódka, the Polish Vodka Association, which in 2013 had "Polish Vodka" defined by law and included in the list of the Geographical Indications in the European Union framework, together with Żubrówka, the herbal vodka aromatized with an extract of bison grass, from the northeastern Podlasie lowland.[1] As a matter of fact, Polish vodka has been included among one hundred Geographical Indications that were granted special protection in an EU-China agreement signed in 2019 (Wight 2019).

The Muzeum Polskiej Wódki is very interactive, with high production value multimedia installations that explain the origins and evolution of vodka production in the country. The exhibits feel expensive. There are fewer historical artifacts than in the Muzeum Wódki: the primary goal is to educate consumers about vodka not only as it exists today but also in its aspirational future as a valuable Polish product with a respectable past. The expected audience is international; the installations are both in Polish and in English. At the end, visitors can explore the sensory complexity and variety of Polish vodkas in a gorgeous tasting room dominated by a metal bar counter with etchings of cereals on its side and striking lighting fixtures hanging above it. The interior conveys a sense of opulence, refinement, and worldliness that is clearly meant to raise the profile of the spirit.

The first museum focuses on the tangible elements of the vodka industry, presenting objects from the past as precursors to current customs. Their sheer number indicates the importance of vodka in Polish material culture and why it deserves attention and care. The second museum draws the visitor's attention to the history of technology, the ingredients, the skills involved in production, and the connection between contemporary brands and an evolution that began centuries ago during the Middle Ages and the Renaissance. Both museums exemplify the centrality of history in the revaluation of traditional products in Poland. Tastemakers, who in this case include food and spirit entrepreneurs, collectors, category associations, professional tasters, interior designers, and museum curators, have assembled materials, narratives, and experiences that they tie to the past to emphasize the prestige of the spirit sector in the present and to support its growth in the future. Raising the profile of the industry is essential to expand sales, especially when it comes to more affluent consumers.

The two vodka museums in Warsaw are not the only food- and drink-themed institutions designed to display the past. In fact, museums have become increasingly important in the processes of revaluation of local, traditional, and artisanal foods. They also favor the circulation of narratives and practices that the public can experience through physical objects, spaces, and virtual information. For example, in a section of the palace grounds of the

TIME · 111

Museum of King Jan III's Palace at Wilanów, Warsaw, chef Maciej Nowicki used to lead culinary events for children and adults in a herb garden that features archaeophyte plants, such as elecampane (Inula helenium) or skirret (Sium sisarum), used in long-ago Polish kitchens.[2] The past is not only remembered, but it is materially brought back through the design of raised beds, the use of gardening tools, and the sensory experience of smells and flavors. Under the guidance of Grzegorz Mazur, head of the Historical Reconstruction Department, the museum uses the Villa Intrata, a gorgeous interwar building on its grounds, for events such as culinary conferences and cooking classes, many of which include a walk through the garden. The institution also collaborates with historian Jarosław Dumanowski, frequently mentioned in this book, to publish critical editions of historical Polish cookbooks.

At the Muzeum Okręgowe (District museum) in Bydgoszcz, curator Anna Kornelia Jędrzejewska highlights food-related artifacts while organizing special activities and lectures on eating and drinking in the past. She also arranges events at the nearby eighteenth-century Ostromecko palace and on the Lemara Barge on the Brda river, a reminder of the city's past as an important node in the distribution of food commodities. Ukrainian scholar Ihor Lylo worked at the Łańcut Palace near the city of Rzeszów in southeastern Poland, not far from the Ukrainian border, to explore culinary artifacts and documents that until the Soviet invasion belonged to the powerful Potocki family. While until recently food was treated as a "low" and "light" topic, academic historians and curators now have fewer qualms about food history projects, confirming the shift in the perception of the role and value of material culture among the Polish intelligentsia (as illustrated in chapter 3).

In some cases, museums have sections in which visitors can manipulate, taste, or otherwise interact with materials presented as faithful derivations or reproductions of the past. The Żywe Muzeum Piernika (Living museum of piernik) and Muzeum Toruńskiego Piernika (Museum of the Toruń piernik) in Toruń, both dedicated to *piernik* (gingerbread), as well as the Rogalowe Muzeum Poznania (Museum of the *rogal świętomarciński* of Saint Martin, a kind of croissant with a white poppy seed filling) in Poznań, all include interactive hands-on experiences that involve children and adults in kneading dough, baking, and tasting. The Muzeum Oscypka (Museum of Oscypek cheese) in Zakopane invites tourists not only to watch how the famed highland cheese is made, but also to make the cheese themselves. These recreational activities contribute to the diffusion and strengthening of stories and legends that reinforce the cultural appreciation of the foods whose origins they explain. Such museums are either close to places of production and consumption or occupy former manufacturing plants. The physical proximity erases the distance in time, connecting current built environments, machinery, and souvenir stores to the history of the products.

Sensory engagement appears central to these experiences. The museums are not archaeological enterprises trying to dig out buried artifacts or to celebrate customs long gone; they are reenactments, less concerned with accurately recreating history as it was than with validating present-day experiences by connecting them with their roots. In doing so, they contribute to the construction of shared cultural memory, a selective form of public knowledge that is produced by groups or institutions through their framing of the past (Tarkowska 2013) and contributes to shaping contemporary perspectives and narratives.

The entanglement of places and historical narratives with materials and their sensory aspects is a recurrent strategy in the tastemakers' efforts to redesign the Polish culinary landscape. In the previous chapter we examined how place, articulated through ideas of nationality, locality, terroir, and nature, has become an important component in the current revaluation and legitimization of food. However, we saw how these approaches may have the side effect of taking food out of history, turning it into a timeless expression of an unchanging, almost eternal and essential Polish spirit. In this chapter we turn to the current dynamics in the Polish food scene that operate in the registers of time. In them, actors with different takes on the present and diverging visions of the future, constantly find themselves negotiating evaluations of historical eras.

For example, tastemakers such as chefs, media professionals, and event organizers may display forms of selective nostalgia that leads to great appreciation of the early modern Polish-Lithuanian Commonwealth or the interwar years of independent Poland between 1919 and 1939. Although actors in the culinary field frequently imagine and represent these periods as rich with culinary splendor, in reality in those years most Poles—with the exception of the upper classes—were plagued by hunger and malnourishment. Other periods, especially socialism, are instead remembered as disasters that constituted a break with a valuable past, causing the erasure of landscapes, objects, and customs that tastemakers consider irrelevant to their revaluation of the Polish culinary world.

Since Polish society and statehood underwent huge transformations during the nineteenth and twentieth centuries, different understandings of historical periods coexist, at times competing with each other (Kwiatkowski

2008; Szpociński 2004). The past turns into a resource to retell history, invent tradition, and define heritage across a political spectrum that spans from progressive aspirations toward openness, inclusion, and multiculturality, to the more conservative categories of canon, nationalistic pride, and even clash of civilizations. Contrasting assessments of history provide the building blocks for diverging interpretations about what the nation was, is, or should (not) be and what sort of transformation it should undergo to achieve the preferred future (Anioł 2015; Kalb 2009; Nowicka-Franczak 2018). The identification and the definitions of Polishness and tradition in the realm of food have broader implications that reflect and indirectly contribute to controversies ranging from the educational mission of museums, the role of art and media, and the centrality of religion and traditional family values in the national identity. The interpretation of history has turned into a crucial arena of political negotiations about the identity and destiny of Poland.

In this chapter we will assess how discourse and practices referring to time contribute to current tastemakers' revaluation of traditional, regional, and artisanal food in Poland. We examine tastemakers' approaches to tradition and its representations in food-related communication and media, from TV shows to food magazines. Our analysis suggests that tastemakers' approaches are far from prevalent: they inevitably interact with a variety of perspectives that reflect diverging priorities and values. We also analyze discourse and practices observed in expert panels and focus groups, which provide a partial representation of the diversity within the Polish culinary landscape.

SAVORING TIME THROUGH TRADITION

Tradition is commonly identified with specific ingredients, dishes, and customs whose origin is in the past, purportedly handed down from generation to generation. Tradition also includes social processes, such the identification and transmission of valuable elements from former times, as well as the current cultural formations that such activities produce (M. Polányi 1962). Little attention is usually paid to these acts of selection, negotiation, and interpretation that determine what constitutes tradition and what does not, linking the past with the concerns and priorities of the present, as well as with visions for a preferred future.

Inevitably, despite the constant reference to tradition and its centrality in their redesign of Polish cuisine, tastemakers display vastly different approaches to assessing, practicing, and transforming it into tangible products and sensory experiences. The preparation of pierogi in three restaurants and a (now closed) shopping center booth from the same area in northern Poland offers a clear example of such a variety of perspectives. Cooking techniques, design, discourse, and hospitality practices all contribute to create different experiences of tradition.

Restauracja Ostromecko, located right outside the large industrial city of Bydgoszcz, may appear to be an unassuming roadside eatery. Close to two gorgeous historical palaces and a well-known mineral water spring, the building belonged to a local socialist association. When its current owner, Waldemar Klorek, bought it, he had to embark on extensive repairs to turn it into a restaurant. Its current interior decor is inspired by Bydgoszcz's past, with oversized fin-de-siecle sepia photographs and beautiful early nineteenth-century bourgeois furniture. Klorek's menu focuses on goose, a local specialty that has recently acquired more countrywide visibility in connection with the St. Martin celebrations. Interestingly, this holiday, which falls on November 11, is also National Independence Day. Poland is one of the largest producers of goose in the world; therefore it also makes economic sense to highlight culinary traditions connected to the fowl industry, which is flourishing in the north of the country.

At Restauracja Ostromecko, smoked goose breast, goose roulade, ground goose fat with onion and herbs, as well as goose-filled pierogi, are presented matter-of-factly, without embellishments or aestheticized plating, just the way people would serve them at home. This apparently informal aesthetic is meant to suggest that the restaurant upholds local domestic traditions. The connection with the community is also reinforced through the choice of purveyors. Klorek knows them personally: they are mostly neighbors, and many of them follow organic regulations. However, the affordable prices at the restaurant sometimes make visitors from the city suspicious, as they are used to much higher bills in establishments that advertise organic food. At Restauracja Ostromecko, pierogi reinforce customers' growing recognition of goose as a local traditional product that has been around for a long time; it is their filling that acquires symbolic relevance, as it is not particularly common around the country.

Forty kilometers east of Gdańsk, the restaurant Gospoda Mały Holender engages with tradition on different terms. While Restauracja Ostromecko builds on dishes that are still prepared in the region, Gospoda Mały Holender (literally "the little Dutchman inn," in reference to the Dutch Mennonite population that settled in the area between the fifteenth and the eighteenth centuries) explores a tradition that needs to be reconstructed from scratch, at times assembled from sparse surviving material and discursive elements. Its sources are communities with centuries of history that no longer exist. The post-migration area of Żuławy, where the restaurant is located, is constantly searching for its own identity (Paprot-Wielopolska 2018) as it was completely repopulated after World War II. The original dwellers of German descent were replaced by ethnic Poles coming from the eastern territories that had been assigned to Lithuania, Belarus, and Ukraine; by Ukrainians; and by inhabitants of the nearby Kaszuby and Kociewie areas. This demographic reshuffling, followed by forty years of socialist regime, erased local customs almost completely and introduced new ones. Emblematically, the eighteenth-century Mennonite wooden farmhouse that hosts the Gospoda Mały Holender inn was transported to the present location after owner Marek Opitz—whom we mentioned in the previous chapter—bought it elsewhere. Opitz at first used the structure to bring back material culture from the local past: among other activities, he organized cheesemaking workshops, building on the few remnants of local traditional practices.

Overtime, however, Opitz became interested in the long-gone culinary culture of the place, and his restaurant began incorporating products and dishes that had basically disappeared. He seems to understand tradition as cultural and physical remains of subsequent groups of inhabitants, gathered and creatively assembled in the present. His mission of historical reconstruction is now continued by his son Jacek, a chef, who offers a streamlined but well-curated menu featuring local specialties such as crayfish soup and *babka ziemniaczana* (baked potato casserole) coming from the eastern regions, together with some adaptations and new creations. The menu included three kinds of pierogi: the classic cheese and onion (*ruskie*) were "made with the twaróg from the dairy in [nearby] Nowy Dwór Gdański." There were also fava and pea pierogi, about which the chefs wrote in the menu: "We use the seasonal availability of fresh fava beans; we have mixed them with the sweetness of young sweet peas." The third pierogi, filled with meat, were—according to the dish description—"inspired by the now no longer existing Szkarpawianka restaurant in Drewnica, which was a cult place among the river sailors traversing the water trails of Żuławy."

While the first two kinds of dumplings activate locality and seasonality, exhibiting strategies employed by many farm-to-fork establishments or Slow Food eateries, the latter explicitly connects the dish with the local past, in this case sailors' traditions. This ethnographic, almost archaeological engagement with tradition has often proved successful in Poland, including from a commercial point of view, as the revival of Jewish eateries in Kraków (chapter 6) and the reconstruction of Tatar culinary customs in the East suggest as well. However, the interpretations offered by chefs and producers can diverge significantly from historical realities, showing that the relevance and the emotional appeal of tradition is rather based on current meanings and practices.

Just a few kilometers northwest of Gdańsk, in the charming coastal resort town of Sopot, celebrity chef Artur Moroz had been working in the restaurant Bulaj since 2004.[3] Previously a fried fish dive of questionable quality, under his tenure the restaurant became one of the most interesting establishments in the so-called Tricity (Trójmiasto) of Gdańsk, Sopot, and Gdynia. Moroz, who has a background in food science and often collaborates with the food industry, is an ambassador of Polish cuisine abroad. He is often sent by the regional and the national government to represent the country in international exhibitions or to cook for diplomatic events. He is proud of Polish cuisine, and he is used to presenting it in its most demonstrative and didactic forms around the world. He is secure in his skills and creativity. In his restaurant, tradition was embraced and celebrated but also expanded, stretched, and experimented with. In our conversation chef Moroz lamented the fact that many young chefs who are striving to elevate Polish cuisine "have started running before learning how to walk."

At his restaurant, we tasted four different kinds of pierogi, all made on the premises: black dough with cuttlefish ink, filled with cod; sweet Kamchatka honeysuckle (*jagoda kamczacka*); wild game; and *ruskie*, with the addition of smoked pork belly (*boczek*) and sunflower and pumpkin seeds on top, instead of onions. In spite of being made with common ingredients, the combinations were original and intriguing. Moroz was proud of the texture of the dough: white, thanks to the flour he uses, and not grayish, as in many other versions; not too thin, resistant to the bite, but still very tender. For his pierogi, both classic and creative, he explained that his inspiration was the texture and thickness of the dough his grandmother used to make. "It does not need to be too thin, it was a poor dish," he stated. He achieves that same mouthfeel not only through kneading skills but also through exhaustive research on flour and milling technology.

On the menu, a traditional but perfectly executed version of *żurek* (fermented rye soup) was featured next to a seafood soup where lemongrass and lime brighten the flavors; a classic venison pâté was served side by side with a stunning beef tartare with seaweed and horseradish sauce. As in other countries with very strong historical traditions and a well-developed restaurant culture, such as France, Italy, Japan, or Mexico, creative chefs like Moroz experience the constant tension between the respect for established customs on the one hand, and their desire for innovation and experimentation on the other. For many of them, if tradition is to be kept alive, it cannot be treated as a fragile, untouchable museum piece.

Although their relationships to tradition are quite different, the tastemakers in these three restaurants all buttress the sensory experiences they offer to customers with connections to past practices, the decor and the built environments, as well as the narrative that chefs and entrepreneurs share with their clients. Their designerly attitudes are quite clear: Restauracja Ostromecko repurposed a building that had nothing to do with food, the owner of Gospoda Mały Holender physically brought a historical construction to the current location, and Moroz took over an existing, though modest, eatery in a popular seaside location, exploring both local and personal traditions to present his interpretation of Polish food. The three entrepreneurs reassembled elements of the past into something new that has to be constantly tested, tweaked, and made accessible in order to achieve success.

Unlike Klorek, Opitz, and Moroz, not all tastemakers have the means to build and open restaurants. Chef Anna Szkaradzińska, a former contestant on the Polish edition of the TV show *Hell's Kitchen*, opened Miastowa (now closed), little more than a food stall in the food court of the Metropolia mall, located in Gdańsk's hip Wrzeszcz neighborhood. The context in which she worked did not scream tradition; the mall was built recently and most of her patrons were relatively young people more interested in a quick bite selected from various "world cuisines" offered throughout the food hall than in enjoying the nuances of her Polish cuisine. Yet she too was working with and commenting on tradition. The sign in front of her stall read "Polski [Polish] street food," partly to describe the eatery, and partly to link its offerings to the international boom in street food, which is newly seen as trendy and exciting.

Szkaradzińska's pierogi were sophisticated and daring in their attempt to shake solid traditions. Her meat pierogi, for instance, came with confit cherry tomatoes, grilled eggplant, and onion rings; pierogi *ruskie* had crayfish instead of bacon. On the menu one could also find pierogi filled with blood sausage, and vegetarian pierogi seasoned with miso. The chef explained that she centered her work on pierogi because they are items that are easily understood by anybody; however, she soon realized she had to explain how her versions were different from what the average client might expect. She even posted large pictures of the dishes in the stall to avoid misunderstandings. Although she did not explicitly claim to be inspired by history or to interpret it, her intention was to add her own personal touch to a common traditional dish. This strategy was not surprising in a former culinary reality show contestant, as she tried to leverage the brand she had built through her TV appearances, decorating her stall with photos and wearing her chef uniform from the show.

TASTEMAKERS' INTERPRETATIONS OF THE PAST

Such a variety of approaches points to the complexity of the tastemakers' relationship with the past and the role it plays in their attempts to redesign Polish cuisine. They find themselves in constant negotiation with current trends and collective memory processes taking place among actors who do not command the same levels of power and access to varied forms of social, financial, and culinary capital within the culinary field. Tradition—or what tradition is thought to be—is not evoked randomly; it is rather appreciated or criticized and included in or excluded from culinary lifestyle projects that consumers constantly put to the test. To get a better sense of tastemakers' take on tradition, we organized five expert panels between March and July 2018 in the cities of Warsaw, Poznań, and Kraków. Experts included chefs, entrepreneurs, producers, journalists, scholars, and activists with whom we later kept in touch through interviews or participation in events.

Although the contexts in which they operate are quite different, a few themes and perspectives recurred, showing how the food professionals' and tastemakers' discourse is relatively uniform across the country. The participants continued to interweave the concept of tradition with Polishness, as though the two were one and the same: for them, the present of their country is deeply rooted in its past—or at least in specific historical moments. In Kraków some participants suggested that Poland may have an advantage when it comes to rediscovering traditions, when compared to countries like the United States, because in Poland the industrialization and massification of the food system connected with the capitalist system and supermarkets started relatively late. "It is easier for us to go back, but we have lost quite a bit in between. . . . We have a living population that remembers things, that has the knowledge, even though the young generation prefers to learn from the internet."

The panels' participants tended to reflect on tradition by discussing specific dishes and practices, rather than the cultural or social dynamics that established them as traditional. Specialties like *powidła* (a spread made by slowly cooking down plums without sugar or additives), smoked fish and meat, *miód pitny* (mead), *nalewki* (spirits made by steeping fruits and herbs in sugar and alcohol), and vodka were mentioned as both traditional and symbolic of what defines Polish food, together with everyday items such as barley and *kasza gryczana* (buckwheat groats). The presence of similar practices and dishes in neighboring countries surfaced only in the Poznań panel, in which the participants brought up the similarity between Polish *pierogi ruskie* and Ukrainian *varenyky* (to which at times they referred with the word *pelmeni*, a Russian term referring to a slightly different dish), as well as *kulebiak*, a pastry shell usually filled with mushroom and cabbage. *Kulebiak* can also be found with similar names and various fillings such as salmon or sturgeon, rice or buckwheat, hard-boiled eggs, mushrooms, onions, and dill, in Russia, Lithuania, Belarus, Ukraine, and even France, where it appeared under the name of *coulibiac* in the nineteenth century.

Most participants deprecated the lack of pride in culinary traditions among their fellow citizens; they only mentioned holidays as an exception, when most Poles cook a well-defined set of well-established dishes with customary ingredients. Easter (*Wielkanoc*) and above all the Christmas Eve (*Wigilia*) meals came up as occasions in which culinary traditions were on display, although admittedly performed in different ways in domestic settings and in restaurants. The experts felt that their own engagement with tradition was qualitatively different from the majority of the population, who were at times described as uninterested in good food. No specific definition of who these other people were was offered and the possible reasons for such differences in approaches were not tackled either. This perception among tastemakers is quite intriguing because both our fieldwork and the existing research (Domański et al. 2015) suggest quite the opposite: Polish food (however that may be defined) was popular and appreciated, in spite of what cosmopolitan chefs, producers, and consumers constantly repeated to us, although in forms the experts may consider unrefined or bastardized.

Panel participants in the three cities expressed excitement about the growing success of fine dining restaurants that emphasize Polish cuisine, with young chefs often proffering their own updated interpretations of traditional dishes. Although these changes were perceived as nascent ("*in statu nascendi*," as one of the experts stated in Latin), they were evaluated as positive and as part of a trend visible in other European countries. However, this inward-looking aspect of cosmopolitanism was never described as purely imitative. Some experts underlined the impact of a growing presence of foreign tourists who are curious to taste Polish specialties beyond "the first wave that started in the nineties with *Chłopskie jadło*, *Polskie jadło* village food, and fake *karczmy*," a reference to low-brow establishments and nationwide chains that offer homey but plain, lowest-common-denominator versions of Polish cuisine at accessible prices and in abundant portions, which are quite successful among consumers outside foodie circles.

Experts were wary of mass-produced goods that commodify tradition by exploiting nostalgia; they seemed to consider them low-quality marketing gimmicks that can distort consumers' perceptions and expectations about "true" Polish traditions. The misuse of tradition by the food industry was examined in one of the Warsaw panels through the example of *kiełbasa lisiecka*, a particular artisanal sausage that cannot be produced on a large scale and yet can easily be found in supermarket chains. According to some panel participants, part of the reason for this dilution of tradition is that although local producers are trying to make genuine products, they are hindered by laws and regulations, requirements from distributors, and customers' preferences, "so they have to find ways to cheat and fake it." Our experts connected the origins of this habit to the socialist years. According to the prevalent narrative, with which participants in all the expert panels seemed to agree, the socialist government got rid of traditional foods; many were taken out of production because they were not financially sustainable, were too slow to manufacture, or used resources inefficiently.

Overall, the intergenerational transmission of knowledge and skills outside of professional fields was not central to the experts' reflections except to condemn the impact of the socialist decades and the Soviet influence, to which we will return later in this chapter. The panel participants also bemoaned the lack of coordination among food producers and other food professionals in identifying, safeguarding, and reproducing traditional food, suggesting that tastemakers perceive tradition as something that may be or should be subject to intentional interventions. At the same time, some experts pointed out that farmers respond to the preferences and demands of their clients, especially the high-paying ones in large cities, and are open to collaborating with activists and other urban actors to bring back interesting crop varieties if they can charge premium prices. Tastemakers' engagement with the past and history through the dimension of tradition seems to be shaped both by the desire of bolstering up ingredients, dishes, and practices for their intrinsic cultural and social value, and by the realities of markets and marketing.

TRADITION IN CONSUMERS' CULTURE

Tastemakers' practices and discourse do not happen in a void, but are constantly interacting with other approaches to tradition, as we saw in the four consumer focus groups. Several participants did not frame tradition in terms of large cultural sedimentation over time or history, as may happen in cosmopolitan discourses and practices, but rather mentioned it in relation to the intergenerational transmission of culinary knowledge and skills within the family, above all among women. Mothers and grandmothers (*babcie*) remain important reference points, both as reliable sources ("when I need something about the old stuff, I call my mother") and targets of competitive jabs ("traditional Polish cuisine is my forte, so of course on the weekend there has to be a classic *rosół* [soup], which is already better than my mother's"). Similarly to what we heard from tastemakers, as discussed in chapter 3, focus group participants brought up childhood flavors with affectionate tones: "Mom is from Warsaw. Basically, I had quite healthy cooking at home and I remember that when I was little, there were all kinds of stewed and baked things, veal, mutton." They also, at times nostalgically, valued the ability to cook "by eye," that is without measurements.

Learning from older women played a central role in the development of many participants' cooking abilities: "I was watching my mother cooking. Because for me it is family above all. This is a family that ... some are there and some are gone, yes. Grannies, aunts and so on. So they just cooked something different every day. They were cooking and eating freaks. So I come from such a family." "It's more when you live with your family. . . . Well, when someone participates in this family life, you also participate in what is happening in the kitchen, yes."

Learning, however, was not always described as a pleasurable interpersonal experience: "No one taught me, because my mother did not have time, it was just 'get out of the kitchen because I have to do it quickly'. . . . I watched Grandma, so I was an observer." Like the tastemakers, focus groups participants highlighted the joys and troubles of the intergenerational transmission of culinary knowledge. These same dynamics are apparent in the documentary *Food: Generations* that cultural operator Monika Kucia (2021) created for the Kultur Symposium Weimar 2021. The film looks at pierogi-making in five families in different places of Poland with diverse socioeconomic and educational backgrounds. For instance, we see an interracial family, a young man with painted fingernails who plays the accordion, and a young woman with her hair dyed green and a nose ring. Definitely not the default uniform Poland to which many of our interlocutors seemed to refer. Yet, grandmothers and grandchildren are together in their kitchens, around the table, cooking.

Cookbooks, both contemporary ones and family heirlooms, were often mentioned in interviews with consumers and in the focus groups as sources of knowledge. Even the cookbooks from the 1980s were remembered with affection as presenting simple recipes that were communicated "with passion." However, for our focus groups participants, cookbooks do not satisfy every need: "Cookbooks, to be honest, for me they are quite a limitation. . . . I prefer the internet because the internet is wide. Unclosed, open." The internet is not necessarily seen in contrast with tradition: "I slowly start reaching to the internet. Because most of the dishes are . . . as if I was brought up on traditional cuisine." Nevertheless, it provides more freedom and opportunities for agency and creativity: "I practically do not cook what my mother does, but from the internet, from Google. I even enter recipes."

The focus group participants from urban milieus, especially those who had not been born in cities, often made reference to foods that for them had some connections with the countryside, such as stuffed duck and duckling ("the duck is the Polish turkey"). They also mentioned everyday foods like fermented cucumber soup (*zupa ogórkowa*), yeast cake with plums (*drożdżowy placek ze śliwkami*), fruit *kompot* (beverages made from boiling fresh or dried fruits in water), buckwheat groats (*kasza gryczana*), cabbage soup (*kapuśniak*), pancakes (*naleśniki*), and potato latkes (*placki ziemniaczane*). Just like tastemakers in the expert panels, the focus groups participants could not separate the idea and practice of tradition from specific dishes originating from the countryside, which they implicitly framed as the place where the past is still alive. Although we may assume they are fully aware of modernization and ongoing changes, rural Poland is perceived—cognitively and emotionally—as frozen in time.

Pierogi were mentioned, either as a family dish or as something that could be offered to foreign guests, together with *bigos* (a hunter's stew both fermented and shredded fresh cabbage with chopped meats), *krokiety* (crepes filled with ground meat and cabbage or mushrooms, breaded and fried), or meat-stuffed cabbage rolls (*gołąbki*). While such dishes were considered important in the performance of Polishness for outsiders, cooking them for Polish friends would be too obvious. Some participants voiced their desire to impress friends with creative dishes or at least with variations on the classics, mostly with the addition of spices and non-Polish flavors including Provençal herbs, oregano, basil, hot chili peppers, and truffle oil. Innovations were presented as welcome aspects of the globalized or at least more international present, better than rote repetitions of an exclusively Polish past. At any rate, the focus group participants could not exactly explain why they felt that certain dishes were traditionally Polish. Among the possible reasons, they mentioned Polish ingredients, cooking methods, and pervasiveness in Polish homes.

Connections with specific geographical areas and their communities also emerged, especially in the case of well-known dishes that nevertheless are not regularly consumed all over the country: these included *czernina* (duck or goose blood soup), *kluski śląskie* (Silesian potato dumplings), *babka ziemniaczana* (savory potato casserole), and *kiszka kartoflana* (pork intestine filled with potatoes with pork or bacon). These were particularly important for individuals who, having grown up outside of Warsaw, were also able to discuss the differences between the products they find in the capital and those from their places of origin. The historical roots of the traditional dishes the focus group participants experienced as quintessentially Polish were not explicitly mentioned, as though the past they learned of in school had little to do with their family stories and their current habits. Tradition seems to emerge from personal experiences rather than from historical events.

SAMPLING THE PAST THROUGH MEDIA

Such a wide range of perceptions and practices is reflected in Polish food media, which display varied—at times clashing—approaches to understanding the Polish culinary past, both in terms of a national cuisine and its regional manifestations (Bachórz and Parasecoli 2023). In some cases Polish tradition is treated as self-evident and familiar; in others as in need of rediscovery and redefinition. Food media representations, of course, cannot be taken at face value as an accurate reflection of shifts in food consumption.

They are rather the expression of ideals and aspirational visions that occasionally interact with and influence audiences' evaluations of the past and tradition. They can also be understood as contributing to collective memory-making processes.

In Polish media we see two main approaches, which are not necessarily directed at different audiences and occasionally overlap. The media that are explicitly connected with the circulation of tastemakers' cosmopolitanism and introduce novel notions and values can be described as "foodie." We especially recognized this perspective in magazines such as *Kuchnia* (subtitled *Magazyn dla smakoszy*, "magazine for gourmets," published since 1995 and currently online only, geared toward high-income urban women), *Usta* (taking a very cultural approach to food, published since 2014), *Kukbuk* (also intended for a sophisticated audience, published since 2012), *Moje gotowanie* (with a twenty-year history, heavily focused on recipes) and *Food & Friends* (lifestyle approach, published since 2010), as well as in TV shows including *Jakubiak w sezonie* and *Jakubiak lokalnie* (which premiered respectively in 2011 and 2013), as well as numerous shows by Robert Makłowicz, one of the first food celebrities to make a name for themselves after 1989.[4] The foodie approach addresses people who link their interest in food to leisure, eating out, and traveling (both in Poland and abroad), presented as highly knowledge-intensive activities. It promotes diversity and a certain aestheticization of food that is often linked to global trends and international circuits of expertise. This perspective is also visible in many cookbooks and food-related books (memoirs, historical reconstructions, and gastronomy essays) that are targeting a foodie readership interested in cultural and social issues.

Other media tend instead to stick to existing, but largely implicit, forms of culinary capital that feel both familiar and natural to audiences. Such media are not immune to the integration of foreign and new elements, but do not explicitly celebrate them as cosmopolitan and multicultural forms of distinction, or as something with the potential to make Polish food better and more worthy of attention. We define this second approach as "pragmatic." It is partly visible in TV shows like *Polska na patelni* (Poland in the pan), with six episodes broadcast in 2019 and focused on "typical" foods, and to a greater extent in magazines like the very popular monthly *Przyślij przepis* (Submit a recipe), which since 2007 has published recipes from readers, and in the food column in the biweekly *Przyjaciółka* (Woman friend), published since 1948 and still the most popular women's advice publication in Poland. Although the differences between the foodie and pragmatic approaches had already emerged in the early 2000s, they became more visible as the culinary field evolved, grew, and became more varied.[5]

The pragmatic approach mostly focuses on forms of cooking that hinge on the idea of "feeding the family" and eating at home. The recipes' rhetoric assumes that readers evaluate them according to the priorities imposed by "family taste" and the preferences of family members rather than following external sources of authority and legitimacy like experts, reviewers, or foreign reference points.

Both the foodie and pragmatic media approaches single out certain elements of the past as important and worth remembering, while condemning others to amnesia. They interact with recurrent trajectories of collective recollection and oblivion that evaluate particular historical periods as good for food production and culinary culture, and others as negative. Through this process they legitimize and attribute cultural value and economic worth to certain food products, manufacturing methods, dishes, and practices. Such strategies also contribute to reinforce different narratives about Poland as a nation and as a community.

In general, pragmatic material tends to embrace a strongly ahistorical approach while finding the foundations of tradition in individual or family-based experiences. In the *Przyjaciółka* food column or in the *Przyślij przepis* recipes, we found very few mentions of the regional or national past, at least in the way official institutions and established experts discuss it; the exceptions were nostalgic personal memories coinciding with the socialist period, which as a result is not completely erased. Elaborated narratives about the roots of culinary techniques, products, and tastes are almost absent. Similarly to what we heard in the focus groups conversations with consumers, in the pragmatic type of media private and intrafamily habits are the most legitimate mechanism for framing past foodways.

Foodie approaches, instead, willingly engage with the collective past and the negotiations that surround its elaboration, and they do it through established forms of expertise based on education and research. In this content, both Polish and foreign history are much more visible. The search for the origins of methods and styles of food production is addressed to readers that are interested in food not only as nourishment and pleasure, but also as competence and knowledge. In general, in foodie material the historical background provides the context to better understand food as an important manifestation of Polish culture (at which more traditional intellectuals still bristle). Tangible traces of the past serve to stylize food as an aesthetic object.

For example, in a 2014 *Kuchnia* article on *faworki*, the traditional deep fried pastries eaten during Carnival, a photograph of a stained page from an old cookbook is used to illustrate the text (Kolondra 2014). Similarly, an article on Easter pastries presents the picture of an old cookbook in the background (Bartelak and Kolondra 2013).

In *Kuchnia*, there is also a regular column explicitly dedicated to food history, in which authors such as food historian Jarosław Dumanowski explore the origins and development of dishes and products. An article by Dumanowski (2013) discussing the Polish tradition of fasting in specific periods of the Catholic calendar was accompanied by recipes based on "old Polish" (*staropolskie*) cookbooks and elaborated by chef Maciej Nowicki, who was in charge of public programming at the Museum of King Jan III's Palace in Wilanów, Warsaw.[6] In *Kuchnia* the past becomes historical knowledge about food that goes beyond the family memories tinted with nostalgia found in more pragmatic editorial content. Such a history-inflected approach contributes to establishing and legitimizing authenticity, interpreted as adherence to an original model that is verifiable by knowledgeable and authoritative experts and experienced as accurate (Selwyn 1996). Such understanding of authenticity and its mechanisms of reproduction are solidly inscribed in the foodie cosmopolitan worldview (Parasecoli 2016).

In an effort to revive these collective memories, foodie media tells the stories of specific people and institutions engaged in reconstructing history-based food products and practices (Grasseni 2017). The figure of "the last person who knows" (or, frequently, who makes), often mentioned in relation to almost forgotten dishes and recipes, is central to these narratives. For example, a *Kuchnia* article in the *Smakowita historia* (Tasty History) section describes the forgotten traditions of the northeastern Kurpie region that are rediscovered and preserved by local enthusiasts (Krzyżanowski 2012). An article published in *Kuchnia*'s *Gwarancja smaku* (Guarantee of taste) section about the traditional *sękacz*—a type of layered cake from the Suwałki region in the northeast—declares that "a real *sękacz* is slowly cooked over an open fire. Krystyna Mosiewicz from Berzniki is one of the last housewives in the Suwałki region to make it using this method" (Nazaruk 2014). What we can observe here is how the media provides legitimation to these saviors of allegedly forgotten traditions: journalists or narrators with the required expertise and culinary capital have to "discover" them to confirm their value. Again, it is not only the practice itself which is important: selecting, naming, and announcing it as newly restored from the past are equally relevant strategies.

This approach also invites readers to reconsider the two centuries in which Poland did not exist as a country but was divided between the Russian, Prussian, and Austro-Hungarian empires. In particular, Makłowicz often refers to the latter two as an antidote to the socialist "destruction" of food culture. Poland's partition and the period before World War II, when the western areas of today's Poland were part of Germany, serve as sources of historical narratives that bridge Polish cuisine with its Western and European roots, rather than with its Eastern heritage. This perspective is also present in Makłowicz's discussions about wine production in former German territories (Food Network 2018b), which touch on the broader, ever-thorny issue of German heritage in Polish culture. Sociologist Tomasz Zarycki (2012, 2014) identifies differences in contemporary Polish memory between Western and Eastern influences: while the Prussian or Austro-Hungarian impact is linked to the idea of civilization, Russian and Soviet dominations are almost always unambiguously associated with stagnation or backwardness. This contrast has become even more central in public debates about Poland's identity after the Russian invasion of Ukraine in February 2022, which has rekindled deep-seated fears. Such a selection of particular narratives and material fragments from former times contributes to Westernization in today's Poland, turning the past into a resource to be leveraged in constructing the future.

THE FLAVORS OF SOCIALISM

History, understood as a shared narrative about the past, generates a variety of evaluations not only because it can be used for different purposes but also because its elaboration involves diverse actors with diverging priorities and values. When referring to periods of the past for which ambivalent interpretations exist, private memories and nostalgia are intertwined with established narratives that become part of broader negotiations and debates about collective identity. This ambivalence is particularly glaring in reference to the years of the socialist Poland's People Republic or PRL.

If mentioned at all in pragmatic media material such as the *Przyjaciółka* food column or the *Przyślij przepis* recipes, the socialist period is framed by nostalgia: "Oatmeal balls: Grandma made them in the '80s when there were no sweets in the stores" (Olewicz 2013). Given the significant role of family memories, as revealed by our focus groups, that is not surprising. Also, as we saw in chapter 3, several older tastemakers attribute a formative function to their youth experiences during socialism, which allowed them to acquire culinary skills and know-how about food. The taste of the PRL is associated with positive sensory memories from childhood that are presented as personal, although widely shared, experiences, rather than discussed and problematized in their broader historical significance.

In some of the foodie magazines and TV shows, the role of the PRL is more central, although unresolved. On the one hand, memories from the socialist period may be the only ones within reach, often colored with childhood longings. On the other hand, nostalgia for PRL products connects individual sensory and affective recollections from one's past with collective history, but the process is not necessarily smooth. When personal experiences are examined through the more abstract lens of national events, the PRL is mostly perceived as a destroyer of culinary traditions, knowledge, and etiquette.

For example, the current lack of fish in the typical Polish diet can be attributed to its overuse as a substitute for meat: "Back then [i.e., under socialism] there was more fish, it was cheaper. But we underestimated it. We used to say: 'eat cod, shit is worse'. . . . Luckily, people are getting acquainted with fish again" (Nazaruk 2013). As historian Jarosław Dumanowski told us, the PRL is also considered responsible for the ubiquity of carp on the Christmas Eve table, although this custom harks back at least to the Renaissance. According to his research, the socialist regime only increased production to make sure that everybody had access to the fish. At other times, the loss of tradition is attributed, by default, to the practices of the socialist food industry: "Smoked meats are a Polish specialty that we should be proud of. A specialty, let's add, which was almost wiped off the face of the earth by the war years and the PPR" (Wójcik 2014).[7]

The experts on the Warsaw, Kraków, and Poznań panels, who are often involved in the production of foodie media material, repeatedly underlined the negative impact of the socialist regime and its centrality in the collective memory. Time and again, participants connected the loss of food tradition and culinary refinement with repression, political ineptitude, economic disarray, and the Soviet influence. Similar considerations, centered however on the actual lack of food, were echoed in our focus groups as well. "There was simply vinegar in the shops and thank you, nothing more." The theme of seafood was also brought up: "Cod was our fish, during World War II; before World War II, we ate cod, fish was inferior. And you could get cod on every corner. There was a flood of cod in the Baltic Sea. It was a poor fish." People had to learn to get by in any way they could: "My grandfather had such a job that sometimes people offered him, for example, half a pig out of gratitude." Mentions of milk, potatoes, and eggs from the villages were frequent: "A guy would open the side of the truck and a melody would be playing; homemade products, from some small butcher's shop. . . . You could buy both raw meat and preserves."

Very few well-known food products from the PRL are recalled as worthy of a revival; in that case, they represent continuity with presocialist times rather than post–World War II creativity. For example, processed fried cheese from Nowy Tomyśl, an industrial product from the PRL period, is described both in *Kuchnia* magazine and in Makłowicz's show as almost artisanal, because it reminds consumers of well-known homemade regional dishes that supposedly predate socialism (Food Network 2018b; Gorlas 2014). In his travels through Poland, chef Jakubiak explored not only individual artisanal productions in the countryside, but also small, semi-industrial plants operating in cities since 1945. In the first episode of *Jakubiak lokalnie* we see him visit a small bakery in Lublin, where we are told that during socialism the owners had to produce bread and *cebularz lubelski*—the typical onion rolls from the region we discussed in the previous chapter—in accordance with official state recipes, while after 1989 they were able to reintroduce their own version, handed down within the family (Canal + Kuchnia 2013). As we discussed, vodka, which was widely available in the PRL, is also undergoing reinterpretation and refinement, with frequent references to presocialist times. In a Polish vodka review in *Kuchnia* we read: "It is a great drink that harks back to the style of exported rye vodkas from the old times" (Klesyk 2012).

However, this ambivalent evaluation of the post-PRL period is further complicated by a certain nostalgia. Milk bars (*bary mleczne*), the popular eateries with a few available dishes at extremely affordable prices supported by the socialist government, are often mentioned with affection. New ones have opened that are inspired by the decor and the style of the old ones, but with more refined, lighter fare and cool, well-appointed interiors that reveal the intervention of architects and designers. Some offer vegetarian and vegan interpretations of common dishes such as *schabowy* fried pork chops and meatballs. The store Rzeźnik z PRL-u (Butcher from the Polish People's Republic) in Gdańsk may surprise those who remember the iconically empty shelves of butcher shops at that time. Perhaps with some irony, the name plays with nostalgia and with the suggestion that production at that time was not industrial and was closer to craftsmanship (their Facebook fan page mentions "cold cuts with a short ingredient list" and "products of Polish origin"). The bar Setka in Warsaw went a step further, using the design of the logo of the PZPR, the Polish United Workers' Party, to create its own logo. Still, its interiors have nothing to do with the period. A good dose of millennial (some would say hipster) irony is evidently at work here: as most Poles are aware of the problems with food during the socialist years, the customers are supposed to be in on the joke.

When it comes to the period following the collapse of socialism, we witness the continuation of a "catastrophic chronology:" the beginning of the post-1989 transformation is interpreted as stagnant in terms of food culture, if not destructive. In this chronology, capitalism entered Poland in the 1990s and intensified the wide distribution of mass-produced, industrial items through supermarkets, erasing what remained of culinary traditions. A story about forgotten cherry trees in *Kuchnia* provides an interesting example. The author of the article writes: "First, they [the cherry trees] were hurt by socialism, because when large-scale state-owned farms were created, cherries growing on bordering paths and roads among fields were cut. Later, under capitalism, trees along the roads are cut down en masse to ensure the safety of drivers, answers the naturalist. Are there any roadside cherry-tree-lined avenues left from before the war?" (Augustyn 2014, 74).

Tastemakers frequently indicate the sudden introduction of ruthless capitalism after 1989 as a cause for the end of artisanal, local culinary culture, the disappearance of plant and animal varieties, and the loss of good taste. However, the same period, with the arrival of the free market economy, is also described as a time of "renewal:" its modernizing power was able to fill empty hills and fields, as well as store shelves. According to the foodie media, the newly introduced capitalist system had some benefits in terms of maintaining food practices. This can be observed in the way carp production and its celebration is described in *Kuchnia*: "It was only thanks to the free market and the growing sense of local identity that the Carp Festival was reactivated several years ago" (Augustyn 2012, 30).

How should we interpret the tension in the contradictory attribution of values and disruptions to historical realities? Without a doubt, references to a vague past give a stamp of authenticity, even when they end up representing an imaginary lost paradise. In such cases, it may not always matter which past is being discussed, because general ideas about it are more important than factual details. Second, alternative or competing food histories express the complex path to the reconstruction of Polish identity after World War II and 1989, which includes controversies on what should or should not be included in the national cuisine. Such debates are clearly linked to the variety of the actors who make references to the past and engage in its reconstruction. The "discovery" of the past by TV-show hosts, magazine writers, and tastemakers in general can be read as a strategy that not only looks down on less authoritative or prestigious citizens and tells them about their own traditions, but also makes choices for them, deciding on the proper identity symbols for the national "we." Third, by juggling historical elements and using them in different configurations, chefs, professionals, and food authors are able to foster creativity in reinterpreting well-known recipes, while remaining within widely accepted culinary knowledge that is considered objective and fact-based.

SIMMERING HISTORY: CHEFS REINTERPRET THE PAST

Not only domestic practices and media discourse show a variegated relationship with the past and tradition. Raw materials from the past—be they documents, archaeological findings, traces in urban design, remains of built environments, or landscapes—have also emerged as resources to transform the present toward a redesigned future. This historical sensibility reveals regret for the destruction of Polish cuisine as a lively and refined (although largely imagined) culinary culture and the desire to elevate it again to its rightful status "alongside that of the French." As more than one of the taste-makers we interacted with has remarked, there was a time when the French talked about cooking something à la Polonaise and not the other way around, a time "before we [Poles] have turned our eyes to France."[8]

Polish tastemakers have picked up and reassembled scattered, often unfamiliar fragments—recipes, techniques, ingredients, and flavors from exotic spices, meant to counter what they often see as the blandness of Polish food in its current form. Popular media avidly pick up stories about the past of Polish cuisine being "based on spicy flavors and resembling Indonesian more than anything else" (Dumanowski and Czarnecki 2009). Chefs around the country use old recipes, history, and geographies of commodity exchanges to enact a more worldly Polish identity, made more intriguing with pepper, saffron, ginger, nutmeg, cloves, cinnamon, cardamom, and turmeric (Łuczaj et al. 2023). In the promotional materials for its redesign, the Mercato restaurant in Gdańsk explicitly framed its Polishness as "cosmopolitan." The staff we interviewed used the colonial term "Spice Islands" to speak of the port city and its past as a member of the Hanseatic league, which was linked to the Maluku Islands through the maritime Via Mercatorum, the trade network that connected Europe with the Far East. Gdańsk's position as an international entrepôt that connected Poland to the rest of Eastern Europe, Western Europe, and the world, became a resource in the attempt to develop a more exciting cuisine, better connected to global networks.

In their search for tradition, the tastemakers who identify politically as liberal, progressive, pro-European, and cosmopolitan, may find themselves in an awkward tension with the nativist "historical politics" of the former nationalist government and more generally, with the nationalist rhetoric that is still circulating under the post-October 2023 government. While they place the ultimate value in the soil and its products, those tastemakers aspire to be in dialogue with cosmopolitan foodie culture and its attention to the local, all around the world. However, they may tend to subordinate local, ethnic, or religious identities to assert a clear and undeniable Polishness as an overarching cultural category, even when they do not identify patriotism with illiberal exclusionary politics. They seem to resolve this contradiction through the notion that the culinary use of local resources is a practice they have observed among European chefs outside of Poland; by embracing it, they indicate their participation in global networks. To illustrate these dynamics, we follow a cultural object that has emerged as an important point of reference for many tastemakers: the annotated edition of the 1682 recipe collection *Compendium ferculorum*, the first cookbook printed in Polish, coedited by Jarosław Dumanowski (Czerniecki, Dumanowski, and Spychaj 2012).

As we mentioned earlier, in collaboration with the Museum of King Jan III's Palace in Wilanów, Warsaw, Dumanowski has undertaken a philological examination of culinary manuals from the 1600s onward that had fallen out of culinary practices and had been lying unexplored in libraries. His work, based on a methodical and scholarly reading of the recipes, also addresses their social and political context, as well as the material culture in which they appeared. His rigorous methodology in analyzing historical texts has granted cultural legitimacy and authority to the culinary arts. Dumanowski is part of a larger effort in Polish academia to increase the visibility and respectability of food history as a legitimate scholarly endeavor (Dias-Lewandowska and Kurczewski 2018; Sikorska 2019). He is also connected to a network of food historians from other Central and Eastern

European countries who organize events and panels, travel to each other's locations, and are eager to collaborate in terms of international publications with the goal of making the food history of their areas better known abroad, especially in Western countries.

Dumanowski also widely discusses Polish food in popular media (Dumanowski and Kasprzyk-Chevriaux 2019). He has appeared on TV with the celebrity chef Karol Okrasa, who cooked reinterpreted historical recipes in his show. He is also the host of the twenty-six-episode series *Historia kuchni polskiej* (History of food in Poland), which premiered in April 2024 on the public TVP Historia and in which coauthors Fabio Parasecoli and Agata Bachórz are featured as experts. However, Dumanowski is not the only tastemaker with an academic background to bring history to the general public. Łukasz Modelski, whom we met in chapter 3, has launched culinary series with historical themes on TVP Historia, focusing on the interwar period, the Jagiellon dynasty (1386–1596), Polish Jews, and the Piast dynasty, the first royal dynasty of Poland (960–1370). In each episode, Modelski— who has a background in medieval art history and hosts a radio show on literature and cuisine—prepares recipes inspired by the period while showing iconography and reading historical citations from documents and memoirs. Modelski's shows demonstrate the undeniable appeal of "serious" history to general audiences.

Copies of Dumanowski's edition of *Compendium ferculorum* tended to pop up wherever we went to explore the redesign of the national cuisine. We saw a well-used copy in Figatella restaurant in the Nowy Wiśnicz castle, where Stanisław Czerniecki, the author of the recipes, lived in the late seventeenth century as a member of the service staff of the Lubomirski family, the local landowners. At Figatella, chef Marcin Pławecki finds inspiration in ancient dishes while reworking them in his personal and creative way. This was the case with his goose pierogi in a goose stock with mace, rosemary, and lime, which evokes one of the recipes of the *Compendium*. While reminiscent of the culinary customs of Polish noble families of yore and their use of spices, the dish is meaningful to contemporary foodies who appreciate current interpretations of traditions. The chef was actually able to quote whole sentences from the book verbatim, showing his familiarity with the text.

Andrea Camastra, an Italian chef whose Warsaw restaurant Senses boasted one Michelin star before its closure during the COVID-19 pandemic, offered another example of the use of *Compendium ferculorum*.[9] The volume stood on a shelf in the chef's starkly lit lab, located right next door to the restaurant, above machinery such as a rotary evaporator that would not be out of place in a biotech facility. Tinkering with air pressure, temperature, and the chemistry at the molecular level, Camastra boldly traversed all registers of Polish cuisine, from the contemporary to the country's past and from the noble to the peasant. He would spend days cooking a pot of *bigos* meat and cabbage stew only to later centrifuge it to extract the essence of the perfect flavor—light and ethereal, with the sourness of fermented cabbage balancing out the umami of forest game—and reintroduce it into other dishes.

As is the case for many other chefs, *Compendium ferculorum* was a source of both inspiration and legitimation for Camastra's experiments. The chef's contemporary recipe for sea trout (*troć wędrowna*) with almonds, green peppers, and saffron uses fragments of the past to creates an homage to the role that Poland played as a cultural hinge between East and West, and as a transit point for spices flowing into Europe. Here Camastra used particular flavors and ingredients to feed patrons a version of Polish history redolent of imperial nostalgia, which some Polish tastemakers display quite uncritically and without self-awareness. This national identity is projected onto the seventeenth century Polish-Lithuanian Commonwealth, which included areas of today's Lithuania, Belarus, and Ukraine ("from the Baltic to the Black Sea") that are almost framed as borderlands at the margins of the core Polish civilization. The Polish word *kresy*, often used to indicate them, suggests that there is nothing beyond such borderlands, expressing a colonial political center's point of view that belittles its peripheries, brushing aside their relevance as cultural entities (Bakuła 2014; Beauvois 1994; Kwaśniewski 1997).

Tastemakers' forays into the deep past of Poland—at times with vaguely colonial undertones that may go unrecognized—are not only a way to add excitement to what is seen as the blandness of contemporary Polish cooking. They are also a strategy to design sensory engagements that counter the current racial, religious, and ethnic homogeneity. The tastemakers' distaste for monotony often stands in for a social critique of the lack of diversity in the postwar republic, while promoting a picture of allegedly conflict-free coexistence of different nations, which could be criticized as an imperialistic fantasy (Bakuła 2014; Beauvois 1994).

Tastemakers sometimes explicitly frame their explorations of national history as an effort toward a more cosmopolitan ideal of citizenship against the political propaganda that stokes xenophobic and anti-immigrant sentiment. Redesigning the dishes and telling new stories, practitioners engage their patrons' bodies in an affective politics of inclusivity and diversity in a largely mono-ethnic country, seeking to materialize a multicultural Poland with Jewish, Tartar, Ukrainian, and Lithuanian contributions. Sometimes, however, this Poland is imagined or manufactured largely for commercial reasons, as in the case of kosher-inspired food establishments that, as we will see in the next chapter, benefit from broad consumer appeal but maintain little to no connection with the surviving Jewish community.

Such interest for materials from the past is also present in the work of chef Aleksander Baron, who studied art and launched his culinary career in Scotland, where he started looking at old recipes. An avid student of culinary history, he even blogged for the Polish National Library's online repository of digitized historical texts, *Polona*. In an interview with us, he compared browsing the archive to "falling into a rabbit hole," as so much inspiring material from the past was available at the tip of his fingers.[10] Baron explicitly declared that "to understand Polish cooking, you must first understand the history of our country" (Baron and Madej 2018), somewhat understating his active role in reimagining Polish cooking and enacting new histories of Poland through food. Baron consulted *Compendium ferculorum*, other historical cookbooks, and Dumanowski in person, to design a sumptuous dinner organized in October 2018 at Zoni, the restaurant where he was the executive chef at the time. The event, which celebrated the food history conference *The Power of Taste: Europe at the Royal Table*,[11] was titled *Dzika historia* (Wild history), and according to the menu it was inspired by the "forgotten wilderness" and the "wild nature of our ancestors."

Dishes included veal brains, beaver tails, and a stunning composition of roasted pheasants, partridges, and quails arranged in what looked like a seventeenth-century Dutch still life painting. The references to wilderness, hunting, and the lifestyle of the great households who could afford such luxuries in the past was activated as a ruse to bring spectacle and wonder and to allow guests, both national and international, to experience an alternate Poland. Neglecting peasant food, it was also a gesture of gentrification, symbolically including members of the new middle class, often two or three generations removed from a rural background, into an imagined post-aristocratic community of *szlachta* (nobility), *ziemiaństwo* (landed gentry), and *mieszczaństwo* (bourgeoisie).

The new generation of library-going chefs-cum-historians is small in numbers but quite influential in cultural circles and visible in the media. During that same 2018 food history conference, Maciej Nowicki and Dumanowski planned two meals composed of dishes from historical cookbooks. In the now closed Gothic Café in the Teutonic Order castle in Malbork, in northern Poland, chef Bogdan Gałązka examined accounting books and warehouse lists found on site to reimagine what the Teutonic knights ate, based on the staples and ingredients they bought. He also created entirely new dishes, like almond milk rice pudding with caramelized violet petals, based on the same historical information. For special events, before dinner guests were entertained with drinks, hors d'oeuvres, and Renaissance music in an outdoor space right next to the castle walls. Guests stood next to the garden where some of the plants and herbs used in Gałązka's recipes were grown.

In Poland, where cultural power is still largely held and distributed by the intelligentsia (Zarycki 2009 and 2019), the culinary field seems intent on building legitimacy by cooperating with academia, a relatively less common phenomenon in culinary powerhouses such as France, Denmark, or the United States. In 2017, Dumanowski collaborated with several local chefs to organize a celebratory event during the Europejski Festiwal Smaku (European festival of taste) in Lublin, featuring dishes—from spiced sturgeon to blancmange—that could have been consumed at the time of the Union of Lublin, the political agreement signed in 1569 that established the Polish-Lithuanian Commonwealth. Such events are a curious elite mirroring of the historical reenactments (*rekonstrukcje historyczne*) recently popularized in Polish middle-brow culture (Szlendak et al. 2012).

Recipes in *Compendium ferculorum* and other early modern cookbooks overflow with apparently overwhelming spices but lack detailed cooking instructions (a common feature in the courtly cookbooks of the past). During a meeting before the dinner in Lublin, Dumanowski helped chefs put the recipes in their historical context, explaining the evolution of taste, the shifts in flavor preferences, and the cultural and political functions of banquets in the sixteenth century. The scholar provided a framework for chefs to operate with novel techniques and unusual ingredients. Because of the flavor profile of the recipes that they were reinterpreting, in their original versions almost inedible by current standards, the priority was to design and cook dishes that could be successfully tasted and tested against the contemporary palate. Ancient delicacies such as blancmange, poached sturgeon, or heavily spiced marzipan were brought back to life for an audience of Lublin notables who, although not all food enthusiasts, thoroughly enjoyed the menu as part of the celebrations for the historical event.

The meals we describe show how tastemakers have been selecting material and discursive elements from the past to craft not only specific dishes but also an evolving version of the culinary history—and history in general—of Poland. The most systematic and focused example to date of this approach is the restaurant Epoka, in the prestigious Raffles Europejski Hotel in Warsaw. Its menus invite guests to travel in time and explore the past of Polish gastronomy. Starting from the elegant foyer, the restaurant aims to impress its customers with impeccable service and grand interior design: history can be enjoyed sensually at the highest levels of refinement. Every detail has been studied carefully; every object has been created by local artists and designers. Even the ceramic napkin ring is a design piece.

At the time of our visit, customers could choose between an à la carte menu and three prix fixe menus, ranging from ten to twenty "recipes." The chef Marcin Przybysz, a winner of the local edition of *Top Chef*, uses the idea of "recipe" rather than dish because each of them is taken from a historical Polish cookbook from a different period, starting in the late seventeenth century. The whole concept is built around culinary history: different historical moments, however, are juxtaposed with each other as if they all could coexist together. As the menu states, the restaurant offers "a creative vision of Polish dining traditions, prepared in a state-of-the-art kitchen." For instance, the recipe from *Compendium ferculorum* for *babka piaskowa*, or sand cake, becomes a tiny petit four filled with a decadent custard in Przybysz's version. He often uses the term "interpretation" to explain his concept (developed together with the restaurant director Antoine Azaïs). While asserting creativity and uniqueness through historical recipes, Przybysz strives to maintain accuracy and legitimacy, as the collaboration with historian Jarosław Dumanowski suggests.

The kitchen in Epoka is not organized according to the traditional scheme of the brigade; instead, each period of time has its own station, where cooks focus on the dishes taken from the cookbooks of that era. Przybysz argues that this structure allows them to experiment and explore constantly. While they are serving one menu, they can test recipes for the next menu and maintain the general approach of that specific epoch. The restaurant is explicitly geared to draw attention on social media. Clients can use a light box, brought next to their table, to take well-lit pictures of the dishes to be posted on Instagram or Pinterest. Guests are invited to visit the kitchen, meet the chef, and take pictures with the whole team. Epoka may be steeped in history, but it is definitely attuned not only to modern taste, but also to the contemporary pressures of the hospitality business.

In this chapter we have examined how discursive negotiations about culinary history, tradition and heritage constantly engage with practices and the materiality of ingredients and dishes. Different approaches to pierogi-making, actualizations of ancient recipes, as well as dinners inspired by historical events require not only archival—at times, almost archaeological—research but also the honing of skills and techniques that often have to be rebuilt from scratch. In their creative and shifting relationship with the past, the tastemakers' approach to Polish cuisine reveals its design-like qualities: insights give way to projects that are prototyped, tested, and constantly subjected to modification. In the next chapter we will continue examining the relevance of materiality in the quest for sensory qualities that can be identified as Polish, focusing on objects, buildings, and landscapes as opportunities for tastemakers to shape the future of the food scene of Poland. We will see how through sustained and project-based interactions with materialities, new discursive frameworks of evaluation emerge that further contribute to the tastemakers' redesign of Polish cuisine.

SIX

Materiality

IN MARCH 2022 CELEBRITY CHEFS Tim Maelzer and Johann Lafer, well-known to the German TV audience, were seen buying food in Hala Mirowska market in Warsaw, one of the few to survive the wave of gentrification that has turned grocery shopping places into sites for leisure with bars and exotic eateries. A camera crew followed them as the chefs explored the market. Coauthor Mateusz Halawa had the opportunity to observe as they tried to interact with grocers in English and whatever Polish they were able to glean from Google Translate on their smartphones. Maelzer asked a fishmonger for carp, then realized it is only available in the Christmas season. He pulled out a lighter and put the flame to a piece of sturgeon, smelling the charred flesh and studying its structure and texture. At a loss for Polish words, he used gestures to ask for a fish with a different, perhaps hardier feel. At the next stall, Google Translate in hand, he asked for buckwheat flour. He bought a few different bags of flour, opening each to touch and get a sniff. Then he spent some time smelling different varieties of dried mushrooms.

The chefs were there to film a German TV show called *Kitchen Impossible*. Framed as a duel, each episode features two chefs traveling to a surprise location and given a box containing cooked dishes that speak to the locale. Then, they compete to recreate the dishes, with no knowledge of the recipes, ingredients, or techniques that went into their making. The entire show is a performance of discerning, debating, and recreating textures and flavors across cultural differences; the chefs depend only on their sensory and culinary skills, and work under the pressure of time and competition.

Even though it was March, they were filming the Christmas episode—hence their interest in carp. The competition box was curated by Polish celebrity chef Wojciech Modest Amaro (whom we met in chapter 4), so it was not so close to common Christmas Eve dishes in Poland. He had chosen mushroom soup, eel terrine in aspic with Jerusalem artichoke, and a dessert made from eggplant and covered in gingerbread powder. The German chefs had tasted it in front of the cameras the previous night and on the following day their challenge was to recreate it. Maelzer put his nose into a bunch of dried mushrooms tied with a string as if to make a necklace. "Hmm," he said out loud to himself, making sure the camera and audio guy captured it, "*das klingt Polnish*" (that sounds Polish). He meant the smell and taste, but the synesthesia revealed the chefs' quest to decode the feel of Polishness encoded by Amaro in the soup and the other dishes.

With many bags of groceries in the trunk of a rental van, the chefs and the crew traveled to Dębówka, about twenty-five kilometers from Warsaw, where Amaro welcomed them. His large house looks like a modern barn, built in an old apple orchard, featuring a private chapel and a giant kitchen that the chefs used throughout the day. As the German chefs toiled in the kitchen, tinkering with mushroom flavors and trying to get the texture of the buckwheat pasta just right, the camera crew asked Amaro to comment on their shopping. "They got 70 percent right," he said. "Nice try bringing shiitake, but they might struggle with the texture, it's too meaty to approximate the boletus. I have no clue why they brought basil, rosemary, and coriander, this stuff will lead them away from Polishness toward a more Mediterranean feel."

In the living room, a group of eleven well-dressed family members and friends of Amaro's—including his wife and some of his former collaborators at the now closed Atelier restaurant—began to gather around the dinner table. They were the jury. To recreate the holiday environment in spring, there was a Christmas tree and a teenage boy playing traditional Polish carols on the grand piano. In a pre-interview the guests said they expected the work of the German chefs to reflect the traditions of the Wigilia (Christmas Eve) dinner, but acknowledged that as foreigners they might not know much. The producers asked them to reminisce about past Christmases, focusing on emotions and kinship. The jurors also acknowledged that the dishes presented to the foreign chefs reflected Amaro's distinct approach to the typical Wigilia menu. They had tasted his take on these dishes before and would judge how the German chefs recreated not only Polishness, but also Amaro's fine dining interpretation.

The soup was served as a first course. "That's not it," the panel soon agreed. "Too salty," "too greasy." "Am I feeling basil?" asks someone. "Yeah, kinda suppressing the taste of mushrooms." "OK, I'm getting carrots, I guess here the point goes to the chefs, but what is up with the *łazanki* noodles?" (*Łazanki* is a kind of square or rhomboid pasta often cooked in one-pot dishes and for Christmas with cabbage and mushrooms.) "They don't feel right." "They don't have this springiness, you know?" "Maybe it's not our kind of flour?" "I think they didn't fry the mushrooms first, they don't have the butteriness." "And the sour cream is missing in the aftertaste." "My mom would always add it and so does Modest. It is fatty, but at the same time light and creamy." "I wouldn't say this soup is Amaro, and I wouldn't say it's very Polish." "The idea of the soup is the taste of the forest. This is the soup of my childhood, I wanted to revisit those memories." The failure of the chefs to meet the challenge is very often the point of *Kitchen Impossible*. It makes for great TV, with frustrated professionals racing against the clock and worrying about being judged. After the whole affair is over, it gives them an opportunity to express wonder and appreciation for other cuisines and cultures, their not-so-easy-to-crack mysteries, and their dishes rich with history and memories.

The spectacle of taste orchestrated by the *Kitchen Impossible* crew draws us into the themes of this chapter: the role of materiality in how tastemakers produce and negotiate the sensory experience of Polishness, while establishing frameworks and categories to evaluate it. This, however, is not a simple case of playing cultural dress-up. The TV audience for *Kitchen Impossible* engages in a conversation not only with "Polish traditions," as codified in cookbooks and reproduced in family rituals, but also with a cosmopolitan fine-dining chef, Amaro, whose cachet and skill transcend the locality. In the show we see "Polish food" through the lens of those techniques, flavors, and experiences that, according to the participants but maybe not for average Poles, bring about a "Polish feel."

These dynamics are also essential to tastemakers' discursive practices and their engagements with materiality, from the flavors and textures of foodstuffs to the characteristics of built environments and landscapes. In this chapter we examine how actors in the Polish culinary scene identify and negotiate sensory elements that they consider quintessentially Polish and that, in their opinion, most Poles could immediately recognize as "theirs." Moreover, we explore how these characteristics are elaborated and communicated among the tastemakers themselves, to their Polish interlocutors, and to the foreign foodies they would like to intrigue. In the words of philosopher Dorota Konczanowicz (2022, 99), "Taste should be explored as a manifestation of the body's integrated activity in its socio-cultural context. . . . While it originates in a holistic, sense-channeled experience, the intensity and character of taste results from the joint work of memory, emotions, associations, and social impacts." Accordingly, we also turn to the regulatory aspects of these dynamics and the processes through which consumers are expected to learn the "right" way to understand and evaluate the sensory characteristics of Polish food.

WHAT IS THE FLAVOR OF POLAND?

Dariusz Barański's menu at the restaurant Warszawska explicitly seeks to identify and highlight uniquely Polish flavors. The restaurant is located in the basement of the prewar Prudential skyscraper in Warsaw, a glamorous historical building that now also hosts the fashionable hotel Warszawa. With its wide dining room, open kitchen, minimalistic wooden tables with black tops, and black metal shelves for tableware and crockery, the decor matches the powerful simplicity of the massive cement foundation pillars of the building. Nothing in the interior design screams traditional Poland. Far from it. The idea is to draw attention to what is on the plate. Barański focuses on local ingredients; for instance, he buys vegetables from the nearby Ludwik Majlert's farm, an extremely popular destination with local foodies. Varsovians can easily drive there and pick their produce from a well-appointed space decorated with old furniture and objects reminiscent of the Polish countryside. At Majlert's, the decor is carefully designed: endearing drawings of vegetables illustrate the posters that list prices, handwritten with charming fonts. The farm has been instrumental, together with upscale urban markets, in educating Varsovians about a certain way of understanding the quality and values of vegetables and fruits, shaping their preferences and expectations.

At Warszawska, Barański does not limit himself to only putting the best from the Polish fields on the menu. He makes sausage and *kaszanka* blood sausage from scratch, using the meat that he buys from pig farms in the surrounding region of Mazuria. He has also outfitted his establishment with a smoking room: characteristically, Poles recognize the scents and the flavors of smoked meats as central to their culinary identity. As flavors are at the core of Barański's cooking, local ingredients are not only used in Polish preparations but also to make non-Polish cured meats like *guanciale* or *nduja*; the latter, however, is slightly fermented and has a velvety texture that is reminiscent of Polish *pasztet* pâté. The chef bakes bread and makes *twaróg* fresh cheese in-house, although he also traveled to Italy to learn how to make ricotta, stracciatella, and burrata, which he now produces in the restaurant using local milk and butter. "I don't copy anyone. . . . I try to think about how Polish people can like it. And then okay, it's so close to Italian, maybe it's too close, let's go like maybe with a more Polish style, you know. . . . so we decided to change a few things a little bit and see how it's going to work." In his experimentation, Barański seems to refer to an inner sensory compass that allows him to tweak flavors toward what he identifies as Polishness. When he does not have access to local products, Barański buys from farther-away locations, even abroad, as in the case of the Hungarian paprika he uses for his cured meats, but the goal is always to achieve flavors and textures perceived as Polish.

Barański told us he developed his understanding of what constitutes Polish taste during his childhood in Zakopane, in the south of the country, where he spent time in the miners' canteen in which his mother worked and his uncle was the chef. He pointed out that they did not serve fancy food but the ingredients were good quality and tasty; those memories have stayed with him and still guide him. When we visited the restaurant, one of the highlights of the menu was the mushroom pâté: impeccable from a technical point of view, it was rich in mushroom flavors, reflecting the passion of many Poles for foraging for mushrooms in summer and autumn. Barański draws on familiar and recognizable sensory characteristics to establish culinary values that align with the expectations of his urban patrons. Although he is well versed in the culinary language of cosmopolitan foodies (like many of his peers he has worked abroad), he does not discount the taste categories of the working class, as the presence of offal or pig feet on his menu suggests.

NEGOTIATING THE VALUE OF SENSORY QUALITIES

In our conversation, Dariusz Barański did not mention fattiness, heaviness, or blandness, which are some of the qualities that tastemakers frequently use to discount old-school and working-class Polish food. These qualities of Polish cuisine are not seen as negative by the whole society. As we mentioned in chapter 2, *schabowy* fried pork chop is still a favorite dish among Poles, including young ones. We suggest that some Poles feel a kind of "cultural intimacy" with foods that possess heaviness or blandness. This experience is one that Michael Herzfeld (1997, 3) described as "the recognition of those aspects of cultural identity that are considered a source of external embarrassment but nevertheless provide insiders with their assurance of common sociality, the familiarity with the bases of power that may at one moment ensure the disenfranchised a degree of creative irreverence and at the next moment reinforce the effectiveness of intimidation." A version of the collective self that the state and cultural establishments (especially the latter, in our case) try to hide from international centers creates a "shame community" that for many is a source of authenticity, security, natural expression, and togetherness. At times, this collective self possesses a "defiant pride." Herzfeld does not suggest a simple binary division between the views of elite and ordinary people, but rather argues that the tension between two types of identity—one domestic and connected to the past, and the other, international, cultivated and desired—is inscribed into the collective experience. Although constantly negotiated, these identities are widely understood across the nation.

In her study of Hungarian socialist and postsocialist built environments, anthropologist Krisztina Fehérváry (2013, 8) argues that certain qualities have the capacity "to appear across a variety of objects, materials, or substances" so that "a variety of seemingly unrelated objects can be united into a coherent style—an aesthetic." In the context of Polish cuisine, sensory descriptors such as fatty, heavy, or bland are used to refer to a whole culinary aesthetic. They seem to transcend any specific food, translating instead the overall assessment that some tastemakers seem to formulate about the backwardness of Polish domestic and old-style cuisine. Such traits are also plainly experienced as class markers; their refusal is a recurrent strategy in middleclassing processes. As Fehérváry aptly notes, for some, certain "colors, textures, and aromas might exude the welcoming warmth of a 'homey' interior, but for others they trigger repulsion, association with the decay of a different generation or the earthy impurity of a different class" (8).

Looking at the changes unfolding in the Polish culinary field, sensory affect and emotional impact appear connected to class, culture, and political outlook. The belief that certain textures and flavors are undesirable can be interpreted as another expression of the inferiority complex that, as discussed in the previous chapters, makes many Poles experience the West as a place with which to "catch up." Fehérváry (2013, 7) observes that "material objects can provoke powerful affective responses with their qualities, designs, or aesthetic assemblages. . . . Such experiences can help constitute, reinforce or challenge shared understanding of the workings of the social, political, and economic order." Fattiness, heaviness, and blandness, and the negative feelings they elicit in tastemakers and their circles, are almost bogeymen that represent the worst of Poland's past and a possible future they strive to avoid.

However, it is not easy to reconstitute a new coherent set of sensory categories that effectively reflect Polish food and drink while materializing the transformations taking place both in the domestic and in the public culinary scene. It is even more difficult to uphold them with pride at the global level. An easy strategy could be using well-known frameworks. In 2021 one of Poland's major retail chains, Biedronka, published a cookbook titled *Kuchnia ŚródziemnoPOLSKA (Jeronimo Martins Polska S.A. 2021)*. The title is a word play on the expression "Mediterranean cuisine," a well-known construct globally associated with health, and the adjective "Polish." The authors of this book recommend that readers "combine the tenets of the Mediterranean diet with locally sourced seasonal produce." The goal is not just a linguistic, but also material, hybrid: it is "to establish a balanced/sustainable diet—the diet of the future—while respecting local conditions." The hidden premise of this didactic publication seems to be an attempt to strip Polish cuisine of its unwanted characteristics, while leaving it understandable and familiar.

However, tastemakers' ambitions seem to go further. As we saw in chapter 3, they cannot totally discard entrenched judgments developed at the table of their *babcie* (grandmothers). Instead they use particular homely dishes and flavors as building blocks while selecting and interpreting which domestic sensory experiences are worth adapting. Looking at Barański's work at Warszawska, as well as at the interactions among the two foreign chefs, the local expert, and the jurors in *Kitchen Impossible,* it would seem that Polish sensory traits resist being squeezed into cosmopolitan categories. Flavors and textures that Polish eaters easily identify appear hard to grasp for non-Poles. Amaro and the jurors find themselves in the position of cultural intermediaries not only for the two German chefs, but also for the foreign TV audiences who will watch the show. Barański leverages his experience and fine-dining techniques to turn provincial flavor categories into valuable assets that appeal to cosmopolitan patrons. In the previous chapters, we have observed tastemakers trying to elevate domestic taste to fit with what they perceive as a more refined sensibility, mostly through discursive uses of time and space. Do attempts at translating sensory categories to make them fit in a different cultural framework change Polish eaters and their sensory experience of the food world with which they are familiar? As Annemarie Mol (2021, 66) has pointed out, "engaging perceptively with an object, while at the same time valuing it, may change the subject."

Ana María Ulloa (2019, 190) observes that when it comes to tasting and sensory acuity, "expertise is processually acquired in a community of practice and is enacted through the quality of interactions with materials, objects, tools, and people." In the *Kitchen Impossible* evaluation of the German interpretations of Polish dishes, we see Polish jurors performing what Spackman and Lahne (2019, 143) define as "sensory labor:" those engaged in collective tasting processes "produce a valuable fact about collective preferences.... [T]he types and modes of sensory labor mobilized in the provisioning, making, and eating food are not neutral—rather they coproduce modes of food production." When tasting and establishing new categories of Polishness or clashing with existing ones, tastemakers can influence individual, collective, and institutional decisions that have tangible consequences. They are engaged in shaping the foundations, if not for a new food system, at least for a burgeoning sector of food production, distribution, and consumption. This Polish culinary "scene" needs to forge a new set of rules to hold its own in the global landscape.

Negotiations around categories of taste interact with the political, environmental, and technological context. Polish tastemakers strive to distance themselves from the flavor and texture standardization that is found in industrial food (Lahne 2016), which suffers from stultifying globalization and a lack of embeddedness. As we saw in chapter 3, they do not claim legitimacy for their judgments by drawing on scientific approaches; instead, they highlight their skills, embodied expertise, relationship with nature, and personal experiences, as well as their connections with foreign sources of knowledge that are considered valuable and more advanced. Observing what is included in the emerging categories of taste evaluation is as important as determining what is excluded (Croissant 2014; Proctor and Schiebinger 2008). That is the case, for example, with offal, which many working-class Poles now consider uncouth and backward, if not outright disgusting; the tastemakers have "reclaimed" it. For instance, the casual restaurant Pyzy Flaki Gorace in Warsaw serves *flaki* (cow tripe) in mason jars to guests seated around metal tables painted in bright primary colors, in full hipster style. While he was cooking at the hip Browar Stu Mostów Brewery in Wrocław, chef Michał Czekajło included all sorts of offal meat on the menu. Served in an informal but well-designed setting, the dishes provided a bridge between old practices and the international trend of cosmopolitan foodies' revaluation of offal. It is a manifestation of the same impulse that caused the rebirth of the *quinto quarto* cuisine in Rome or the comeback of oxtail in the United States. Also in Poland, similar negotiations are taking place around what counts as good and bad and who can determine the correct categories

MATERIALITY • 147

through which such judgments can be legitimately expressed. Following Spackman and Burlingame (2018), we can describe these dynamics as "sensory politics;" reflecting power relations within the culinary field, they reveal the clash of divergent projects about the future of Polish food.

The exposure to cosmopolitan standards, which come with more prestige and cultural capital, is influencing taste categories and value standards in Polish foodie circles. The opposite process, in which Polish foodies would influence global cosmopolitan standards, appears harder to set in motion. Our tastemakers' attempts to uphold a recognizably Polish sensibility in global contexts require a certain flexibility and adventurousness on the part of non-Poles. Can the experience of eating *żurek* fermented rye soup or *kiszony sok* (pickled vegetable fermentation juice) by those not used to these flavors usher in changes in global cosmopolitan categories? Polish tastemakers are betting that, because of their desire for fresh experiences and their interest in local flavors, foreign eaters will learn to accept unfamiliar Polish flavors and textures and incorporate them in their own sensory worlds.

FERMENTATION

Humans are not the only actors involved in the sensory politics currently unfolding in Poland (Kopczyńska 2021). As we discussed in the introduction, materials have their own agency: they can have an impact and produce tangible effects. As anybody who has fermented, dried, or salted food knows all too well, materials and living organisms may be stubborn or pliant. It takes work on the part of tastemakers to coax ingredients, microorganisms, and even soil to do their bidding and reflect their goals and preferences. In political theorist Jane Bennett's (2010, ix) words, things have a "vitality," as they can "act as quasi agents or forces with trajectories, propensities, or tendencies of their own." Moreover, materials, microorganisms, and humans do not interact in a void: certain productive choices are more or less viable because of the existing administrative statutes and the public institutions that manage the sector. As we will see, in the world of *nalewki* (spirits made by macerating fruits and herbs in alcohol and sugar), the regulatory framework determines not only how the spirits are produced and what ingredients can be used in them, but also their quality assessment, the sensory categories used to evaluate them, and the networks through which spirits circulate among Poles (Stasik 2018). Matter, human actors, and institutions are all involved in these negotiations.

The process of fermentation and the discourse around it offer some of the best examples of sensory politics in the Polish culinary field. The technique, which is well represented all around the world, probably originated from the observation that some materials change their texture and flavors when left to themselves. Although the role of microorganisms like yeasts, bacteria, and fungi has only relatively recently become the object of intense study, through trial and error humans have learned how to take advantage of these processes, which at times were so mysterious to be considered a sign of divine intervention (Fruton 2006). In fermentation, microorganisms "not only contribute a kind of labor to the production of cheese and other fermented foods but also confer vitality on them" (Paxson 2008, 38). The interaction between living organisms, the objects used in fermentation, and the environments where the process takes place, colonized by different bacteria, molds, and yeasts, influence the final results in terms of safety, quality, and flavors. These dynamics provide the foundation for complex sensory politics in which experts, administrative bodies, and laws also participate in determining not only what is good or bad from the flavor point of view, but also what is safe, what is legal to consume and to sell, and what is worthy of admiration and prestige.

As in other Central and Eastern European countries (Jasarevic 2015; Quave and Pieroni 2014; Sõukand et al. 2015), in Poland fermentation is central to the production of a wide range of products, from spirits and drinks to kefir, cheese, bread, and pickles (*kiszonki*). Fermentation used to be a common preservation method in a country whose vegetable harvest is bountiful but limited to a few months a year. Fermented rye and other cereal flours are the base for the ubiquitous *żurek* soup, whose characteristic sour taste many Poles recognize as quintessentially Polish. The same sour notes also dominate in *kwas chlebowy*, the mildly alcoholic drink obtained by soaking bread in hot water and fermenting it for a few hours. Fermented dill cucumbers, sauerkraut, and beets are mainstays in Polish kitchens. They can also be used in soups such as *ogórkowa* with pickled dill cucumbers, the summer cold soup *chłodnik*, and *kapuśniak* with sauerkraut. They can also be incorporated in bigos and in pierogi fillings. *Zsiadłe mleko* (curdled milk) often accompanies cold summer meals, while the relatively newcomers yogurt and *kefir* can be found virtually anywhere (Mętrak-Ruda 2023).

If in the past fermentation was a largely domestic affair, from the late nineteenth century onward it was slowly transformed by mechanized processes. It was during socialism that mass production really took over in the beer, bread, cheese, and pickle sectors, among others. The increase in industrialized fermentation does not mean that the technique disappeared from the domestic and artisanal spheres, where it thrived as a strategy to bring variety into the limited diet that for many Polish citizens marked the Cold War years. Having a few jars of *kiszonki* stored in the pantry was an insurance policy against scarcity, a source of sensory variety in a diet otherwise perceived as boring, and a means to participate in lively gift and economic exchanges that thrived besides the official distribution networks (Dunn 2004). The juices from vegetables' fermentation were and still are appreciated for their nutritional value and for their bright if sour flavor. As Poland and the whole region moved into its postsocialist era, these practices lost some of their appeal, but continued at the domestic level. The *słoiki* jars that many Poles still receive as gifts from countryside friends and family (Mroczkowska 2018) often contain fermented foods.

As most Poles grow up consuming pickles, they are in general very fond of the taste and also quite knowledgeable about the varieties, flavors, and quality. Popular categories of judgment determine not only the culinary merits of pickles but also their economic value. In many informal street markets, homemade pickles are sold out of big tubs and packaged in small transparent plastic bags, embodying an accessible model of entrepreneurship that thrives mostly beyond the government's control. Women all over the country still churn out large batches of pickles for their families, or at least in the pastoral fantasies of many urban dwellers, they are imagined to be doing so. Beyond the long-standing national fondness for pickles, in the 1990s and 2000s many Poles did not find anything particularly exciting about their production.

However, as fermentation surfaced as a global trend among foodies (El-Sheika 2022), it acquired new positive connotations in Poland as well. It is now embraced as a DIY practice that anybody can enjoy at home. It is also extolled for its health benefits, which are becoming increasingly clear as our understanding of the human microbiome develops. Fermentation became one of the identifying traits of hipster culinary culture, with kombucha as one of its most internationally recognizable symbols (Parasecoli and Halawa 2021). At the same time, interest in fermentation traditions from around the world grew, leading to the renewed popularity of sauerkraut, tempeh, and miso (Katz 2021). US author Sandor Katz emerged as one of the key figures in this phenomenon. His books *Wild Fermentation: The Flavor, Nutrition, and Craft of Live-Culture* (2003) and *The Art of Fermentation* (2012) turned into international hits. A gay AIDS survivor born in New York City to an Ashkenazi Jewish family of Belarussian descent, Katz started dabbling with fermentation while living in a back-to-the-land community in Tennessee. His influence is felt all the way to Poland. His worldwide fame, his Eastern European origins, his persona as a provocateur, and his straightforward and experimental approach to fermenting all combine to make him a compelling figure to a new generation of Polish tastemakers. They finally see something that is deeply ingrained in their culture getting recognition in cosmopolitan foodie circles around the world. This is neither grandma's pickling nor a side-of-the-road production.

Although at times lacking the home pickle producers' expertise, young tastemakers felt that there was a whole wild world to explore, new experiments to be conducted, and a fresh language to be built around fermentation, with categories that in their dialogue with cosmopolitan preferences often did not overlap with traditional ones. The new fermentation style that emerged as a hybrid between Polish *kiszonki* and western approaches was embraced by the well-known Zakwasownia company, established in Gdańsk by career-changers Magdalena and Mikołaj Bator around 2016 (Muraszko 2019), together with many other producers of different sizes such as FermentuJEMY, Zakiszony, and Kiszone Specjały. They offer classic and popular fermented cucumbers or cabbage, partly forgotten products like beetroot *zakwas* or fruit vinegars, and fermented goods previously unknown in Poland like kimchi and kombucha.

Whether traditional Polish or foreign, fermentation products are wrapped in fresh aesthetics and stories about health, taste, and craft. Aleksander Baron, whom we met in the previous chapter, emerged as a leader of this new trend. His restaurant Solec 44, which closed in 2018, turned into a lab in which all kinds of experiments took place. When entering the establishment, one could not but notice the scent of fermentation, always lingering in the various rooms. Whole walls were covered in huge jars that contained vegetables at all different phases of fermentation. This design choice gave the interiors a grungy, low-key vibe. Incidentally, this restaurant started a style trend. After Baron decorated his restaurant this way, those jars became a widespread element of interior design throughout Poland, used by both restaurateurs and artisan producers. Baron did not only work with the traditional cucumbers (*ogórki*), but also with tomatoes, berries, and fruit, which most Poles would find unusual. His 2016 book *Kiszonki i fermentacje* (Pickles and fermentations), which includes a note by Sandor Katz, solidified his fame as a pioneer in the rediscovery of fermented foods in Poland. Katz visited Solec 44 in June 2017 for a public talk and book signing, further consolidating Baron's position in the emerging field.

However, it was clear that Baron was creating something that differed considerably from the *kiszonki* found in markets and stores all over the country. In fact, in a video produced in 2020 by the Polish Cultural Institute in New York, he stated that fermentation "was almost forgotten" and that as a chef he was rediscovering the timeless tradition and its sour flavors (Polish Cultural Institute in New York 2020). *Żurek* made of fermented buckwheat, pumpkins fermented in buttermilk with garlic, radishes in black salt, and pumpkin cream in buttermilk take inspiration from existing practices but establish a different language and unfamiliar categories whose validity not everybody acknowledges. While tastemakers and foodies embraced and saluted Baron's work as an opportunity for Poland to play a visible role in this global trend, dishes like fermented melon sorbet with sage or kale fermented in yogurt with juniper probably came across as quite foreign to most Poles. These dishes seem to be a far cry from the abundantly consumed homemade and store-bought *kiszonki*.

The value of Baron's new fermented creations and their unusual flavors derives from his dialogue with cosmopolitan trends and at the same time his desire to reclaim forms of Polishness that he can translate for audiences outside of the country. He embodies a hip Polishness that is expressed in his innovative approach to fermentation that vegetarians and vegans can enjoy too; furthermore, those concerned about health and nutrition can also happily embrace it. The connection between the emerging fermentation trend and cosmopolitan foodie culture is apparent in the craze for kimchi, which started being produced in Poland before the COVID pandemic. Its popularity only grew during the lockdown period. After all, kimchi has both the familiarity of fermented cabbage and an exoticness that many Polish foodies appreciate; moreover, it is also part of a broader interest in Asian cuisines, as suggested by the enduring success of ramen shops. Kimchi consumption in Poland is so significant that some Korean producers have chosen Poland as the European base for their enterprises (Tilles 2022).

BREAD AND CHEESE

Katz's influence extends beyond pickles. Therefore, it was not a surprise when, during an interview with Arek Andrzejewski, a bread maker whom we met in chapter 3, also known on social media as Chlebodawca (the breadwinner), he showed us a well-used copy of Katz's *Wild Fermentation* (2003), which he described as a major inspiration for his own work. Sourdough bread (*chleb na zakwasie*) has become another focus in Poland's fermentation boom. While today sourdough bread made with rye flour (*chleb na zakwasie żytnim*) is quite common, bakers are also experimenting with new kinds of loaves inspired by the traditions and trends popular in other countries. Rye sourdough bread is part of Andrzejewski's childhood memories but he stopped eating it after he moved to the capital. It wasn't until he was advised to give up anything containing industrial yeast because of health issues that he started buying sourdough loaves again, in the hope they were yeast-free. However, he soon discovered that these industrial products were not 100% sourdough and actually also contained yeast. He attributes the lowered standards in breadmaking to Poland's accession to the EU and the arrival of international food enterprises and supermarket chains that killed small bakeries. Andrzejewski's narrative is one of the rediscovery of familiar traditions that, according to many tastemakers, had been forgotten in the first decades of postsocialist Poland.

This experience inspired him to learn how to bake his own sourdough bread through trial and error. "I was stubborn. I was looking for recipes. I traveled all over Poland. I looked everywhere where bread was baked, in villages, with old housewives, where there was a tradition and it was still baked at home." He has named his starter Hieronim (Jerome), a recognition that he sees this culture as an active agent in his breadmaking. He has become part of a network of aficionados that exchange knowledge and sourdough starters, each with their own microorganisms, their history, and their sensory traits. "We do things that some have already forgotten, and we bring it back to life and study these recipes. I contact people all over Poland and it's more or less the same. It goes toward quality. This is a common feature of this new movement, which is already very visible, and has multiplied." He also gives frequent classes to amateurs who want to bake at home, contributing to spreading the culture of sourdough bread. Andrzejewski's work is part of an attempt to change what Poles consider good bread in terms of textures, flavors, and quality, moving away from categories of taste imposed by industrialized mass production toward those considered to be coming from a past that only survives in fragments.

Her experiences abroad are quite central to Monika Walecka's personal path toward becoming a baker. After working as a TV producer, she slowly moved to the food sector, at first working as a food photographer and recipe developer, then as a blogger (Walecka 2016). When she moved to San Francisco, she dove into the local baking culture, taking classes, making bread at home, and doing internships in well-known establishments. Back in Warsaw, she opened the Cała w Mące (A woman all in flour) bakery. At the time of this writing in the fall of 2023, she has also opened a sandwich store and a French-style pastry store. In our conversation, she painted herself as a part of an expanding baking scene in Poland that is deeply influenced by American sourdough trends; she mentioned several times that the style of Tartine bakery in San Francisco is a point of reference for local bread makers.

In Walecka's opinion, only some of the new Polish bakers are truly artisanal, while others are semi-industrial enterprises that are trying to jump on the bandwagon without having the necessary know-how. In her work, she tries to rely on what she calls an "ecosystem of artisans." She buys organic flour from a local producer, offers natural wines, and in her pastry store sells objects made by designers she knows personally. This network reflects not only business connections, but also a community of taste composed of individuals who are trying to introduce new aesthetic categories in Poland; they may work in different fields, but their approaches all reflect the same desire to be part of an internationally relevant and responsive scene.

Fluent in the emergent cosmopolitan foodie culture, Walecka can chat about bakeries in Rome and pastry stores in Paris. She acknowledges that starting her bakery was not an easy endeavor. However, she took it on with the fervor of an educator, embracing the didactic mission that many tastemakers share. Talking about her local customers, she observed: "At first they saw the prices and they balked, then they saw the bread and thought it was burned. I had to educate them that it is fermented and caramelized, sweet and delicate. It was quite a process." Although explicitly influenced by foreign trends, it is important to Walecka to buy Polish flours, including organic whole grain spelt, rye, and emmer. In this way, she fits into the hybrid formula of the new Polish gastronomic scene that combines the foreign with the domestic. She hopes one day to have a mill in her own bakery.

Moreover, she describes her style as "nostalgic," harking back to the time when people consumed artisanal bread, before industrialization introduced the 100 percent white flour bread that most Poles are now used to. Having successfully translated flavors and textures she learned abroad into the Polish context, Walecka understands herself as part of a budding national baking movement. It is too early to say what these "new traditional" breads will taste like, but they will likely be supported by the community of tastemakers. What remains to be seen is whether consumers outside of the tastemakers' circles will embrace these flavors.

Similar developments are also taking place in the cheese sector. Until recently, in most Polish stores the options were the mostly industrial *żółty ser* (yellow cheese), with a few main varieties, and a *twaróg* fresh cheese called *biały ser* (white cheese). They were unremarkable, but familiar and reliable. Their taste was not challenging, but ubiquitous and affordable. However, the growing number of successful artisanal cheese producers demonstrates that there is room for products with stronger, unique flavors. Producers such as Janina Rzepka, Tomasz Strubiński, and Wojtek Komperda frequently attend events and food fairs, at times dressed in traditional garb, making artisanal Polish cheese more accessible to consumers beyond tastemakers. Traditional local cheeses such as the smoked sheep milk *oscypek* from the Tatra mountains (now protected by a Geographical Indication) have acquired new visibility. Goat milk is also enjoying renewed appreciation. Some industrial companies have started to differentiate their production both by launching imitations of foreign cheeses and by creating products that claim connection with traditional Polish cheese.

Tastemakers have played a key role in this increased interest in artisanal cheeses. Gieno Mientkiewicz has emerged as a relevant cheese expert and critic. A former actor, he is able to connect with the public directly and without fuss. Together with culinary consultant Zbigniew Kmieć, he is behind the initiative to make June 2 Twaróg Day (disclaimer: coauthor Fabio Parasecoli was among the signatories of the proclamation document) (Mientkiewicz and Kmieć 2020). This initiative is emblematic of the conversations taking place in the Polish culinary scene around taste and evaluation of quality. As Mientkiewicz explained to us, *twaróg* is made by heating milk that has been acidified with lactic acid bacteria, which changes its taste to sour. The curd is then cut and fermented, affecting the structure of proteins, fats, and sugars. The traditional process is undergoing some changes, especially due to the growing use of rennet, which makes the milk coagulation faster and leaves less protein in the whey. However, according to Mientkiewicz, the rennet-based version loses some of its health properties and shows different culinary characteristics. *Twaróg* is traditionally used to make pierogi, pancakes, cheesecake (*sernik*), pies, breakfast spreads, and *gzik* (*twaróg* paste served with warm potatoes), among other recipes. *Twaróg* can be further processed through drying, smoking, salting, and aging.

The Twaróg Day proclamation starts with a call "on cooks, gourmets, cosmopolitans and patriots to study and meditate on cheese." This statement both lays out who the expected protagonists are and underscores that there is no contradiction between being patriotic and cosmopolitan. The cheese is described as a "symbol of the freshness of Polish culinary thought and the purity of Polish nature." The document continues: "We want twaróg to emerge from the shadow of mediocrity and frequent anonymity. To proudly bear names derived from their creators, the places they come from, the time with which they are created, the techniques of production and processing." Expertise, fueled by cosmopolitan awareness, is meant to transform a product that many Poles eat every morning for breakfast: a central element of Polishness and Polish taste that, however, can become mediocre and anonymous if due attention is not paid to locality, temporality, and know-how.

The goal is the establishment of "canons of its production, consumption and assessment of its quality." However, it is still unclear through which processes and by whom these canons will be determined, especially as differences within *twaróg* are underlined in terms of origins, authorship, and producers' names. The unruliness of both producers without expertise and microorganisms, which need to be disciplined by rules and human intervention to ensure the expected results, can damage the profile of the cheese. Much *twaróg* is still manufactured domestically, especially in the countryside, embodying preferences, sensory categories, and evaluation standards that may not meet the approval of some tastemakers. It is not difficult to imagine future debates about its flavor profile and texture among consumers, industrial and artisanal producers, critics with tastemaker's approaches, distributors, and retailers that do not have the same access to culture, means of communication, and social status.

THE BURGEONING WINE INDUSTRY

The interactions between people, plants, microorganisms, and landscape is evident in another product of fermentation (and aging): wine. As Colleen Myles (2020, xix) observes in her research on "fermented landscapes," fermentation processes allow consumers "to consider the macro consequences of micro(be) processes of socio-environmental transformation" and to examine "the excitement, unrest, and agitation evident across shifting physical-environmental and sociocultural landscape" (16). Such vitality can easily be detected in Poland's wine industry.[1]

Although quite small compared to other food and spirit sectors, the wine industry provides ample opportunities to understand how sensory politics

156 · CHAPTER 6

develop around materials, living beings, landscapes, and institutions. Its novelty (Kopczyńska 2014), to which we have already drawn attention in chapter 3 when describing the emerging social network of wine producers, makes the elaboration of sensory and evaluation categories clearly visible, revealing the constant interactions between domestic dynamics and inputs coming from abroad. At the time of writing, there are fewer than four hundred wineries in Poland (Puzio 2023). As a great number of them are quite small, economies of scale are in many cases virtually impossible, keeping production costs high. Polish wines are often more expensive than foreign ones and, according to most tastemakers, also of variable quality. Nevertheless, there is a strong sense among food professionals that investing in Polish products is exciting and worthwhile. Moreover, as wine is important in prestigious cuisines like French or Italian, many tastemakers have mentioned in conversation that the local wine production may support Poland in achieving greater visibility on the international culinary scene, and as such it is worth supporting it. Polish bottles from the most renowned producers now come recommended not as a fun but risky novelty, but as a legitimate choice in establishments stocked with premium labels.

Polish wine has come to the fore in restaurants that pride themselves on offering interpretations of Polish cuisine ranging from the vaguely national to the regional. The entire Polish wine culture is being built from the ground up, leveraging forms of design such as landscaping, branding, and service design. Polish consumers are gently being eased into the new, cosmopolitan, and relatively expensive custom of discussing local wines and visiting wineries.

Although in certain parts of the country a few producers have managed to successfully grow *Vitis vinifera* grapes, most local vintners produce wine with German-engineered hybrid grapes that thrive in colder climates. These varieties are obtained by crossing plants of the grapevine species, *Vitis vinifera*, with *Vitis labrusca* or *Vitis rupestris*, with the goal of combining the aromas and flavors from the former with the natural resistance to diseases and harsh climate conditions of the latter. At the moment, the most common varieties include solaris, johanniter, and hibernal for white and rondo and regent for red. At first, such varieties were looked down upon by local wine experts whose professional training followed international standards and the aesthetic categories borrowed from English-language wine writing and critique. However, this attitude appears to be changing.

Taking advantage of climate change, producers are now also trying their hand at the more prestigious *Vitis vinifera*, still at the center of the age-old wine cultures of Italy, France, and Spain. Although some wine was historically produced in Lower Silesia, near the Czech border, and in the Zielona Góra region (the historical Ziemia Lubuska), other areas have recently emerged in the warmest regions of Poland. Probably because of the novelty of the wine industry's resurgence, some producers are keen to reconnect with history and, when possible, ecologies from the past that confirm the ties between local geographies and human communities. Today, vineyards cover only small areas, with low yields. The reestablishment of winemaking is a project that has required the acquisition of new skills and techniques that range from taming soils to handling grapes, controlling fermentation processes, assembling wines, aging them, and learning the language to speak about all of this. New and seasoned entrepreneurs plant vineyards, modify landscapes, design labels, build or adapt production and tourism infrastructures. Their role as tastemakers is thus deeply entangled with the materialities of the wine industry.

Many small producers are self-taught amateurs and enthusiasts (one of them proudly told us that he had learned how to make wine from YouTube). Not surprisingly, as we observed in chapter 3, a few go abroad to gain experience and establish professional networks, or hire expert consultants who can import their knowledge to Poland. In some cases, foreigners with vine-growing and winemaking experience have bought land in Poland and started vineyards, bringing with them notions of connoisseurship and distinction, as well as practices, values, and sensory categories that can be translated into local concepts of *terroir*. Vintners and winemakers are trying to establish their own terroirs by identifying the places where grapes give the best results. Some of these areas overlap with old viticultural regions, as several producers are quick to point out (the parts of the country where their vineyards are located used to produce wine under the Austro-Hungarian and Prussian empires). Nevertheless, neither socially nor biologically is there much continuity of cultivation. To better understand the sensory politics and the current conversations emerging around wine, we embarked on an exploration of wineries around Kraków, one of the best-known and most rapidly developing viticultural areas in the country. The financial and logistic efforts to launch a new industry go together with interventions on landscapes and built environment, as well as with decisions on growing techniques, winemaking choices, and marketing strategies that are determining the sensory profile of the local wines. Mirosław Jaxa Kwiatkowski and Mikołaj Tyc, owners of the Srebrna Góra winery (introduced in chapter 3) have put locality and its traditions at the center of their project. Their winery is located in the Camaldolese monastery of Bielany in the outskirts of Kraków. As they state in their website, "wines from Srebrna Góra are closely related to the place they come from. At the stage of their creation, we made a lot of effort both to reflect the individual character of the grape varieties and the uniqueness of the Bielany habitat." However, they also point out that their goal was "not so much to recreate a fragment of the past, but to make the spirit of wine come alive in a new, modern version." We met Kwiatkowski at the monastery, where he showed us the production plant that was located within the old monastic buildings: a fascinating location with plenty of logistical challenges. He also walked us through the nearby vines, growing on beautiful south and southeast facing slopes with magnificent views over a river.

Proud to share and excited about his and his business partner's achievements, Kwiatkowski recalls that the beginnings were not easy. For years subsidies from the EU could not be used in wine production. The regulations have changed, and Kwiatkowski and his business partner have taken advantage of the new opportunities to finance their expansion, both in terms of built infrastructures, barrels (acacia and oak), and land. Over time they have developed two market approaches: they launched monovarietal lines which sold at higher prices and a blend line called Polka (Polish woman), which instead at first they distributed at lower prices in the Lidl supermarket chain and now maintain under the name Cuvee Blanc and Cuvee Rouge. The Srebrna Góra business model reveals the entanglements between market requirements, a steep learning curve in winemaking, the desire for the industry to acquire respectability, the attempts at establishing connections between vineyards and the land, and last but not least the need to create consumers with enough knowledge and enthusiasm to support budding industry.

When it first started, the Winnica Srebrna Góra winery relied on the proximity of local winemaker Agnieszka Wyrobek-Rousseau, who with her partner Piotr Jaskóła is among the best-known protagonists of the Polish wine scene. We met Wyrobek-Rousseau in her Winnica Wieliczka winery, not far from Kraków, which is the first vineyard in Poland with an EU organic certification. We had the opportunity to visit the vineyard and taste the wine right in the field where the vines are grown. Wyrobek-Rousseau, a native of these lands who went on to become one of the first female graduates of the Montpellier enology school, rents the land from the Congregation of Saint Michael the Archangel. Before making such a momentous business

MATERIALITY · 159

decision, Rousseau examined the local environment to assess its suitability to her project: the forest in the north of her land would protect the vineyard from cold northern winds, while the west to east winds would help control mildew; the sloping position would ensure sun all day; the presence of hibiscus bushes on neighboring properties signaled the absence of prolonged freezes in the cold season. Eventually, she chose the land not only for its position and microclimate—allowing her to grow *Vitis vinifera*, rather than hardy hybrids—but also for its proximity to the John Paul II Kraków-Balice International Airport, which makes her international consulting engagements more manageable.

From the start, Wyrobek-Rousseau and Jaskóła decided to embrace biodynamic growing methods, avoiding monocultures and allowing other herbs and plants to grow between the vines in order to take away excess nitrogen and keep the soil loose for the vine roots to expand. Understanding the ecology of the land and respecting biodiversity is central to both their style of work and the sensory characteristics they want to achieve in their wines. Besides the vineyard, they planted a bee-friendly buckwheat field and an orchard with around 2,000 trees of all kinds of fruit, among which are twenty varieties of apples that they use to produce cider without artificial enzymes. They do not apply artificial pesticides; they prune and harvest by hand. Wyrobek-Rousseau does not subscribe to cookie-cutter winemaking styles: "You just make something that is really not so much different from ketchup." She prefers to allow each grape variety to express its specificities in the environment of her vineyards, embracing the philosophy of natural wines but applying the know-how she has acquired through her international experience to produce the best wine possible. She believes it is necessary to eliminate the flavor defects which many natural winemakers leave in their wines for what could boil down to ideological choices or lack of knowledge.

CREATING A WINE CULTURE

As we illustrated, the Polish wine industry is the tangible result of a deliberate assemblage of discursive elements, practices, landscapes, and materialities that translate into sensory characteristics and judgments of quality. The protagonists of these dynamics are not only winemakers, but also sommeliers, critics, vendors, wine shop and wine bar owners, marketing agencies, and even supermarket chain buyers, whose activities impact how wine is experienced, talked about, evaluated, and eventually consumed. Sommelier, instructor and wine critic Monika Bielka-Vescovi exemplifies the role played by such professionals in the wine industry. The owner of a sommelier school in Kraków since 2011, Bielka-Vescovi also teaches online courses, both in English and Polish, aimed at restaurateurs, wine professionals, and consumers. She established her international credentials by earning diplomas from the International Sommelier Guild in Denver and from the Wine and Spirit Education Trust in London; she now coaches candidates for the latter. As a founder of the Stowarzyszenie Kobiety i Wino (Women and wine association), she is working to bring more women into the wine business. Her concurrent involvement in education, association activities, and writing is not unusual. As wine experts are still relatively few, they have opportunities to play different roles; this allows them to have an outsized influence in the industry in terms of determining its direction, its standards, and the language and the categories used to appreciate wine. While deeply embedded in an international network of wine connoisseurs, Bielka-Vescovi is in turn forming a new community of Polish experts to join the international network, with which they share perspectives, approaches, and evaluation categories.

The restaurant sommelier is a relatively new role in Poland, and because of this it is particularly important. These professionals function as educators for consumers who may be unfamiliar with the flavors and scent of wines. They often find themselves in the position of translating the evaluation categories elaborated by other tastemakers such as instructors, wine critics, and producers to patrons who are not involved in the industry and are not necessarily interested in its subtleties. We discussed these dynamics with sommelier Łukasz Głowacki, who works at the one-Michelin-star restaurant Muga in Poznań. Głowacki admitted that he sold Polish wines primarily to foreign tourists and businessmen who are curious to try local productions and have the financial means to afford them. These diners are interested in learning more about a world which they may not know. In our conversation, his familiarity with evaluation categories shared with the global wine world was evident through his descriptions of the sensory traits of wines, the expressions he used to present his pairings with the dishes on the tasting menu, and his explanations of technical issues from soil quality to winemaking. This body of knowledge indicated that he has been trained in an international network of experts with English as their common language. As in the case of Wyrobek-Rousseau and Bielka-Vescovi, the participation of Polish wine tastemakers in a transnational community of professionals has a huge impact on this nascent industry, providing legitimacy and shaping its internal dynamics and future outlook.

Sharing knowledge about wine is also a crucial part of the job for the vendors who sell wine to stores and restaurants. In a conversation with Robert Komosa, who entered the wine business in the early 2000s and now represents Polish and foreign wineries in the Warsaw area, his role as a cultural intermediary emerged in its complexity. Sales representatives often find themselves educating their clients, who in turn use the concepts, language, and evaluation categories that they have learned to sell wine to their customers. Komosa is aware of this connection and has built a social media presence as an influencer, which allows him to directly reach a younger audience. Through images and text, he introduces curious potential consumers to the language and customs of wine aficionados by inviting them to an online community that supports wine drinking as a cultural space and a field of social practice. Social media allows trends such as natural wines and their pairings with food to become hallmarks of this community, causing the preferences and expectations of young Polish enthusiasts to align with those of their peers around the world. The flavor profiles of natural wines, which younger drinkers seem to appreciate in Poland as in other parts of the world, reflect other categories of evaluation such as locality, artisanality, and authenticity,

Because of its novelty and its still-limited size, as well as the relatively high cost of its products, the Polish wine business witnesses ongoing debates about the industry composition and governance, which in turn have an impact on distribution, access, and affordability. Tightly connected to such structural issues but never directly addressed, class, education, and financial status influence the development of the sector in terms of how it elaborates sensory categories and quality standards. The sensory politics surrounding the rise of Polish wine also suggests an attempt at rethinking and expanding the flavors of Polishness.

In the case of other fermented products such as pickles, bread, and cheese, established evaluation categories already exist, so storytelling strategies are necessary to "elevate" these products to a "new level," that of the cosmopolitan worlds in which Polish tastemakers aspire to participate in as peers. Raw materials, microorganisms, chemical transformations, and the practices become tools to differentiate and define these products. Bread's caramelization needs to be translated from "burned" into "flavor depth;" *kiszonki* fermented vegetables become part of daring and unfamiliar pairings; *twaróg* cheese is freed from "mediocrity and anonymity" through expertise, authorship, and good taste. These shifts, which have evident class connotations, get entangled in economic competition (who produces the best? which products are worthy of higher prices?), institutional interventions (who decides the quality standards?), and national(ist) cultural tensions (what represents the best of Poland?). In the case of wine, however, there are no pre-existing categories of taste native to Poland, no standards of evaluation, and no language to talk about it. The product itself still comes across as foreign and classed to many Poles, so that it represents a sensory expression of upward mobility. Is it possible to include it in the taste of Polishness? The ongoing efforts to promote Polish wines show that tastemakers believe they can. While borrowing many elements from abroad, they are tweaking categories and standards to adapt them to their own context, as the support for hybrid grapes suggests.

TASTING *NALEWKI*

The sensory politics surrounding a prestige product like wine have had an impact on *nalewka*, a traditional spirit that most Poles are likely to recognize as familiar. *Nalewki* (the plural) are not the result of a fermentation process but rather of the maceration of fruits, flowers, herbs, spices or honey with the addition of sugar syrup and alcohol. The spirit is closely connected to foraging from forests and plains. *Nalewki* might be flavored with berries like rowan, dogwood, and buckthorn, which are quite exotic to non-Poles. These products confer to the spirit an unequivocal taste of place.

The manufacture of *nalewki* as an artisanal activity originates, like *kiszonki*, from home productions that Poles still practice. It operates in the gray area between legality and bootlegging, yet it is appreciated all over the country. With some noticeable exceptions, its distribution seems limited to informal networks of production and exchange in order to avoid taxation by the government and other regulatory headaches. Precisely because of these connections with rural culture and domestic environments, lively and at times heated conversations about manufacturing techniques, standards of quality, evaluation processes, and sensory categories abound. Many tastemakers are attempting to elevate the spirit to the same level of prestige and credibility enjoyed by a foreign import like wine. The need to better define *nalewka* is made more urgent by the marketing of drinks with the same name that in reality are just alcohol industrially mixed with natural and artificial flavors. These spirits have nothing to do with the traditional product.

The term *nalewka* probably comes from the Polish words *nalewać* or *nalew*, which refer to the process of pouring alcohol over fruits and other ingredients. The term became common around the mid-nineteenth century, apparently to distinguish this uniquely Polish product from other spirits made through maceration, such as French liqueurs, Italian ratafias, and cordials of all kinds, which were especially popular among the upper classes. Part of the current debate is due to the fact that it is difficult to determine the exact proportions between macerated ingredients and the amount of alcohol: fruits, berries, and roots have different water and sugar contents, as well as essential oils of varying intensity. This variability makes deciding the duration of the maceration for each batch an art. In general, the longer the maceration, the more intense the color and the flavor, which however can be spoiled by the ingredients' acidity.

To better understand these processes, we visited Karol Majewski, who owns and runs the Nalewki Staropolskie ("old-Polish *nalewki*") company out of his home in the outskirts of Warsaw. Nalewki Staropolskie is a tax-paying, fully legal operation that sells its products to the public, and as such it has acquired national visibility. Most of the production happens in the garden behind the Majewski family home, where huge glass demijohn-like jars filled with macerations of all colors sit on display. Majewski keeps track of each batch to ensure a certain uniformity in his product, which is then bottled, labeled, and packaged. To make fruit *nalewki*, Majewski covers the ingredients with alcohol and allows it to macerate for a length of time ranging from a couple of weeks to over a month. He then filters and sets aside the alcohol before covering the remaining ingredients with sugar. After a few weeks, the resulting syrup is combined with the alcohol from the maceration. However, some producers add sugar and honey at the same time they pour the alcohol over the ingredients, which can cause some fermentation to take place. Zbigniew Sierszuła, widely considered one of the most respected *nalewka* experts, told us that this second method produces "vodka with fruit juice."

Sierszuła was the head judge in two *nalewka* competitions that we had the opportunity to witness, the first during the 2017 Gruczno Festival of Taste and the other during Poznań's 2018 Food Festival. Coauthor Fabio Parasecoli was invited to participate in the first one as a member of the tasting panel: the participants were curious to hear his take on the drink as a foreign culinary expert who had not been exposed to *nalewka* before. While the Gruczno contest was more informal, the one in Poznań was noticeably more structured, with over seventy entries, most of which had been delivered to the organizers the day before. Small shot glasses with *nalewki* were placed on grids with numbers, which allowed the judges to give marks anonymously. At first the marks were jotted on paper. Later, when the judges had been able to better calibrate their evaluation after having tasted all the entries, they were transferred to a software that tallied the final scores.

Those who had submitted their spirits were mostly male hobbyists. We were told that women frequently make *nalewki* at home, but it is just for their family's and friends' consumption; they do not join the hobbyists' networks that go foraging together, discuss good places to find berries, and share tips. The men in these networks use the word "organic" not in the sense of certi-fied, but meaning far from the road, clean, free from pesticides. Shared cat-egories of taste evaluation may emerge here and there within and among these networks, based on personal and communal memories; however, some of the contestants expressed their creativity by working with unusual flavors like pineapple, dried lemon, or honey and salt. Their perception of what is good and bad at times clashes with the standards and expectations of the judges, who claim legitimacy and expertise. We could not detect any exten-sive vocabulary being explicitly articulated. Some general evaluation criteria that came up included: not too much sugar; clarity; purity of flavor; color; good quality alcohol and good extraction. The goal was to discern quality in the production method rather than giving primacy to particular flavors.

Some spirits were deemed too weak, disparaged with jokes about *nalewki* for kids and *kompot*, a beverage obtained by boiling fruits in water. A judge sarcastically quipped: "It would taste really good if it were mixed with alco-hol." Other *nalewki* were too sweet: "It would help this *nalewka* if the gov-ernment went back to rationing sugar like back in the day." Excessive reliance on sugar was seen as incompetence and as an attempt at masking defects. A criterion that was explicitly discussed, however difficult to define, was the presence of "natural" and artisanal characteristics. Some of the entries were criticized as factory-produced candy or as tasting like hospital medicine, as opposed to herbal.

The conversations among judges differed from those that usually take place in wine or beer tasting where the vocabulary and the parameters are relatively established and clear due to a higher degree of institutionalization in terms of training, books, and connection with international and authori-tative networks. In the *nalewki* contest, the evaluation appeared to be based on claims to embodied experience rather than articulated discourse. Although contestants and experts seem to recognize certain *nalewki* flavors as unquestionable expressions of Polishness that do not even require discussion, it is unclear if contests have any effect in introducing widely shared and uncontested evaluation categories. "Some people like oranges, some other people like when their feet are stinky," one of the organizers said, citing his grandmother. The joke pointed to the relatively arbitrary nature of evaluations in a newly-emerging field that is trying to achieve recognition and respectability by establishing shared standards of quality.

THE TASTE OF THE URBAN

The tastemakers' efforts to define the new taste of Polishness have given rise to emerging categories of sensory evaluation in products as diverse as *kiszonki*, wine, and *nalewki*. Although these categories vary product by product, they all reflect the same investment in excitement, originality, artisanality, and locality that tastemakers hope will raise the profile of Polish cuisine both domestically and internationally. Tastemakers may also intervene on urban landscapes to generate a sense of place. Although many Poles live in the countryside and in small urban centers, where a shared sense of unadulterated Polishness may be less contested and more integrated into everyday life, the growing urban population increasingly expresses a desire for a Polishness that can be experienced in what they eat and what they see in cities. However, although connected to local identities, materialities, and the stories people tell, the urban perception of culinary Polishness tends to be different from what rural contexts take for granted. Despite exceptions like Pszczelarium, relying on bees and the pollens from local flowers to provide a taste of the city (see chapter 4), it is built environments, rather than soil, flora, and fauna, that contribute to shaping such identities.

Markets have played a central role in solidifying urban food cultures by reaffirming their role as magnets for good products from the countryside. After World War II, markets mainly supplied the population with agricultural products. They flourished again in the nineties as spaces of bottom-up unrestrained entrepreneurship (Zuzańska-Żyśko and Sitek 2011) but started to decline later on when opportunities for Poles to shop in Western-style supermarkets and discount stores increased. In 2021 there were more than two thousand markets in Poland, with this number slightly declining in the years since (Statistics Poland 2022). However, all markets are not equal. Nowadays, old-school markets still thrive, providing fresh food to wide segments of consumers who are attuned to convenience, familiarity, and good prices (Maciuła-Ziomek 2023; Malinowska 2016). At the same time, up-and-coming farmers' markets and food stores offer more curated, upscale environments with broader varieties of products that tend to have higher price tags.

They greatly vary in typology, ranging from the former military garrisons of Forteca Kręgliccy in Warsaw and the grand structure of Hala Targowa in Wrocław,[2] to the large, apparently temporary but actually permanent tents of Bazar Natury in Gdańsk and the mix of open spaces and old utilitarian buildings for Targ Pietruszkowy in Kraków, the first farmers' market in Poland with an explicit connection to the Slow Food international association. The oldest indoor farmers' markets maintain a certain shabby air that reflects the pioneering times in which they were launched. Located in an unassuming prewar building with some more modern additions and a small bistro beside it, Bazar Olkuska in Warsaw has been operating uninterruptedly since the late 2000s. Open six days a week, it presents a mix of aesthetics ranging from the elegant to the casually thrown together; shoppers can find Hungarian products, French cheese, and exotic spices next to artisanal breads, handmade jams, and organic produce. Despite some structural renovations and design interventions here and there, Bazar Olkuska feels relatively unpretentious and inclusive, with prices that are higher than in common markets but still affordable.

The visual and sensory contrast between old and new markets can be striking. In Warsaw, Hala Mirowska—built at the turn of the nineteenth and twentieth centuries, destroyed during World War II, and rebuilt afterward—is one of the oldest locations to buy food in the capital. Most stalls are simple, the experience straightforward and utilitarian, but basic groceries are available at reasonably affordable prices (at least until recently), together with non-food products like shoes, clothes, tableware, and cheap electronics. Some new stalls are popping up here and there offering more expensive, less common products, but Hala Mirowska has overall maintained its approachable character. However, it has been threatened by attempts at redeveloping and beautifying the bazaar that every day pops up around it. People from all walks of life shop in it, creating a visual, auditory, and olfactory landscape that reinforces the shabby but lively feel of the place.

Right across the street, Hala Gwardii was built in the same period as Hala Mirowska, as part of an extended complex of shopping halls. It too was destroyed during World War II, after which it was rebuilt as a bus depot and later, in the 1950s, transformed into an important center for Polish boxing. A ring and displayed pictures from past fights hearken back to that period. With its metal and glass architectural features and soaring roof, Hala Gwardii now fits into a contemporary vision of urban middle-class leisure, with stalls selling food that can be eaten around long shared tables and spaces for cultural events and exhibitions, as well as shopping for high-end food and non-food products. The clientele is quite different from the nearby Hala Mirowska: during our visit, we only saw fashionably dressed people, mostly young, who moved at ease among the stalls, chatting with vendors with whom they share not only languages and mannerisms, but also ideas about food and eating. While we were there, we observed one elderly lady who entered the space and immediately made a U-turn to exit, apparently feeling uncomfortable and out of place. Contemporary music played in the background (we were told that at times there is a live DJ).

The aesthetics of the stalls and the overall vibe of the place reflected the style that we have elsewhere described as "Global Brooklyn" (Parasecoli and Halawa 2021). As the market's web page explains, "The creators of today's Hala Gwardii draw inspiration from the history of Hala Mirowska and from such places as Lisbon's Mercado da Ribera, London's Borough Market, New York's Chelsea Market, Lyon's Les Halles De Bocuse, and Mercado Boqueria in Barcelona." This is a space that is easily recognizable to cosmopolitan foodies, both Polish and foreign; it is part of a "leisurization" of former utilitarian and production spaces that is recurrent in contemporary urban renewal projects in postindustrial societies (Parham 2012).

However, the fascination with such spaces only works if its origins and previous uses are still readable to customers, who want to feel they are experiencing an "authentic" connection with their roots. Architectural structures and interior design are maintained and restored, while new elements are added to increase a sense of novelty and excitement for visitors. In Warsaw, another old market, Hala Koszyki, has become a hotspot for shopping and dining, with one of the busiest bars in town located at its center. Smaller stalls and larger stores take advantage of the wide space, with shared tables and seatings made of upcycled wood and pipes echoing the metalwork details of the structure. The market is busy during the day with shoppers and at night with revelers. Food entrepreneur and restaurant owner Justyna Kosmala told us that in 2013 she and her collaborators had come up with the idea of a food place in the then-abandoned and run-down market. Confirming the importance of foreign influences in the Polish food scene, she felt it was very Williamsburg and Brooklyn in inspiration and vibe. At the time, their intentions were met with great skepticism; although the pop-up food court they set up became a hit, they were not given permission to continue. It was not until later that real estate developers renovated the place as it is today.

An old decommissioned train station in Warsaw has become the location for the summer Nocny (night) Market. Metal tables and chairs in bright colors have been added to the preexisting benches to provide seating for young customers who buy food and drink from the stalls located around the platforms. The vendors mostly sell interpretations of exotic foods, from ramen to baos, with some Polish options sprinkled here and there. Here, the sense of place is created by affordable, accessible cosmopolitanism rather than by local food traditions. Similarly, in Poznań an old repair pavilion belonging to the public railways, always at the brink of being torn down, is home to the Nocny Targ Towarzyski, a night market where food is sold out of food trucks while dance parties and cultural events happen on the main floor.

At times urban renewal tackles whole industrial areas, as in the case of Fabryka Norblina in Warsaw. This market occupies a former metal factory that was founded in 1820 as a private enterprise, nationalized after World War II, and shut down in the 1980s. The wide and soaring pavilions have been gutted and redecorated in a contemporary style with exposed bricks, metal, wood, and glass as prevalent materials, gesturing to the location's history. Brick chimneys, portions of production lines, and large pieces of machinery (lit in red to evoke the heat of furnaces), have been turned into impressive decorative pieces devoid of any function except to connect the contemporary leisure and shopping space with its past. These attempts to establish a sense of continuity with history while suggesting the excitement of a lively urban place are most visible in the blue and red murals on one of the whitewashed external walls that represent the factory as it used to appear in its productive heyday.

One of the main attractions in Fabryka Norblina is Food Town, a food court located inside one of the largest pavilions with stalls, stores, and food trucks offering Polish and foreign fare. A nearby pavilion has been transformed into a Biobazar for organic products and ready meals to go. All the vendors display their food on the same racks and shelves made of streamlined, light-hued wood reminiscent of both Swedish 1950s furniture and Ikea; a wooden roof with glass skylights, hanging lamps, and exposed bricks all reflect the hip, contemporary "Global Brooklyn" aesthetic. Similarly, the old cellars of the nearby decommissioned Browary Warszawskie brewery, with high barrel vaults lined in red exposed brick, hosts a bustling food court, where the stalls present a prevalence of metal, wood, glass, and neon assembled in a minimalist style that is also reflected in the small wooden tables and stools for the customers.

These initiatives of urban renewal are not limited to the capital. The *Dolne Młyny* complex in Kraków was located in the former State Cigar and Tobacco Products Factory. Its small, low buildings were transformed into restaurants and events spaces from 2016 to 2020, when the foundation that managed it sold it to a real estate developer. During this short period, the compound became a hit among locals and tourists that enjoyed its postindustrial flair, with slightly dirty whitewashed walls enlivened by wood cafe terraces, doors and window fixtures painted in bright colors, whimsical neon signs, and pieces of contemporary art. The best example of a new use of a liminal, semi-abandoned former industrial district is arguably the Gdańsk shipyards, where the Solidarność movement started in the 1980s. The huge area is peppered with buildings and heavy machinery that are still partly functioning, although not as a state-owned enterprise any longer. Amid these machines, abandoned spaces have been turned into art studios, exhibition galleries, shops, cafés, and other leisure spaces. The high ceiling structures still show their original use for industrial production, representing both the ambivalent legacy of socialism and the prewar German history of industrialization (Stacul 2018). Cement, brick, glass, and metal establish a postindustrial atmosphere, amplified by the use of wood pallets and other recycled materials in the interior design. Hanging plants and neon signs in bright colors underlie the hip atmosphere.

It needs to be clarified that all of the renovations we have described are the initiative of private entrepreneurs and real estate developers. Although they may embrace an aesthetic that in other parts of the world may be connected with squatting and other anticapitalist activities aimed at reclaimed unused spaces, in Poland the phenomenon is mainly commercial, with designers and architects leveraging the material traces of working-class activities to create a sense of place for young, educated, upwardly mobile clients who want to enjoy the same experiences as their peers elsewhere. These locations contribute to establish new aesthetic categories whose effect spills over in domestic and institutional environments.

The renovations evoke localized bygone eras to generate an exciting sense of urban place that is both the expression of a recognizable local history and the reflection of the global circulation of foodie preferences and practices.

170 · CHAPTER 6

International and exotic menus reflect the sense of novelty and excitement that these initiatives are supposed to convey. Of course, quite often the flavors, aromas, and textures of foreign fare are heavily adapted to meet the expectations and the preferences of the local customers. Meanwhile, Polish food is presented in creative ways, often in street food style as in the case of the UOBIOD pop-up (similar to the Polish word *obiad*, dinner, but in dialect) by culinary creator Magiczny Składnik (Tomek Czajkowski); in this version, it embodies the "new" light and intriguing taste of Polishness that our tastemakers seem keen on developing. The visual dimension is central to these spaces and the sensory experiences they afford: videos and pictures easily reach potential customers around the world and establish transnational expectations about what passes for cool and trendy. It is not by chance that such locations are designed to be Instagrammable.

RECREATING JEWISHNESS

The desire to use food as a catalyst to generate a sensory Polishness that reflects the priorities and aspirations of urban dwellers has also given rise to the rediscovery of a Jewish culinary culture which had almost completely been erased in the twentieth century. The current absence is particularly strident when compared to the past liveliness of Jewish communities both in rural and urban environments and their contribution to local economies, culture, and social life. The role of Poles in the annihilation of the Polish Jewish population, either through lack of protection against the horror of Nazism or episodes of collaboration that allowed some Poles to take possessions of Jewish land, homes, and money, has become the object of heated political debates that reverberate in academia, museums, and public memory-making processes. In 2018, the conservative government passed a law—the Amended Act on the Institute of National Remembrance—that outlawed any public reference to crimes committed by Poles during the Holocaust. Authors and academics had to face investigations and trials for highlighting historical facts whose very authenticity became the object of debate (Gessen 2021; Kończal 2020).

While tastemakers do not appear to intentionally reflect on these tensions when launching their initiatives, it is against this fraught background that the desire to bring back remnants of Jewish life in Poland, or to create simulacra of it when nothing is left, has been incorporated in the emerging culinary scene. Flavors, sounds, visual clues, and built environments are all activated to establish an often-nostalgic Jewish sensory landscape. Tastemakers appear intent on highlighting elements that can present Poland as diverse, multicultural, and non-uniformly Catholic. The interest in Jewish cuisine is part of a larger Polish phenomenon that has been variously described as "Jewish revival" (Just 2015), "virtual Jewishness" in the absence of Jews (Gruber 2009), and "philosemitism" (Zubrzycki 2022). For Geneviève Zubrzycki (2022, xiii), it consists of "performative solidarity and empathetic forms of cultural appropriation" that is "evident in the gentrification of Kraków's Jewish Quarter, Kazimierz; the slow but steady growth and increased visibility of that city's festival of Jewish culture, and the creation of local 'Jewish Days' throughout the country" (xiv). Such philosemitism implies "various degrees of objectification and instrumentalization of Jews" (10).

Artists and public intellectuals reflect on Jewish-Polish relations in the past and the present. For instance, in 2001 artist Doug Fishbone installed an enormous pile of bananas in the main square of the small town of Piotrków Trybunalski. The main inspiration for this piece was, in the words of the artist, "the mountains of possessions looted from Jews in the death camps— the piles of shoes and heaps of eyeglasses that haunt old photos" (Fishbone 2002). Quite different from the banana-focused protests we discussed in chapter 2.

Commercial and cultural activities geared toward non-Jews are organized and conducted mostly by non-Jewish Poles, who also engage in scholarly research and musealization, at times with the support of Jewish experts. Polin, the museum of the history of Polish Jews, opened in Warsaw in 2013 with Barbara Kirshenblatt-Gimblett, a performance studies scholar previously at New York University, as chief curator (Grudzińska-Gross and Nawrocki 2016). At the same time, the small contemporary Jewish community of Poland has become more visible and organized (Aust 2022). Since 2013 the café of the Warsaw Jewish Community Center has been organizing very popular Sunday brunches, offering both Mediterranean and Polish Jewish dishes to fashionable crowds that may include local Jews (Koenig 2019). The center also offers cooking classes meant to introduce younger generations of Jews to their own culinary traditions (Rakowiecka 2018). During the COVID pandemic, they published *Boker Tov: JCC Warsaw Kosher Vegetarian Recipes and Stories*, a recipe book both in Polish and English (Musidłowska 2021).

Curiosity about Jewish cuisines is growing well beyond the community. Zubrzycki observed a cooking class during Kraków's Jewish Cultural

Festival, in which most sessions were dedicated to explaining the rules of kashrut and how they impact cuisine (Zubrzycki 2022, 122). The participants were apparently eager to learn how to cook Jewish dishes, some out of fascination for a form of domestic exoticism, others because they suspected Jewish ancestry in their families. Such interest is also reflected in Jewish cooking books, such as *Dietojarska kuchnia żydowska* (Dietoyar Jewish cuisine) (Lewando 2020) by vegetarian Fania Lewando, arguably the best-known figure in prewar Polish Jewish cooking, and Hanna Merlak's *Żydzi od kuchni: Opowieści wokół rodzinnego stołu* (Jews from the kitchen: Stories around the family table) (Merlak 2019).

The lack of knowledge about Jewish culinary heritage prompted the Polin museum to organize in 2022 the special exhibition *Od Kuchni: Żydowska Kultura Kulinarna*, translated into English for the many foreign visitors as "What's Cooking? Jewish Culinary Culture." As curator Tamara Sztyma pointed out during our visit, "this exhibition is the opportunity to explain something, because of course, when Jewish people come, they all know what kashrut is. For Polish people, it's something like magic." Using kashrut as an entry point to examine the past, contemporary Jewish life in Poland, and the diaspora, the exhibition touched on Jewish history, law, culture, and holidays. To engage the youngest visitors, a dedicated playroom contained very large and tactile interactive installations that allowed children to "braid a challah" or to "cook cholent."

Pursuing the goal of education, every year since 2018 the museum has organized the TISH Jewish Food Festival. Through talks, hands-on cooking workshops (which often take place in a museum space named after Lewando), walks, and film screenings, the festival aims to familiarize Poles with Jewish culinary traditions. In 2019, among the various activities was a Shabbat dinner at Charlotte Menora, a Jewish-themed café that offers rugelach, poppyseed cookies, and challah to a mostly young, well-heeled customer base. US Jewish cookbook author Leah Koenig participated in it: "The dishes served were a mix of Ashkenazi classics—roasted chicken, pear and plum kugel, honey cake, and Hungarian egg and onion spread—and Sephardi dishes like Moroccan roasted carrots and *marak katom* (Israeli "orange soup"). But the gathering of more than 80 people in a room to light candles, toast l'chaim, and celebrate Shabbat dinner in Warsaw felt quietly staggering. For generations, this was what Jewish life in Warsaw felt like. Now, it was a novelty" (Koenig 2019). In fact, many of the dishes of the menu would probably have come across as unfamiliar to older Polish Jews.

The emerging taste for Jewish cuisine in Poland is part of the similar sensory politics that exist around wine, *nalewki*, or bread, in which education and other forms of cultural capital, class identity, location, economic interests, and institutional interventions all contribute to shifting categories of taste and values. The new Polish Jewish cuisine tastes to non-Jewish Poles like modernity, pluralism, and cosmopolitanism, regardless of whether it is kosher or not. In fact, tastemakers are aware that this reconstruction of an almost disappeared cuisine is different from what it used to be. In early 2024 Chef Aleksander Baron opened the restaurant Kapłony i szczeżuje (Capons and duck mussels) in Kraków's former Jewish neighborhood, with the vision of exploring the past Jewish culinary traditions of Poland, to highlight their contributions to Polish cuisine, and to reinterpret them with a contemporary flare (although without following kashrut rules).

Justyna Kosmala, the entrepreneur behind Charlotte Menora with her sister Basia Kłosińska, explained to us that when they were planning the cafe, they collaborated with Erez Komarowsky, considered the initiator of artisanal breadmaking in Israel in the 1990s. A gay, liberal chef who published a recipe for suckling pig on Yom Kippur and routinely collaborates with Arab chefs, Komarowsky aligns with the contemporary approach that the sisters wanted to introduce at Charlotte Menora. However, although it was their intention from the beginning to highlight Jewish culinary traditions, the baked products in the café are not strictly kosher because there are not enough clients who keep kosher to justify the expense and effort. Their formula has been so successful that in 2023 they opened a second Charlotte Menora in Kraków. At the same time, kosher grocery stores (*koszerne sklepy*) are popping up here and there—mostly in large urban centers—to cater to the Jewish population.

Not all Jewish-themed eateries have Baron's or Charlotte Menora's cultural inspiration. It is enough to take a stroll in Kraków's Kazimierz area, which until World War II used to be a thriving area for the local Jewish community but has now been turned into a "Jewish theme park" (Jochnowitz 2004, 99) both for Polish and foreign tourists. Walking in the streets of the neighborhood, one is often hailed by waiters trying to entice visitors, frequently with the claim that theirs is the oldest Jewish restaurant in town. When the weather is nice, non-Jewish musicians play klezmer on restaurant terraces to add an auditory dimension to the experience.

Most restaurants in Kazimierz do not follow kosher rules, as they are fully aware that the majority of their clients are not Jews. Some try, but in most cases they do not have kosher certificates. Those who do tend to offer Mediterranean fare like hummus and falafel, popular among Israeli customers, or Jewish American mainstays like pastrami; they appear to cater to the growing numbers of tourists from the Jewish diaspora who visit Poland to discover the history of their ancestors. Kazimierz restaurants mostly offer traditional Polish dishes, at times with supposedly Jewish-style twists (*po żydowsku*) such as the addition of garlic, raisins, or almonds. More recognizable Jewish dishes may include *gefilte fisch* (spelled in Yiddish), *gęsie szyjki nadziewane* (stuffed geese necks), *gęsi pipek* (goose stomach), *czulent* (cholent), *gicz jagnięca* (lamb knuckles), kugel, hamantaschen, and charoset. Other dishes present some variation, such as the *kawior żydowski* (Jewish caviar, chopped chicken livers and eggs) with "truffle aroma" and *cymes* (a Shabbat fruit and vegetable stew) served with lamb.

Some restaurants post outdoor menus with pictures of the dishes, to avoid misunderstandings; others mark Jewish specialties with a recognizable symbol, such as a menorah, similarly to how they indicate vegetarian or gluten free items. To increase the credibility of their Jewishness, some establishments use Hebrew lettering or fonts inspired by it on their menus, while vintage Jewish pictures, memorabilia, and objects are exhibited. In fact, the interiors are often intentionally cramped and overdecorated to add to the supposed authenticity of the experience.

Virtual Jewishness, however, is not universally celebrated or acknowledged. The connection with Jewish culture of certain dishes, such as *placki ziemniaczane* (latkes), *obwarzanki krakowskie* (a boiled and then baked braided ring-shaped bread, often sprinkled with sesame or poppy seeds, quite similar to bagels) and *bajgle* (bagels), is frequently glossed over. The picturesque town of Kazimierzy Dolny, on the Vistula river near Lublin, is acquiring national notoriety as the birthplace of bagels; numerous stores sell them, at times in versions that remind us quite a bit of American styles, both in texture, shape, and accoutrements. However, the possible connection between the presence of a lively pre-World War II Jewish community and the bagel tradition is only vaguely mentioned.

Historically, heated debates have raged over ritual slaughtering, in which culture-war arguments were entangled with political strategies and economic interests as Poland is a major exporter of kosher and halal meat (Dyda 2020). The legal disputes were resolved only with the intervention of the Constitutional Court of Poland, revealing the tensions underlying the integration of the Jewish community in the national project (Rzhevkina 2022).

Nevertheless, the exotic aura of Jewishness maintains an appeal, especially when contained as a consumable and controlled experience, as the success of kosher vodkas suggests. These spirits have always circulated in Poland (see chapter 5), as in pre-Partition times Jewish communities were able to receive authorization from noble landowners to produce and sell alcohol (Ingall 2003). Although kosher certification is legally required only for wine, vodkas with rabbinical approval often carry emphasized Jewish visual elements on their labels. In fact, the urban legend that kosher vodkas are healthier and leave no hangover is quite widespread.

As we opened our book with premium vodka in an upscale Warsaw bar, it is only fitting that vodka appears again at the end of our exploration of the tastemakers' role in the dynamics that are meant to change contemporary Polish cuisine. Both examples point to the centrality of materiality and the taste judgments around it in the shifts toward the more cosmopolitan and "elevated" taste of Poland that tastemakers are trying to promote. Soils, microorganisms, plants, and animals all contribute to create products that are also influenced by—and at times influence—landscapes, objects, architecture, and graphic design. Although the foods and spirits we analyzed in this chapter are clearly different, transversal categories of evaluation are emerging. They generate the overall sense that the Polish culinary field is moving away from a sensory world connoted by heaviness, boredom, unhealthiness, backwardness, and lack of refinement to one that is full of excitement, newfangled or rediscovered flavors, intriguing textures, and beautiful environments that will allow Poland to hold its own on the global foodie scene.

Such aspirations, however, are rife with intense sensory politics in which class, education, financial status, geographical location, and exposure to the world outside of Poland are crucial components. The economic competition to capture growing segments of affluent consumers has inevitable repercussions not only on the discursive worlds of media, marketing, and advertising, but also on the political negotiations that shape institutions, legal frameworks, and administrative regulations. Tastemakers' reinvention of Polish food to appeal to cosmopolitan appetites is far from being a done deal, and it is still unclear to which extent it will succeed.

Conclusions

POLAND'S GASTRONOMY HAS BEEN DEALING with a "pierogi problem." Most foreigners regard this stuffed dumpling as the sole Polish dish of note. While for the majority of Poles this may not be an issue, a new category of food professionals, experts, and entrepreneurs has been trying to change this state of affairs. We call them "tastemakers," as their often-explicit intention is to transform their fellow citizens' experience and evaluation of food, introducing new standards of quality and categories of judgment. Their ultimate goal is to improve Polish gastronomy and its image abroad, while establishing an autonomous and legitimate culinary field in which cultural values, economic priorities, and power positions are constantly negotiated.

While similar dynamics have been observed in other postsocialist Central and Eastern European countries, as the literature on the topic indicates, Polish tastemakers are happy and eager to point out the elements that distinguish Poland from its neighbors, including the variety of its natural and agricultural bounty and its unique history. One of their main strategies is to "rediscover," "bring back," or "elevate" local, traditional or historical, and artisanal foods that from their point of view were too boring and casual, or had been almost erased during the socialist years, or are currently at risk of disappearing because of the influx of industrial food in the marketplace, which is wholeheartedly welcomed by the vast majority of Poles. The tastemakers we have followed are trying to challenge two basic pillars of the contemporary Polish foodscape: familiar homely fare, which presents elements of a simplified and unified version of Polish cuisine, and the widely purchased generic products of the global food industry.

Tastemakers tend to partly attribute the predominance of these pillars to structural factors, including globalization, the expansion of (often foreign) retail chains, the ubiquity of mass-produced goods, as well as stifling bureaucracies and regulations, together with a lack of effective government involvement in the gastronomy sector. They also lay the blame on cultural and social dynamics, such as the scarce interest on the part of the average Pole toward their own culinary customs (which would justify tastemakers' role as experts and educators). However, this last claim is not supported by what we have seen and heard around the country.

Our research suggests that contrary to a widely held belief among tastemakers, Poles have not abandoned their culinary customs. It is not that traditional or artisanal foods do not exist any longer; they are simply not prevalent in the form that tastemakers and their growing foodie audience appreciate. Cheesemakers, bakers, and fermented food producers often operate in modalities that tastemakers perceive as underdeveloped, unrefined, and uncomfortably associated with shades of undesirable Eastern-ness. Since the end of socialism, consumption patterns have included foreign and "modern" food, but our research indicates that the majority of the population also feels a profound emotional attachment to traditional Polish foods, from *rosół* noodle soup to *schabowy* fried pork chops and, yes, pierogi. These foods may not be a constant presence on most Poles' tables, and nowadays not everybody knows how to make them—or to make them properly—but they still mark special occasions and holidays. In the fall of 2023, the internet was awash with pictures of the former president of Poland Lech Wałęsa blowing out candles placed on an unusually large *schabowy* for his eightieth birthday. Many Poles are likely to find this image, as exaggerated and performative as it is, not only "normal" and representative of their own habits, but also endearing. Those who instead discount this kind of Polish cuisine as predictable, backward, and unhealthy, may read this image as ridiculous or even embarrassing.

Tastemakers and foodies berate domestic home cooks, and professional cooks in the thousands of unpretentious eating establishments that still thrive across the country, for offering versions of Polish food that in the connoisseurs' eyes are bland, heavy, fatty, unoriginal, and uninteresting. Alternatively, these cooks may be discovered as hidden gems that tastemakers help refine, elevate, and bring to the attention of their audiences. These processes are not exclusively discursive: materials, services, and practices evolve to allow for acceptable food experiences that deserve being featured in the emerging culinary field. Tastemakers often show designer-like attitudes in their involvement with projects that extend to products and their sensory characteristics, recipes, objects, built environments, and even landscapes. This mode of material production also requires sustained interaction with soils, animals, plants, bacteria, and fungi that need to be cajoled into collaboration.

Despite their similarity to the local intelligentsia in terms of education, social backgrounds, and cultural attitudes, Polish tastemakers willingly engage with manual activities that until recently would be discounted as too blue-collar for any individual with middle-class aspirations. Nevertheless, they may frame their initiatives as didactic, thus implicitly declaring their involvement with the civilizing efforts that Polish intellectuals have often embraced as their mission. Tastemakers position themselves as cultural intermediaries connecting producers, artisans, and food entrepreneurs with a growing foodie community that is largely composed of educated and upwardly mobile individuals, city-dwellers, and professionals, including those who have recently moved to the countryside in search of a different life. For them, food anchors a culinary field through which they strive to establish their middle- or upper-class status, performing what we describe as "middle-classing" efforts.

Foodies are sensitive to tastemakers' advice, points of view, and aspirations because they often share their social and cultural backgrounds. They tend to speak the same language and partake in similar values. For both tastemakers and their audiences, food is part of an experience economy where stories and narratives connected to products are as important as their quality and sensory traits. Digital and social media—especially visual platforms—have become central to the tastemakers' mission to reimagine Polish food. As this emerging culinary culture is incessantly mediated, objects, spaces, and experiences are designed to be Instagrammable and sensually pleasurable.

In the hands of tastemakers, eating gets detached from the daily, tedious chores of reproductive labor aimed at nourishing bodies and providing basic social connectivity; it instead tends to reflect a dimension of leisure that requires not only financial means but also cognitive involvement. The foods and spirits that tastemakers promote and foodies enjoy tend to be knowledge-intensive: enlightened eaters are supposed to know the provenance of what they consume, the most appropriate ways to serve it, the best time of the year to eat it, and which varieties to seek out. To properly function, this circulation of culinary capital needs to be legitimated by specialists that claim authority and expertise within the culinary field. They do this by accessing external sources of cultural, social, economic, and political power to which they ascribe a superior status. Our research shows that Polish tastemakers and foodies tend to identify such sources of legitimacy from within the global community of food experts, producers, and professionals, from whom they strive to achieve full recognition.

In their attempts at redesigning the Polish culinary landscape, local tastemakers build a complex relationship between the global and the local. They borrow from international discourses, practices, and forms of engagement with materialities, to generate an inward-looking cosmopolitanism that, as in other postindustrial societies, extol local cultures and traditions as an antidote to globalization and its supposed tendency to erase difference. This paradoxical entanglement of external values with attitudes rooted in the local context is a fundamental feature in the transformation of the Polish culinary landscape we describe in this book. Comparable transformations are taking place in neighboring countries, but Polish tastemakers appear to be more preoccupied with finding acceptance and validation in Western-inflected culinary cosmopolitanism than in looking at similarities with other Central and Eastern European countries, which are often ignored as relevant points of reference.

It is important to acknowledge that the inward-looking forms of cosmopolitanism do not erase or replace its more outward-looking expressions, which have been prevalent among well-off Polish consumers since the end of the socialist regime. Tastemakers can appreciate native breeds of trout or local breadmaking techniques while enjoying ramen, kimchi, or risotto. In fact, both inward- and outward-looking forms of culinary cosmopolitanism are an expression of the same disposition toward omnivorousness that is observed in all strata of society, as is happening also in other postsocialist countries. Anybody can now enjoy affordable kebab, pizza, and donuts without giving up kiełbasa, *kopytka* potato dumplings, or *pączki* deep-fried desserts. This apparent democratization, however, does not stand in opposition to the classed dimension of the shifts taking place in the Polish culinary field: not all Poles have access to or can afford the same products in the same way.

These dynamics build on the widespread sense—shared by many tastemakers and foodies—that they have been detached from a West to which they legitimately belong, an element they feel implicitly differentiates Poland from other Central and Eastern European countries. The acknowledgment that Poland has been stuck in the geopolitical and cultural periphery of the world for decades engenders a certain inferiority complex. Polish tastemakers often express the desire to "catch up" with the rest of the world and make up for wasted time. Their efforts to connect to external sources of authority—in the hope of achieving the same level of prestige as their Western neighbors— is at the core of the way tastemakers embrace cosmopolitanism.

Food becomes a domain through which to claim a right to global power and modernity. Tastemakers benefit from the free flow of people and ideas that has taken the country by storm since the end of the socialist regime. They tend to position themselves among those who contribute to the Europeanization of Polish society. This is a part of their educational mission. In this context, food consumption turns into a form of both embodied class affiliation and participation in debates about what Poland was, is, and should be in the future. Statements about what is worthy of appreciation at a market, a store, or a restaurant can become part of the broader political controversies that have shaped Poland since the beginning of its postsocialist transformation.

Such political tensions have intensified with the turmoil that accompanied the conservative PiS (*Prawo i Sprawiedliwość* or Law and Justice) party's rise to power in 2015 and its attempts to impose its cultural and social tenets on civil society and public opinion. These events took place more or less at the same time as the emergence of tastemakers, cosmopolitan foodies' culture, and the overall culinary field in Poland. While it is not possible to claim direct causality between these phenomena, our research suggests that they are indeed connected and probably inscribed in the same culture wars, no matter how much certain intellectual circles may still underestimate the importance of food. While not all tastemakers resented or opposed the PiS's ideological stance and policies, many of them did not subscribe to the party's vision for the future of Poland, which was nevertheless espoused by large segments of the population. Because most Poles tend to support or at least approve of the revitalization of their country's food, both culturally and economically, Polish culinary traditions constantly get caught in ideological battles about the country's place in the world and the form of the national community.

As in other countries in the area (in particular Hungary and Slovakia), substantial numbers of Poles subscribe to nationalistic positions that aim to defend native social customs, religion, and cultural identity against internationalism and pressures from the West—the EU in particular. For this segment of the population, Polish food is an expression of the eternal spirit of Poland. They favor the establishment of canons and clear boundaries. Unlike Hungarian and Slovakian leaders, Polish PiS conservative leaders also felt a

CONCLUSIONS · 181

clear threat from the East, especially after Russia's attack on Ukraine and Belarus's support of the Kremlin's actions. This sense of urgency about a need for greater European defense integration is shared by the coalition that took power after the October 2023 election. The new government is composed of political forces that oppose PiS but that, at the time of writing, have embraced continuity with previous policies in terms of criticism of the European Green Deal and caution about immigration.

Progressive Poles hope for a more open, multicultural, and inclusive society in which patriotism does not necessarily mean nationalism (although at times the lines are quite blurred). For them, Polish food deserves respect and appreciation, but does not sit in opposition to other culinary cultures. They uphold local traditions not in contrast to Western hegemony, but as a remedy against globalization. Progressives—and many tastemakers and foodies among them—feel that Poland should claim its place as a peer among world gastronomies while staying open to the global circulation of ideas, values, and attitudes. This latter approach is instead painted as elitist and out of touch by those who have not reaped the benefits of the postsocialist transformation and the country's opening to the world.

However, even progressive tastemakers often seem to act under the implicit belief that an objective and unwavering essence of Polishness, which Poles are supposedly able to intuitively identify and understand, exists. Probably due to their efforts to assert the legitimacy and value of Polish cuisine, many tastemakers tacitly operate on the assumption that Polishness is indigenous, given, and recognizable, a horizon to which local, ethnic, and religious identities are implicitly subordinated. They tinker with history and tradition; they acknowledge, define, and integrate regional food customs; they use their own biographies as an important source of legitimacy and professional expertise; and they challenge authenticity by adding contemporary or foreign ingredients to local food. In other words, they select the building blocks for their current projects, while claiming that they are upholding all that is Polish. However, the landscape is far from monolithic: different understandings of the nation and national culture coexist, allowing the emergence of a variety of approaches to local, traditional, and artisanal food.

The political landscape is too complex and contested to allow for unequivocal correlations between conservative–progressive tensions and the culinary dynamics we have identified. As in other Central and Eastern European countries, we are not dealing with clear-cut dichotomies but rather with a spectrum on which one position can gradually morph into the next. For

182 · CONCLUSIONS

example, our analysis of Polish media indicates that seemingly contradictory attitudes can find expression in the same TV show, magazine, or even in the work of the same writer. Our research has also revealed a widespread no-nonsense apolitical pragmatism that freely borrows elements and themes from both conservative and progressive ideologies. These pragmatist consumers make value choices and practical decisions around food while thinking of their family and close community, rather than the nation as a whole. For them, cost, accessibility, and convenience constitute central motivations.

The future of the tastemakers' project remains open. On the one hand, inward-looking forms of cosmopolitanism may cease to be attractive to the more progressive sectors of society, because they might align too closely with nationalistic attitudes that have prevailed in neighboring countries and even in the "eternal enemy" Russia. If this is the case, a new turn toward worldliness may become a remedy against a surfeit of nationalist discourse. On the other hand, a sustained focus on local production and practices can remain relevant as possible solutions to climate change, economic crises, and the excesses of globalization. This outlook may be appealing not only to cosmopolitan tastemakers but also to those trying to oppose overconsumption, as well as to the more pragmatic sectors of the populations that equate tradition, in any way it may be conceptualized and experienced, with family and stability.

Future studies should examine how the classed dimension of the changes we explore in this book will evolve over time. To what extent will the Polish tastemakers' project remain an elite one? We started our research eight years ago. Since then, COVID-19 transformed the world, followed by high inflation, the war in Ukraine, and the transit of millions of refugees, many of whom have settled in Poland. Through all this, Poland's domestic political world has remained in constant turmoil. Walking through Warsaw or any major city, we are struck by the number of restaurants—which, however, a large sector of the population can no longer afford. Shifting socio-political circumstances, in particular growing inequalities, could make the tastemakers' vision impossible to achieve. In today's climate, their attempts to redesign the Polish culinary landscape may come across as more elitist than they did before, inaccessible even for the intelligentsia and the most affluent circles. It might not be possible to democratize an "elevated" Polish cuisine.

This resistance to progressive culinary change is likely to unfold in similar ways in other Central and Eastern European countries, which like Poland may be experiencing various degrees of postindustrialization. In the whole area, the impact of growing inequality on the potential for local cuisines to evolve is amplified and intensified by the structural consequence of COVID in terms of shifts in production and exports, the weaponization of the food trade accompanying the Ukrainian conflict, the negative impact of climate change, and the extreme weather events that are taking place with increasing frequency. In Poland's case, wine production may expand as temperatures rise, while some traditional crops—from mushrooms to wild berries and cold weather grains—that we have seen play such an important role in defining culinary and sensory Polishness may be affected. As the research on the food cultures of Central and Eastern Europe expands, it will be interesting to see how future developments converge or diverge, and to what point Polish tastemakers will be able to claim the uniqueness and distinctiveness of their culinary landscape. Moreover, as the country's economy develops—partly due to its sheer size and its crucial geopolitical role—the case of Poland should be further examined in comparison with other mid-income countries in other regions of the world, especially those that have embraced various forms of gastrodiplomacy as expressions of soft power.

Finally, we want to emphasize that our book does not only examine the influence of global food culture on Poland, but also how Polish tastemakers strive to achieve visibility and legitimacy on the international culinary scene, in order to eventually leave their mark on it. We argue that important insights can emerge from observing the international circulation of values, trends, and practices in the culinary field of countries that find themselves at the periphery of that world. How will the attempts by tastemakers and foodies to be incorporated into global circles impact the future of local crops, food production activities, and evaluation of existing culinary cultures in countries outside of the supposed core? Will the growing emphasis on locality, tradition, and artisanality constitute a valid antidote to the disasters inflicted by neoliberal models of globalization around the world? How will foods from the periphery be integrated into the circulation of specialties that is characteristic of the international foodie culture? Will these products be so expensive as to become unaffordable for the very communities that produce them? Will growing demands for those specialties encourage the expansion of their production to the point that they may cause environmental and social damage?

These are crucial questions that may be difficult to address from the core locations in global foodie culture. In high-income countries, despite growing inequalities, larger sectors of the population have relatively easy access to artisanal and certified foods, especially as their production increases and prices become more affordable. In Italy, France, and Spain, for instance, supermarket chains already sell geographical indication products under discounted labels, a situation which is still unthinkable in Poland (also due to the lesser interest in adopting these forms of intellectual property). Monitoring the evolution of the culinary scene in Poland, especially in terms of its connection with local social and political dynamics, may offer insights to better understand the present and the future of other "peripheral" postsocialist and mid-income countries, as well as their dialogue with the core countries in global foodie culture.

Appendix

EXPLORING FOOD IN POLAND: LITERATURE AND AUTOETHNOGRAPHIC REFLECTIONS

The research project from which this book originates was a rewarding experience not only in terms of our engagement with Poland's rapidly changing culinary landscape, but also because it has provided us numerous opportunities for broader and deeper reflections about knowledge production in a country that, despite its rapid economic development, still suffers from a sense of peripherality, if not inferiority, on the global intellectual and academic scene. These tensions emerge not only in our specific research but also in ethnography in general, its role in producing culture, and the power dynamics that inevitably underpin it. Our collaboration, which involves scholars from distinct backgrounds, with different experiences, and at various stages of their professional careers, has encouraged us to turn the ethnographic approach on ourselves, even when it was not comfortable, and examine how our own project has engaged with these underlying issues (Bachórz and Parasecoli 2020). In this appendix we share autoethnographic considerations that can be useful to those planning to conduct research in an international and interdisciplinary team. We believe that self-awareness and constant dialogue are necessary to assess power relations in this kind of collaboration, as well as other culture, gender, and class dynamics.

Addressing these imbalances also convinced us about the need to highlight Polish scholars' research about food, which due to language is often not accessible to outsiders. This relative insularity has contributed to a certain sense of isolation that a new generation of Polish researchers has resisted, making their work more available and interacting with intellectual debates outside of their country. However, a certain number of Polish intellectuals resist the pressure to produce research in foreign languages, notably in English, which they resent as yet another example of foreign imperialism. For this reason, we start this appendix with a discussion about differences, misunderstandings, and potential for collaboration among scholarly literatures on food originating in Poland and from outside the country. We also examine the expansion of food-related research both inside and outside food studies, an academic field that is relatively established in the United States and other Western countries but has not achieved intellectual and institutional autonomy in Poland.

THE LITERATURE ABOUT FOOD IN POLAND

It is not without significance that a number of sociological and anthropological studies on "food in the Eastern Bloc" and "food in Poland" before and after 1989 have been carried out by Western European and American universities and publishing houses. After 1989 the "postsocialist framework" was applied to replace and redefine the former East-West division, (e.g. Caldwell, Dunn, and Nestle 2009; Yung, Klein, and Caldwell 2014); however, this did not necessarily entail a shift in power relations between Eastern and Western scholarly perspectives about food in Poland. In the field of food-related research, the use of postsocialism as the main framework runs the risk of positioning "everyday," "working-class," or "peasant" food as the only foodways worth studying in Poland, which introduces the possibility of an orientalist othering of blue-collar and rural segments of the population. This approach has often considered gourmet food and fine dining as relevant only to the West.

For these reasons, amongst others, the use of postsocialism as a framework is controversial (Gracjasz 2024; Kopczyńska and Bachórz 2018; Müller 2019). While for some the "postsocialism" terminology allowed for a focus on agency, with the goal of recognizing the value of local resources (Dunn 2004), others claimed it maintained a binary picture of Europe under a new name and did not give a voice to representatives of the former Eastern Bloc (Červinkova 2012). Moreover, this kind of study often revealed a problematic international division of labor in which theoretical frameworks and analytical concepts were developed in dominant academic centers in the West, and local scholars played the role of those who provided empirical data and "local knowledge" (Buchowski 2004; Buchowski and Červinkova 2015). Recently, however, Central and Eastern European scholars have been highlighting their original theoretical contributions, which derive precisely from doing research in the periphery (Jehlička et al. 2020).

As limited scientific literature on Polish food exists in languages other than Polish, our work builds on the extant and extensive research that local scholars have produced in Poland within disciplines such as sociology, ethnology, anthropology, history and, in particular, in the budding circles of scholars focusing on food across a variety of disciplines. The book's references include sources both in English and in Polish, which have often been omitted in Western scholarly conversations. To make such sources more accessible, we have provided translations of titles in Polish.

Despite the many continuities in food preferences and practices between contemporary times and postwar everyday life (Domański et al. 2015a), food in Poland, as in other postindustrial societies, is an increasingly relevant site for the formation, negotiation, and performance of new individual and collective identities. As diverging evaluations exist of the economic and political transformation processes, in recent years a growing interest in food-related issues as part of these broader dynamics has become visible in Polish academia (e.g. Jarecka and Wieczorkiewicz 2014; Straczuk 2016b).

Polish scholarly journals have dedicated special issues to food in the humanities and social sciences (Bielenin-Lenczowska and Hryciuk 2018; Hryciuk and Król 2020; Kopczyńska and Bachórz 2018). Scholars have published several academic monographs about food (Domański et al. 2015a; Goszczyński 2023; Kopczyńska 2021; Straczuk 2013). Collaborations among researchers working on food and a series of seminars have emerged since the late 2010s under the Food and Drink Research Network frame (Sieć badaczek i badaczy jedzenia i picia). A Food Seminar (Seminarium Jedzeniowe) was conducted in the Institute of Ethnology and Cultural Anthropology of Warsaw University between 2013 and 2016. The Nicolaus Copernicus University in Toruń has established a Research Center for Food History and Culture, while the University of Social Sciences and Humanities (SWPS) in Warsaw has launched a postgraduate program in food studies.

This resurgence of interest has deep roots. Food has been a relevant topic of inquiry throughout the history of Polish ethnography, especially in terms of the study of foodways as part of the material culture of the peasantry. In the nineteenth century, when the country was partitioned among three empires, the results of this research were used in nation-building projects (Kolberg 1857–1890). This tradition was continued after World War II by younger generations of Polish ethnographers who predominantly focused on food traditions in the countryside and used regionality as an analytical category (e.g., Szromba-Rysowa 1978). Contemporary approaches to the study of food have been more recently incorporated into folklore studies, although many ethnographers and folklorists still investigate food primarily in the rural context, emphasizing notions of tradition, the sacred dimensions of food, and its festive or ritual uses. Many such studies have a regional character, with great attention especially dedicated to the food traditions of Silesia and Eastern Poland (Gomóła 2011; Karpińska 2013; Mroczkowska 2016; Przymuszała and Świtała-Trybek 2021; Szelągowska 2004; Tymochowicz 2019).

Food has also been examined by ethnologists and historians interested in heritage (Karpińska 2014; Kleśta-Nawrocki and Kleśta-Nawrocki 2017; Świtała-Trybek 2007). Projects conducted by Polish anthropologists from academic centers such as Warsaw, Łódź, Poznań, and Katowice (Boni 2015, 2016, 2024; Burszta and Kuligowski 2005; Zadrożyńska 2002) are in dialogue with developments in the international field of food studies, even when such work does not specifically focus on Poland (Caldwell 2004; Caldwell, Dunn, and Nestle 2009; Jehlička 2007; Mincyte 2011). Interest in material culture and in particular in the cultural politics of food has emerged in studies about Central and Eastern Europe, which have highlighted a variety of attitudes toward the contemporary market-based food system, ranging from embrace to refusal, from the continuation of preexisting food networks and infrastructures to the creation of alternative food networks (Bach 2017; Goszczyński et al. 2019; Gracjasz and Grasseni 2020; Gracjasz 2024; Mincyte 2012; Mroczkowska 2019; Blumberg and Mincyte 2020). Our research also builds on the theoretical contributions of scholars engaging with the role of food-related traditions and memory play in the construction of postsocialist individual and communal identities in Central and Eastern Europe (Ries 2009; Shkidrova 2021; Sōukand et al 2020). The attention to food offers unexplored venues for ongoing research about cultural participation in Polish society (Drozdowski et al. 2014; Krajewski 2013; Szlendak and Olechnicki 2014), which has been reframed along more anthropological lines in terms of everyday practices of living culture (Bachórz et al. 2014; Fatyga 1999; Sulima 2000).

Investigation on food in Poland has also been conducted within the discipline of sociology, exploring both the recent past and the present. Jacek Kurczewski (2004), for example, describes the political and social dynamics of food shortages during the socialist period. Others study various coping strategies in the contemporary food system (Bachórz 2018b; Kopczyńska 2018, 2021), focusing particularly on alternative food networks (Bilewicz and Śpiewak 2015; Goszczyński, Wróblewski, and Wójtewicz 2018; Goszczyński et al. 2019; Goszczyński 2023; Kopczyńska 2021). Henryk Domański and his collaborators used surveys and interviews to explore contemporary eating patterns in Poland, evaluating to what extent they reflect existing inequalities and stratification, and how they have been affected or influenced by social transformations. Domański's team particularly focused on the new phenomenon of omnivorism, or the willingness to try unfamiliar (mostly foreign) foods and to adopt them in one's dietary patterns as an expression of social mobility. Their research indicates that omnivorism is adopted by the upwardly mobile as a form of distinction that maintains the cultural separation between highbrow and lowbrow cultural expressions (Domański 2017; Domański and Karpiński 2018; Domański et al. 2015a, 2015b).

Historians in Poland have turned their attention to food as well (Stegner 2003). Jarosław Dumanowski from the Nicolaus Copernicus University in Toruń has published critical editions of historical Polish cookbooks in collaboration with the Museum of the King Jan III's Palace ad Wilanów in Warsaw (Czerniecki, Dumanowski, and Spychaj 2012; Dumanowski 2010; Dumanowski, Dias-Lewandowska, and Sikorska 2016). His work has precipitated the formation of a new generation of food historians (Dias-Lewandowska and Kurczewski 2018; Sikorska 2019). Until recently, the examination of recent periods, in particular the socialist decades, has been relatively under-emphasized, with some attention being paid to the state management of the food system and to the food shortages it caused. A new spate of studies is now expanding the range of such research (Milewska 2022; Piotrowski 2024; Stańczak-Wiślicz 2020).

While no English-language scholarly monographs exist on contemporary Polish foodways, a few English-language books exist on the history of food in Poland. Notable here are Maria Dembinska's (1999) *Food and Drink in Medieval Poland: Rediscovering a Cuisine of the Past*, a translation of her 1963 book, which focused on a specific (and quite remote) period, and the English translation of Jarosław Dumanowski's critical edition of the *Compendium Ferculorum* (Dumanowski 2014), a culinary treaty from the seventeenth century. *Old Polish Traditions in the Kitchen and at the Table* (1979), the English translation of a book by Maria Lemnis and Henryk Vitry (a pen name for the late noted musicologist Tadeusz Żakiej), has historical sections that provide information to introduce recipes, without scholarly pretense.

THE POLITICS OF INTERNATIONAL ETHNOGRAPHIC RESEARCH

The center-periphery dynamics we found ourselves facing in our project is not limited to scholarly literature distribution. As in any ethnographic project, it has been important for us to reflect on our own attitudes and positionality regarding the locality we operate in, the topic itself, and the politics of ethnographic fieldwork, including within the team. This assessment is particularly important as our research team straddles intellectual worlds with very different access to visibility, prestige and, ultimately, power. Our research is the result of the collaboration between Fabio Parasecoli, a food insider but cultural outsider in the Polish context; Mateusz Halawa, conversely a food outsider and cultural insider; and Agata Bachórz, a Polish scholar who is primarily a sociologist and a food researcher second. Parasecoli was the principal investigator in the project, funded by a grant from the Narodowe Centrum Nauki (the Polish National Science Centre); Halawa and Bachórz were coresearchers, with Bachórz joining the team after the research had started. While leveraging both the outsider and insider perspectives, we have tried to constantly maintain awareness of the power dynamics among us and with our interlocutors, as well as the impact of Parasecoli's position as a well-known food scholar and writer in granting access but also in influencing existing conversations.

The power relations between the societies and the academic worlds from which we come constitute the background of our collaboration. A center-periphery frame (Zarycki 2009) is an accurate conceptualization of this relationship. While Parasecoli is a full professor in an internationally renowned university in a global center of knowledge production, the United States, Bachórz and Halawa are instead connected to Polish institutions that enjoy varying levels of domestic visibility. We constantly found ourselves dealing with the ramifications of this unequal and symbiotic relation, both in the interactions among ourselves and in the field. Such dimensions cannot be omitted when examining the individual and collective achievements of scholars who engage in knowledge production (Wagner 2012). We have been straightforward in discussing the power relations among us, determined by factors inherent to the research administrative organization, different phases in our careers, distinct education backgrounds, gender dynamics (which, however, we think did not impact the collaboration), local and international visibility inside and outside academia, and previous experiences both in terms of research and of relationships with peers and individuals in higher and lower hierarchical positions. In our case there are two distinct but connected issues that impact each of the three coauthors differently. The first is a question of the authors' positionality in academia at large and more specifically in food research. The second one is the dynamics within the research field: access to the field, availability of information, and perceptions by the interlocutors in the study which may help or disturb ethnographic work.

Parasecoli identifies primarily as a food scholar and works as a tenured full professor in a prestigious (and rich) American institution, New York University. His position allows him to enjoy great independence in his choice of research projects, publications, and relationships with actors in the local food worlds and with academics. In our fieldwork we have noticed how our interlocutors often asked Parasecoli about emerging trends, up-and-coming chefs, or new media, revealing their sense of Poland as a periphery. As his very presence generated some changes in the reality we were studying, we were constantly reminded of the elusiveness of observing such reality as existing untouched by interference.

Interlocutors were not used to receiving attention from academics in general; they tended to be flattered by our interest in their activities. We observed that local actors desired access to Parasecoli, hoping to confirm, through his interest, the value of Polish food, and to obtain clarifications about the shifts taking place in the Polish culinary landscape from an external, more expert, and more objective point of view. A challenge associated with Parasecoli's visibility is that interlocutors sometimes expected a quid pro quo, which at times made ethnographic research complicated. His notoriety has been leveraged to turn him into a Polish food ambassador of sorts; he has often been invited to give talks about Polish food in events organized abroad by or in collaboration with Polish institutions.

Inevitably, Parasecoli's position as a foreigner with a recognizable position both in academia and the food world made his interactions with our interlocutors more noticeable and distinctive. As a result, we have assessed them at greater length compared to Bachórz's and Halawa's experiences. While this might appear to replicate and reinforce the power dynamics that we are exploring, it is important to underline that all along we tried to be self-aware of what the various occurrences we discussed indicated in terms of our positionality and power relations both among us and with the surrounding environment.

While Parasecoli belongs to a clear and distinct academic environment with food at its center, Bachórz's entry into the field of food research is relatively recent. Moreover, her career will likely take many forms in the coming years. Having studied food patterns as a sociologist, she has previously focused on questions of cultural participation, tourism, and leisure, including using a postcolonial framework to examine East-West relations—and for this reason she is sensitive to the power relations hidden behind seemingly minor issues. She comes from an academic context in which institutional food studies, in the sense of an identifiable field of research, pedagogy, and structured programs, has not developed, and scholars conduct valuable research on food in a variety of disciplines and departments. She represents a rather peripheral field of research (food) inside a semi-peripheral academic world (Polish academia), which makes her particularly sensitive to structural constraints.

Bachórz's role and interventions in the research are more difficult to describe: there are not as many vivid ethnographic facts to recall as in Parasecoli's case, which is not to say that her presence in the culinary landscape is so transparent that she does not need to be self-reflexive. On the contrary: she considers her involvement in the field to be on par with her other extensive research experiences, asserting that it must adhere to the same standards expected of sociological work. So far, she does not have experiences of engagement with food-related activities in nonacademic roles. It is interesting that her role was never linked to the evaluation of food in terms of taste, quality, or authenticity. As a sociologist, sometimes she was asked to comment on eating patterns, but not on food. We link this to the fact that Bachórz primarily identifies as a sociologist, while in Parasecoli's case his food expertise constitutes his public identity.

Bachórz is usually well received by participants in her research, but her presence in the field is not particularly celebrated. Her limited public visibility has many benefits in spite of the fact that it does not give her such free access to the culinary field; for example, her presence causes fewer doubts about her position when doing fieldwork. Perhaps it is merely the illusion of transparency, but it seems that the motivations of her interlocutors are less instrumental and the relations between researcher and interlocutor are less hierarchical. For example, only sometimes— when her role was misunderstood and not clearly linked to academia—did she have the impression of being expected to increase the visibility of the interlocutor's business. In general, she has not felt she had any debt to (symbolically) pay back, which is good for the critical stance she considers crucial in a sociological approach.

Halawa's role as coordinator of the project, without previous experience in food-related research and without visibility in the culinary landscape, has positioned him in yet a different way. His previous connection with the Polish Academy of Science and his professional experience in marketing commanded varying levels of respect depending on the interlocutors. His long residence in the United States configured him as somebody with knowledge of the world outside of Poland, even though not specifically food. There is a cachet in Central and Eastern Europe about returning from the West, and Halawa has built on it in terms of cultural, social, and economic capital. Having lived many years abroad, Halawa is particularly sensitive to (amused and sometimes irritated about) provincial and parochial attitudes about Parasecoli's presence, recognizing the Polish preoccupations about "how they see us" and the general concerns of the peripheries about status and recognition. At times it was disappointing and uncomfortable for him as a Polish person to see how his compatriots treat the foreign expert.

Having lived and worked for a long time in Warsaw as well, however, Halawa had social connections with actors in the local culinary landscape that allowed us some behind-the-scenes access and proved very fruitful in establishing lasting relationships with some of the tastemakers we mention in the book. Unlike Parasecoli and Bachórz, much of whose research relates to food, Halawa's focuses are on design as an approach for anthropological research, and on the way Poles experience economics (from mortgages to luxury) in their everyday lives. Parasecoli and Halawa's previous collaboration in GIDEST, the New School's Graduate Institute for Design, Ethnography, and Social Thought in New York City, allowed them to address the project also in terms of design, an approach that is still marginal in food studies. Their collaboration generated a parallel project that eventually led to the publication of the edited volume *Global Brooklyn: Designing Food Experiences in World Cities* (Parasecoli and Halawa 2021). Halawa's presence in the project has brought theoretical insights and methodological solutions that have enriched Parasecoli's already multidisciplinary point of view and Bachórz's sociological analysis. In many ways, the fact that Halawa's main focus is not food per se has been productive in terms of objectivity and diversity.

Both Bachórz and Halawa have been essential in clarifying situations and contexts that Parasecoli would have misinterpreted by building on assumptions, bias, and previous experiences that are not relevant in Poland. Despite the clear advantages of working in an international team, our professional and academic interlocutors often struggled to read our collaboration. They could not seem to accept that we worked as peers in the design of the research and its development in the field or that we would actually write together. We all bring different skills and competences to the project. However, some interlocutors seemed to have a hard time acknowledging the contributions of the Polish coauthors.

Bachórz and Halawa participate in debates in Polish civil society and understand how the local intelligentsia functions. They are more concerned than Parasecoli about how the research project, and this book in particular, will resonate in Poland, both inside and outside academia. The Polish coauthors are also very aware of how the trappings of the Polish middle class emphasize Western competence and knowing how things are done in the West. As we mentioned, we also had to constantly remind ourselves of our own positionality in terms of class. We are urban, upwardly mobile, and educated individuals, just like many of the interlocutors whose practices and discourse we are studying in our project. We have been very careful when stating that lifestyle elements are trickling down, because our own background may influence our perceptions and even the topics we are drawn to. Class, access, gender, age, and other sociocultural factors can generate bias and various forms of "blindness" to dynamics of which we ourselves are a part.

NOTES

INTRODUCTION

1. Poland did have culinary celebrities and well-known gastronomy professionals before the period we examine in this book. The changes in Polish food culture that have accompanied the postsocialist transformation have been happening incrementally rather than suddenly. Examples of pre-2010s celebrities abound. In her decades-long career, restaurateur, entrepreneur, and TV host Magda Gessler has opened various successful restaurants and café-patisseries. Her restaurant U Fukiera, opened in Warsaw in 1990, provided a template for upscale restaurants focusing on Polish food. Since 2010, she has hosted *Kuchenne Revolucje* (Kitchen revolutions), a popular local adaptation of Gordon Ramsay's *Kitchen Nightmares*. Since the late 1990s chef Kurt Scheller, a native Swiss, recognizable for his impressive white mustache, attained notoriety in Poland thanks to his role in establishing the Polish Association of Chefs and Confectioners (*Polskie Stowarzyszenie Szefów Kuchni i Cukierni*) and in launching a well-known cooking academy that since 2002 has partially filled a vacuum in culinary education. From the early 1990s Tessa Capponi Borawska's column on the weekend insert of the new daily paper *Gazeta Wyborcza*, and later in the Polish edition of *Elle* magazine, familiarized consumers and home cooks in Poland with new foreign recipes (often Italian). Starting in 2003, TV producer Mirosław Bork introduced a young and still unknown chef from Podlasie, Karol Okrasa, to viewers of Polish public TV with the show *Kuchnia z Okrasą* (Cooking with Okrasa, which is also a pun as *okrasa* means "topping," like fried onions or bacon on pierogi). Its success inaugurated a new TV format, and established Okrasa as a household name and a culinary celebrity. For years, food critic Robert Makłowicz hosted successful TV shows introducing Polish audiences to the pleasures of foreign gastronomies. Food magazines such as *Kuchnia* (in Polish, both "kitchen" and "cuisine") and *Moje gotowanie* (My cooking) have been published for more than twenty years.

2. We use the concept of transformation rather than transition because the latter, indicating a finite movement towards a predetermined point, has teleological

connotations suggesting there is only one way for a country's development after socialism (Chavance 2002; Verdery 1996).

3. According to the World Bank, in 2002 Poland's GDP growth rate was 5.3 percent, compared to an EU average of 3.4 percent, Germany's 1.8 percent, and the USA's 1.9 percent.

4. Poland's 2023 population of 37.6 million is much larger than any other post-socialist country in Central and Eastern Europe with the exception of Russia. It was around 24 million after World War II. The growth has happened mostly in urban environments, while the total number of people living in the countryside has remained more or less the same. However, Poland has been experiencing a demographic downturn since 2012 (Statistics Poland 2024).

5. In Polish, *gastronomiczny* mostly points to the production and distribution aspects of the field, while *kulinarny* also includes the discursive elements like recipes and media. As many of the tastemakers are engaged in various forms of storytelling and embrace some traditional attitudes of the local intelligentsia, the expression "culinary field" better reflects the variety of the stakeholders we examine.

6. The visit was funded by the Adam Mickiewicz Institute, a public institution charged with promoting Polish culture abroad. In the past few years, the institute has emphasized food, understanding its great appeal for audiences outside of the country. Their English-language website, *culture.pl*, often features food-related stories.

7. The event was organized by Monika Kucia with Agnieszka Rudzińska for the Adam Mickiewicz Institute.

8. These authors are in close dialogue with Polish culture and their books are translated into Polish, as in Zak's case, or have Polish adapted editions, like *Rozkoszne: Wegetariańska uczta z polskimi smakami* (Delicious: A vegetarian feast with Polish flavors) (Korkosz 2020b).

CHAPTER 1

1. Before Czerniecki's work, *Kuchmistrzostwo* (The art of cookery), a Polish version of Czech cookbook from 1535, was printed in Kraków around 1540. Although no original copy survives, its content has been recently published, based on a later manuscript (Dumanowski and Bułatowa 2021).

2. The work of Paul Tremo, cook of Stanisław August Poniatowski, the last king of Poland, offers a well-known example of the synthesis of local traditions with French cuisine (Dumanowski 2022).

3. At times, in a parallel to Hungary's "goulash socialism," this period is also referred to as "bigos socialism," from the name of the popular cabbage- and meat-based hunter's stew, pointing to modest but stable levels of consumption.

4. Kuroń's son, Maciej, was one of the first publicly visible chefs on TV, and his grandsons Jan and Jakub, and granddaughter Grażyna, are also active in the culinary field: an interesting legacy through which history meets the present (Kuroń 2013).

198 · NOTES

CHAPTER 2

1. Marek Sawicki, then Minister of Agriculture, depicted Polish farmers as victims of Putin's trade schemes (Kowalska 2014). Observing that the greater domestic availability of apples would lower prices and eventually damage Polish farmers, he implicitly suggested that consumers should be ready and willing to pay more for the fruit to support the sector (dziennik.pl 2014). In the meantime, the minister expressed the need for the Polish government to look for new markets, including in Eastern Asia (KAIEN, RS, ASL 2014).

2. At the time of writing, the Institute continues to exist under the government that emerged from the October 2023 elections. It is still unclear how its mission will morph under the supposedly more progressive stance of the new political coalition in power.

3. In the 1980s the Orbis restaurant had been part of a state-owned travel agency and chain of hotel with roots in prewar Poland.

CHAPTER 3

1. The ethnographic material was gathered for a variety of purposes during our six-year long research project and with different rules of anonymization. In order to avoid repetitions, only some of the interviewees appear in this chapter, while others are featured elsewhere in the book. Interview quotes should be treated as examples and illustrations of wider phenomena.

2. The Wyższa Szkoła Hotelarstwa i Gastronomii (Higher school of hotel management and gastronomy) in Poznań, the Uniwersytet Przyrodniczy (University of natural science) in Lublin, and the Warmińsko-Mazurski University in Olsztyn now offer courses in gastronomy and the culinary arts.

3. Łukasz Cichy from Gavi restaurant in Kraków, Grzegorz Gręda from the Romantyczna in Wzgórza Dylewskie, chef consultant Tomasz Welter (who also has a unique experience as an army chef and took part in an international army-cook competition), and Paweł Stawicki, previously at Mercato restaurant in Gdańsk, are among these.

4. In 2024, the industry organized collective actions to combat frosts in vineyards.

CHAPTER 4

1. Known as *Koło Gospodyń Wiejskich* (circle of rural homemakers), they are voluntary, self-governing women's organizations operating mainly in rural areas since the late nineteenth century. For the entanglements of politics tradition in these organizations, see Andriichuk 2024.

2. These included for instance the Krajowa Rada Izb Rolniczych (National council of agricultural chambers), Polskie Mięso (Polish meat association), Izba Zbożowo-Paszowa (Grain and feed chamber), and Polska Izba Produktu Regionalnego and Lokalnego (Polish chamber of the regional and local product), which connects producers, the nation government, and local government administrations with the goal of building a Polish system for traditional regional and local products.

3. At the end of 2022, as part of the efforts to promote the Silesian language, a few stores belonging to the Kaufland supermarket chain in Silesia posted aisle signs both in Silesian and in Polish: for instance *sery żółte* (hard cheeses) became *kyjzy*, reminiscent of the German *käse*, and *musztardy* (mustards) were *symfty*, similar to the German *senft* (Ptak 2022b).

4. The restaurant changed location since our visit in 2018 and then closed. The COVID-19 pandemic disrupted the functioning of many of the gastronomic initiatives we discuss.

5. Fiedoruk has written extensively on the history of the local cuisine, restaurants, and artisanal traditions; he has also produced a series of videos where he explores stores, bakeries, and restaurants in today's Białystok to find traces of traditional regional cuisine.

6. Words such as *kresy* and *kresowa* also have postcolonial connotations. *Kresy* indicated "the end" at the time of imperial Poland, an undifferentiated area lacking culture and history. However, Fiedoruk did not seem to base his critique on this specific meaning.

CHAPTER 5

1. Poland has also registered four fermented beverages produced from mead (*Czwórniak, Dwójniak, Półtorak,* and *Trójniak*) in the Traditional Specialties Guaranteed (TSGs) EU category.

2. Chef Maciej Nowicki was studying history and philosophy when he moved to London to gain cooking experience abroad and, after that, started to work in Wilanów. The chef recently left the museum for other history-related projects.

3. After nineteen years, in late October 2023, Moroz announced he would close the Bulaj we visited. He has now opened a new restaurant with the same name, located just a few hundred meters from the first location.

4. These include *Makłowicz w podróży* ("Makłowicz in travel"), broadcast between 2008 and 2017, *Makłowicz w drodze* ("Makłowicz on the road," 2017–2020), the locally-oriented *Makłowicz w Polsce* ("Makłowicz in Poland," 2018), and his current, extremely popular Youtube channel arranged around the idea of travels around Poland and other countries.

5. To sample the discourses of the two media approaches, in previous research we closely analyzed the magazines *Przyślij przepis, Przyjaciółka,* and *Kuchnia,* as well as the TV show *Makłowicz w Polsce,* besides *Jakubiak w sezonie* and *Jakubiak*

lokalnie. We focused on the 2011–2019 period, which we argue marked the beginning of the visible participation of our tastemakers on the Polish food scene. We selected these media according to three criteria: popularity in a quantitative sense, thematic angles and content, and diversity of assumed audiences (Bachórz and Parasecoli 2023).

6. Among historians, the expression *kuchnia staropolska* refers to what we know about Polish cuisine from the past as learned through actual analysis of documents, artifacts, and archaeological remains. This is quite far from the popular perceptions about *kuchnia staropolska* which, as we discussed in chapter 1, are often connected with the idealization of rural cuisine in the socialist years.

7. The "PPR" is the *Polska Partia Robotnicza* or Polish Workers' Party, which actually since 1948 has been called the Polish United Workers' Party (*Polska Zjednoczona Partia Robotnicza)* or PZPR.

8. As we saw in previous chapters, this approach to foreign cuisine is not that far from the more nationalistic statements of conservative politicians, including PiS party leader Kaczyński. Although with different ideological connotations, both measure Polish cuisine against standards from abroad to find it valuable and interesting.

9. Nuta, Camastra's new restaurant in Warsaw, also has obtained one Michelin star.

10. Popular cookbook author Marta Dymek, known for her work on Polish vegan cuisine, *Jadłonomia po polsku* (Foodonomy in Polish) (2020), also mentions the National Library as a central locus for her work. In a newspaper interview she mused: "I had been working on *Jadłonomia po polsku* for two years. I spent the first year entirely at the National Library. I searched through old cookbooks, newspapers and other materials. I really like old leaflets and posters, but not to look for old vegetarian recipes. I wanted to understand even better how the social reality shapes our tastes, how the flavors reflect ideologies and how this affects our culinary practices. And vice versa. I wondered about it in the reading room, occasionally—without any special assumptions—finding many phenomenal and completely forgotten dishes" (Nogaś 2020).

11. The conference, which saw the participation of food historians from France, Italy, England, Russia, and Turkey, was organized by Jarosław Dumanowski, together with Andrzej Kuropatnicki from the Pedagogical University in Kraków and coauthor Fabio Parasecoli. The proceedings were published by the Wilanów museum (Kuropatnicki, Parasecoli, and Dumanowski 2020).

CHAPTER 6

1. After the end of socialism, growers could only produce grapes to make wine for their own consumption; commercial production was legally authorized only in 2008, although advertising of wine is still prohibited, which makes marketing relatively difficult for producers. Many vineyards have been planted quite recently,

taking advantage of the milder temperatures connected with climate change. In 2004, Poland was classified in the EU as part of the coldest wine-growing region; due to the already abundant wine production in Europe, the Union gave Poland the choice between limiting the number of future vineyards in exchange for funding or not limiting them, in which case the union would not have provided funding. The Polish government chose the second scenario. However, funding is available for structural investment, such as production plants or tourism infrastructure.

2. The market was built between 1906 and 1908. Its design, by famed architects Richard Pluddemann and Heinrich Kuster, fuses a brick, traditional-looking facade with the concrete, quite grandiose elliptical arches of the interior.

REFERENCES

Albala, Ken, ed. 2013. *Routledge International Handbook of Food Studies*. New York: Routledge.

Amaro, Wojciech Modest. 2014. *Natura kuchni polskiej* [Nature of Polish cuisine]. Warszawa: Wydawnictwo Zwierciadło.

Andriichuk, Yuliia. 2024. "Traditional Polish Roasted Duck from the 'Dino' Supermarket: Politicizing and Negotiating Tradition through Culinary Competitions for Rural Housewives' Clubs." 2024 Dublin Gastronomy Symposium.

Anioł, Włodzimierz. 2015. "On Three Modernisation Narratives in Poland after 1989." *International Journal of Social Economics* (42)9: 777–790.

AP News. 2016. "Polish Official: French 'Learned to Eat with a Fork from Us.'" October 12, 2016. https://apnews.com/article/57273edd765349358d041d84 bce1a4cb.

Appadurai, Arjun. 1988. "How to Make a National Cuisine: Cookbooks in Contemporary India." *Comparative Studies in Society and History* 30(1): 3–24.

Atzmon, Leslie, and Prasad Boradkar. 2017. *Encountering Things: Design and Theories of Things*. London: Bloomsbury Academic.

Augustyn, Aneta. 2012. "Pan hrabia i jego karp" [Lord count and his carp]. *Kuchnia*, November 2012, 22–30.

Augustyn, Aneta. 2014. "Piknik z ogoniara" [Picnic with a cherry]. *Kuchnia*, July 2014, 72–75.

Aust, Cornelia. 2022. "Burying the Dead, Saving the Community: Jewish Burial Societies as Informal Centres of Jewish Self-Government." *Polin Studies in Polish Jewry* 34: 203–223.

Ayora-Diaz, Steffan Igor, ed. 2021. *The Cultural Politics of Food, Taste, and Identity: A Global Perspective*. London: Bloomsbury.

Bach, Jonathan. 2017. *What Remains: Everyday Encounters with the Socialist Past in Germany*. New York: Columbia University Press.

Bachórz, Agata. 2018a. "'It's Just a Constant Exchange of Containers': Distribution of Home-Made Food as an Element of Polish Family Lifestyles." *Etnografia Polska* 1–2: 131–145.

Bachórz, Agata, 2018b. "Hidden Resources? Households' Strategies for Maintaining Control over Food: Between Continuity and Discontinuity." *Studia Humanistyczne AGH* 17(2): 97–109.

Bachórz, Agata. 2023. "'Rzuciła pracę w korpo i zajęła się ... gotowaniem': Praca z jedzeniem, nieoczywiste transformacje zawodowe i poszukiwanie alternatywnej relacji ze światem" ['She quit her job in corporate and took up ... cooking': Working with food, unobvious professional transformations and the search for an alternative relationship with the world]. *Studia Socjologiczne* 1: 59–86.

Bachórz, Agata. 2024. "'Kiedy nasze jadłospisy będą racjonalne'. Książki kucharskie z okresu PRL i nowoczesny styl życia" [When our menus will be rational: Cookbooks from the Polish People's Republic era and modern lifestyles]. In *Kuchnia (w) PRL* [Cuisine in (of) the Polish People's Republic], edited by Grzegorz Piotrowski, 129–166. Gdańsk: Europejskie Centrum Solidarności/European Solidarity Center.

Bachórz, Agata, and Fabio Parasecoli. 2020. "Why Should We Care? Two Experiences in the Politics of Food and Food Research." *Ethnologia Polona* 41: 13–31. https://doi.org/10.23858/ethp.2020.41.2301.

Bachórz, Agata, and Fabio Parasecoli. 2023. "Savoring the Future of Polishness: History and Tradition in Contemporary Polish Food Media." *Eastern European Politics and Societies and Cultures* 37(1): 103–124.

Bachórz, Agata, Karolina Ciechorska-Kulesza, Sławomir Czarnecki, Martyna Grabowska, Jakub Knera, Lesław Michałowski, Krzysztof Stachura, Stanisław Szultka, Cezary Obracht-Prondzyński, and Piotr Zbieranek. 2014. *Punkty styczne: Między kulturą a praktyką (nie)uczestnictwa* [Tangent points: Between culture and the practice of (non) participation]. Gdańsk: Instytut Kultury Miejskiej.

Bachórz, Agata, Karolina Ciechorska-Kulesza, Sławomir Czarnecki, Martyna Grabowska, Jakub Knera, Lesław Michałowski, Krzysztof Stachura, Stanisław Szultka, Cezary Obracht-Prondzyński, and Piotr Zbieranek. 2016. *Kulturalna hierarchia. Nowe dystynkcje i powinności w kulturze a stratyfikacja społeczna* [Cultural hierarchy: New distinctions and duties in culture and social stratification]. Gdańsk: Instytut Kultury Miejskiej.

Bakuła, Bogusław. 2014. "Colonial and Postcolonial Aspects of Polish Borderlands Studies: an Outline." *Teksty Drugie* 1: 96–123.

Baranowski, Bohdan. 1979. *Polska karczma. Restauracja: Kawiarnia* [Polish *karczma* eatery, restaurant, cafe]. Wrocław: Zakład Narodowy im. Ossolińskich Wydawnictwo.

Bardone, Ester, and Astra Spalvēna. 2019. "European Union Food Quality Schemes and the Transformation of Traditional Foods into European Products in Latvia and Estonia." *Appetite* 135: 43–53.

Baron, Aleksander. 2016. *Kiszonki i fermentacje* [Pickles and fermentations]. Bielsko-Biała: Wydawnictwo Pascal.

Baron, Aleksander, and Baśka Madej. 2018. "Aleksander Baron: 'W Polsce najbardziej smakuje mi polska wódka'" [Aleksander Baron: "In Poland, I like Polish vodka the most"]. *Lounge Magazine,* September 9, 2018. https://loungemagazyn.pl/aleks-baron-w-polsce-najbardziej-smakuje-mi-polska-wodka-wywiad.

Bartelak, Zdzisław, and Paulina Kolondra. 2013. "Masz babę i placek" [A sand cake and a pie]. *Kuchnia,* April 2013, 22–23.

Beauvois, Daniel. 1994. "Mit 'kresów wschodnich', czyli jak mu położyć kres" [The myth of the 'eastern borderlands,' or how to put an end to it]. In *Polskie mity polityczne XIX i XX wieku* [Polish political myths of the 19th and 20th centuries], edited by Wojciech Wrzesiński, 93–105. Wrocław: Wydawnictwo Uniwersytetu Wrocławskiego.

Beck, Ulrich. 2002. "The Cosmopolitan Society and Its Enemies." *Theory, Culture & Society* 19(1–2): 17–44.

Belasco, Warren. 2002. "Food Matters: Perspectives on an Emerging Field." In *Food Nations: Selling Taste in Consumer Societies,* edited by Warren Belasco and Philip Scranton, 2–23. New York: Routledge.

Bendix, Regina. 1997. *In Search of Authenticity: The Formation of Folklore Studies.* Madison: University of Wisconsin Press.

Bennett, Jane. 2010. *Vibrant Matter: A Political Ecology of Things.* Durham: Duke University Press.

Bentley, Amy, Fabio Parasecoli, and Krishnendu Ray. *Practicing Food Studies.* New York: New York University Press.

Bestor, Theodore C. 2004. *Tsukuji: The Fish Market at the Center of the World.* Berkeley: University of California Press.

Białoszewski, Miron. 2014. *A Memoir of the Warsaw Uprising.* Trans. Madeline Elvine. New York: The New York Review of Books.

Bideleux, Robert, and Ian Jeffries. 2007. *A History of Eastern Europe: Crisis and Change.* New York: Routledge.

Bielenin-Lenczowska, Karolina, and Renata Hryciuk. 2018. "Jedzenie i mobilność w perspektywie antropologicznej—wprowadzenie." *Studia Socjologiczne* 4(231): 75–76.

Bilewicz, Aleksandra, and Ruta Śpiewak. 2015. "Enclaves of Activism and Taste: Consumer Cooperatives in Poland as Alternative Food Networks." *SOCIO:HU* 3: 145–66.

Bilewicz, Aleksandra, and Ruta Śpiewak. 2018. "Beyond the 'Northern' and 'Southern' Divide: Food and Space in Polish Consumer Cooperatives." *East European Politics and Societies: and Cultures* 20(10): 1–24.

Bill, Stanley, and Ben Stanley. 2020. "Whose Poland Is It To Be? PiS and the Struggle between Monism and Pluralism." *East European Politics* 36(3): 378–394.

Bivand Erdal, Marta, and Aleksandra Lewicki. 2015. "Polish Migration within Europe: Mobility, Transnationalism and Integration." *Social Identities* 22(1): 1–9.

Błaszczyk, Mateusz, and Michał Cebula. 2016. "Uczestnictwo w kulturze a uczestnictwo w mieście. O kapitałach kulturowych i różnorodności stylów życia mieszkańców dużego miasta [Cultural participation and use of the city: On cultural capitals and diversity of lifestyles of city dwellers]." *Studia Socjologiczne* 1: 99–126.

Blazyca, George. 1980. "An Assessment of Polish Economic Development in the 1970s." *European Economic Review* 14(1): 101–116.

Bluhm, Katharina, and Mihai Varga, eds. 2019. *New Conservatives in Russia and East Central Europe.* New York: Routledge.

Blumberg, Renata. 2022. "Engendering European Alternative Food Networks through Countertopographies." *Anthropology of Food,* April 9, 2022. http://journals.openedition.org/aof/12865.

Blumberg, Renata, and Diana Mincyte. 2019. "Infrastructures of Taste: Rethinking Local Food Histories in Lithuania." *Appetite* 138: 252–259.

Blumberg, Renata, and Diana Mincyte. 2020. "Beyond Europeanization: The Politics of Scale and Positionality in Lithuania's Alternative Food Networks." *European Urban and Regional Studies* 27(2): 189–205.

Boltanski, Luc, and Arnaud Esquerre. 2017. *Enrichissement: Une critique de la marchandise.* Paris: Editions Gallimard.

Boni, Zofia. 2015. "Negotiating Children's Food Culture in Post-Socialist Poland." *Anthropology of Food* 9 (Special Issue on Children's Food Heritage). https://aof.revues.org/7782.

Boni, Zofia. 2016. "Reflections on Food in Food Research." *Anthropologies* 22 (Reflections on Food in Food Research). http://savageminds.org/2016/08/07/anthropologies-22-reflections-food-research.

Boni, Zofia. 2023. *Feeding Anxieties: The Politics of Children's Food in Poland.* New York: Berghahn Books.

Bourdieu, Pierre. 1984. *Distinction: A Social Critique of the Judgment of Taste.* London: Routledge and Kegan Paul.

Bourdieu, Pierre. 1993. *The Field of Cultural Production: Essays on Art and Literature.* New York: Columbia University Press.

Bouty, Isabelle, and Marie-Léandre Gomez. 2013. "Creativity in Haute Cuisine: Strategic Knowledge and Practice in Gourmet Kitchens." *Journal of Culinary Science & Technology* 11(1): 80–95.

Boym, Svetlana. 2007. "Nostalgia and Its Discontents." *Hedgehog Review* 9(2): 7–18.

Brzezinski, Michal, Michał Myck, and Mateusz Najsztub. 2021. "Sharing the Gains of Transition: Evaluating Changes in Income Inequality and Redistribution in Poland Using Combined Survey and Tax Return Data." *European Journal of Political Economy.* https://doi.org/10.1016/j.ejpoleco.2021.102121.

Brzostek, Błażej. 2010. *PRL na widelcu* [The PRL on the fork]. Warszawa: Wydawnictwo Baobab.

Brzostek, Błażej. 2015. *Paryże innej Europy: Warszawa i Bukareszt, XIX i XX wiek* [Parises of another Europe: Warsaw and Bucharest, 19th and 20th centuries]. Warszawa: Wydawnictwo W.A.B—Grupa Wydawnicza Foksal.

Buckley, Neil. 2014. "Tapes Scandal Rattles Sikorski." *Financial Times,* June 23, 2014, 6.

Buchowski, Michael. 2004. "Hierarchies of Knowledge in Central-Eastern European Anthropology." *Anthropology of East Europe Review* 22(2): 5–14.

Buchowski, Michał. 2006. "Social Thought & Commentary: The Specter of Orientalism in Europe: From Exotic Other to Stigmatized Brother." *Anthropological Quarterly* 79(3): 463–82.

Buchowski, Michael, and Hana Cervinkova. 2015. "Introduction: On Rethinking Ethnography in Central Europe: Toward Cosmopolitan Anthropologies in the 'Peripheries.'" In *Rethinking Ethnography in Central Europe*, edited by Hana Cervinkova, Michael Buchowski, and Zdenêk Uherek, 1–20. New York: Palgrave Macmillan.

Bukowski, Paweł, and Filip Novokmet. 2021. "Between Communism and Capitalism: Long-Term Inequality in Poland, 1892–2015." *Journal of Economic Growth* 26: 187–239.

Bukowski, Paweł, Jakub Sawulski, and Michał Brzeziński. 2024. *Nierówności po polsku. Dlaczego trzeba się nimi zająć, jesli chcemy dobrej przyszłosci nad Wisła* [Inequalities in Polish/Polish style: Why they must be addressed if we want a good future on the Vistula River]. Warszawa: Wydawnictwo Krytyki Politycznej.

Bunda, Martyna. 2022. "Schabowy pobił pizzę, kebab przegrał z sushi: Sprawdziliśmy, co jedzą Polacy" [Pork chop beats pizza, kebab lost to sushi: We checked what Poles eat]. *Polityka,* August 3, 2022. https://www.polityka.pl/tygodnikpolityka/spoleczenstwo/2175723,1,schabowy-pobil-pizze-kebab-przegral-z-sushi-sprawdzilismy-co-jedza-polacy.read.

Burrell, Kathy. 2003. "The Political and Social Life of Food in Socialist Poland." *Anthropology of East Europe Review* 22(1): 189–195.

Burrell, Kathy. 2016. *Polish Migration to the UK in the 'New' European Union: After 2004.* London: Routledge.

Burszta, Wojciech J., and Waldemar Kuligowski. 2005. *Sequel: Dalsze przygody kultury w globalnym świecie* [Sequel: Further adventures of culture in a global world]. Warszawa: Warszawskie Wydawnictwo Literackie Muza S.A.

Byrkjeflot, Haldor, Jesper Strandgaard Pedersen, and Silviya Svejenova. 2013. "From Label to Practice: The Process of Creating New Nordic Cuisine." *Journal of Culinary Science & Technology* 11(1): 36–55.

Caldwell, Melissa L. 2002. "The Taste of Nationalism: Food Politics in Postsocialist Moscow." *Ethnos* 67(3): 295–319.

Caldwell, Melissa L. 2004. *Not by Bread Alone: Social Support in the New Russia.* Berkeley: University of California Press.

Caldwell, Melissa L. 2014. "Digestive Politics in Russia: Feeling the Sensorium beyond the Palate." *Food and Foodways* 22(1–2): 112–135.

Caldwell, Melissa L., Elizabeth C. Dunn, and Marion Nestle, eds. 2009. *Food and Everyday Life in the Postsocialist World.* Bloomington: Indiana University Press.

Calhoun, Craig. 2002. "The Class Consciousness of Frequent Travellers: Toward a Critique of Actually Existing Cosmopolitanism." *South Atlantic Quarterly* 101(4): 869–897.

Canal + Kuchnia. 2013. "Jakubiak lokalnie: Sezon 1—Cebula." Video file, 1:05. Player.pl. https://player.pl/playerplus/programy-online/jakubiak-lokalnie-odcinki,13266/odcinek-1,S01E01,111035.

Cappeliez, Sarah, and Josée Johnston. 2013. "From Meat and Potatoes to 'Real-Deal' Rotis: Exploring Everyday Culinary Cosmopolitanism." *Poetics* 41(5): 433–55.

Červinkova, Hana. 2012. "Postcolonialism, Postsocialism and the Anthropology of East-central Europe." *Journal of Postcolonial Writing* 48(2): 155–63.

Chase, Charles. 1983. "Symbolism of Food Shortage in Current Polish Politics." *Anthropological Quarterly* 56(2): 76–82.

Chavance, Bernard. 2002. "Why National Trajectories of Post-Socialist Transformation Differ." *Journal of Economics and Business* 5(1): 47–65.

Chumley, Lily Hope, and Nicholas Harkness. 2013. "Introduction: QUALIA." *Anthropological Theory* 13(1–2): 3–11.

Ciarko, Marta, Greta Poszwa, and Mustafa Caner Timur. 2022. "Geographical Indications as a Local Development and Differentiation Strategy Tool: The Case of Poland." Conference Proceedings, *Determinants Of Regional Development* 3: 135–154.

Cienski, Jan. 2015. "A Polish 'Game of Tapes.'" *Politico,* June 10, 2015. https://www .politico.eu/article/a-polish-game-of-tapes.

Clarke, Alison J. 2018. *Design Anthropology: Object Cultures in Transition.* London: Bloomsbury Academic.

Contois, Emily, and Zenia Kish, eds. 2022. *Food Instagram: Identity, Influence, and Negotiation.* Champaign-Urbana: University of Illinois Press.

Croissant, Jennifer. 2014. "Agnotology: Ignorance and Absence or Towards a Sociology of Things That Aren't There." *Social Epistemology* 28(1): 4–25.

Cseh-Varga, Katalin, and Adam Czirak. 2018. *Performance Art in the Second Public Sphere: Event-Based Art in Late Socialist Europe.* London: Routledge.

Czekalski, Tadeusz. 2011. "Przedsiębiorstwa żywienia zbiorowego w realiach PRL: Model żywienia zbiorowego w warunkach przyspieszonej modernizacji i jego realizacja" [Catering enterprises in the realities of the People's Republic of Poland: Model of mass nutrition in the conditions of accelerated modernization and its implementation]. *Annales Universitatis Paedagogicae Cracoviensis. Studia Politologica* 5: 78–90.

Czerniecki, Stanisław, Jarosław Dumanowski, and Magdalena Spychaj. 2012. *Compendium ferculorum albo Zebranie potraw* [Compendium ferculorum or collection of dishes]. Warszawa: Muzeum Pałacu Króla Jana III w Wilanowie.

Dąbrowska, Anna. 2023. "Kiełbasa wyborcza z robaka: PiS przekracza kolejne granice absurdu" [Election worm-sausage: PiS exceeds further limits of absurdity]. *Polityka,* February 22, 2023. https://www.polityka.pl/tygodnikpolityka/kraj /2202516,1,kielbasa-wyborcza-z-robaka-pis-przekracza-kolejne-granice-absurdu .read.

Daniel, Ondřej, Tomáš Kavka, and Jakub Machek. 2015. "Popular Culture and Post-Socialist Societies in East-Central and South Eastern Europe." *Mediální studia* 9(2): 99–103.

Davies, Norman. 2001. *Heart of Europe: The Past in Poland's Present.* Oxford: Oxford University Press.

Defoe, Daniel. 1705. *The Dyet of Poland: A Satyr. Consider'd Paragraph by Paragraph.* London: Ben Bragg.

Del Secco, Stefano. 2012. *Cook It Raw Poland 2012: Searching for the Distinctive spirit of Suwalszczyzna.* https://vimeo.com/51508392.

Dembinska, Maria. 1999. *Food and Drink in Medieval Poland: Rediscovering a Cuisine of the Past.* Philadelphia: University of Pennsylvania Press.

de Solier, Isabelle. 2013. *Food and the Self: Consumption, Production and Material Culture.* London: Bloomsbury.

Dias-Lewandowska, Dorota, and Gabriel Kurczewski. 2018. *Wino i historia: Studia z historii wina w Polsce* [Wine and history: Studies in the history of wine in Poland]. 2 vols. Warszawa: Stowarzyszenie Historyków Sztuki Oddział Warszawa.

Dorzeczy.pl. 2019. "Do Rzeczy nr 42: Kto chce nam zakazać jedzenia mięsa?! Nowe szaleństwo lewicy" ["Do Rzeczy" No. 42: Who wants to prohibit us from eating meat ?! The new madness of the left]. *DoRzeczy.pl,* October 13, 2019. https://dorzeczy.pl/kraj/117113/do-rzeczy-nr-42-kto-chce-nam-zakazac-jedzenia-miesa.html.

Domański, Henryk. 1998. "Dwie transformacje w krajach Europy Srodkowo-Wschodniej a Ruchliwosc Spoleczna" [Two transformations in countries of Central and Eastern Europe and social mobility]. *Studia Socjologiczne* 1(148): 27–55.

Domański, Henryk. 2002. *O ruchliwości społecznej* [On social mobility]. Warszawa: Ifis PAN.

Domański, Henryk. 2012. *Polska klasa średnia* [The Polish middle class]. Toruń: Wydawnictwo UMK.

Domański, Henryk. 2017. "Omnivorism of Eating and 'Highbrow–Lowbrow' Distinction: Cultural Stratification in Poland." *Polish Sociological Review* 3(199): 299–313.

Domański, Henryk, Zbigniew Karpiński, Dariusz Przybysz, and Justyna Straczuk. 2015a. *Wzory jedzenia a struktura społeczna* [Food patterns and social structure]. Warszawa: Scholar.

Domański, Henryk, Zbigniew Karpiński, Dariusz Przybysz, and Justyna Straczuk. 2015b. "Social Stratification and Eating." *Research & Methods* 24(1): 3–18.

Domański, Henryk, and Zbigniew Karpiński. 2018. "Intergenerational Mobility and Omnivorism in Eating." *Appetite* 121: 83–92.

Drace-Francis, Alex. 2022. *The Making of Mămăligă: Transimperial Recipes for a Romanian National Dish.* Budapest: CEU Press.

Drinóczi, Timea, and Agnieszka Bień-Kacała. 2020. "COVID-19 in Hungary and Poland: Extraordinary Situation and Illiberal Constitutionalism." *The Theory and Practice of Legislation* 8(1–2): 171–192.

Drozdowski, Rafał, and Michał Morchat. 2014. *Praktyki kulturalne Polaków* [The cultural practices of the Poles]. Toruń: Wydawnictwo Naukowe Uniwersytetu Mikołaja Kopernika.

dziennik.pl. 2014. "Sawicki krytykuje markety: Jabłka za złotówkę to prezent dla Putina" [Sawicki criticizes supermarkets: Apples for PLN 1 are a gift for Putin]. *dziennik.pl*, September 4, 2014. https://gospodarka.dziennik.pl/news/artykuly /468811,marek-sawicki-jablko-za-zlotowke-to-wsparcie-dla-putina.html.

Duczmal, Wojciech. 2006. "The Rise of Private Higher Education in Poland: Policies, Markets and Strategies." PhD diss., University of Twente, Center for Higher Education Policy Studies (CHEPS). https://doi.org/10.3990/1.9789036524179.

Dudek, Antoni. 2020. "Spór wokół programu gospodarczego w rządzie Tadeusza Mazowieckiego" [Dispute over the economic program in the government of Tadeusz Mazowiecki]. *Politeja* 16: 373–394.

Dumanowski, Jarosław. 2010. "Monumenta Poloniae Culinaria. Edycja staropolskich książek kucharskich i program badań nad gastronomią historyczną" [Monumenta Poloniae Culinaria: Editing of Old Polish cookbooks and a research program on historical gastronomy]. In *Historie kuchenne. Rola i znaczenie pożywienia w kulturze* [Kitchen stories: The role and importance of food in culture], edited by Ratislava Stolična and Anna Drożdż, 121–132. Cieszyn—Katowice—Brno: Uniwersytet Śląski.

Dumanowski, Jarosław. 2013. "Polskie posty" [Polish posts]. *Kuchnia,* February 2013, 58–65.

Dumanowski, Jarosław. 2014. *Compendium Ferculorum or Collection of Dishes.* Warszawa: Museum of the King Jan III's Palace ad Wilanów.

Dumanowski, Jarosław. 2021. "Old Polish Fasting: Discourse and Dietary Practices in the 16th–18th Century." In *Gruppen identitäten in Ostmittleleuropa,* edited by Bogusław Dybaś and Jacek Bojarski, 93–116. Göttingen: V&R Unipress.

Dumanowski, Jarosław. 2022. *Przepisy Paula Tremo.* Warszawa: Muzeum Pałacu Króla Jana III w Wilanowie.

Dumanowski, Jarosław, and Switłana Bułatowa. 2021. *Zbiór dla kuchmistrza tak potraw jako ciast robienia wypisany roku 1757 dnia 24 lipca* [A collection for the chef of both dishes and cakes, written on July 24, 1757]. Warszawa: Muzeum Pałacu Króla Jana III w Wilanowie.

Dumanowski, Jarosław, and Maciej Czarnecki. 2009. "Polaków ostra wyżerka (wywiad z Jarosławem Dumanowskim)" [Poles' spicy binge (interview with Jarosław Dumanowski)]. *Wysokie Obcasy (Gazeta Wyborcza),* December 8, 2009. https://www.wysokieobcasy.pl/wysokie-obcasy/1,53668,7328565,Polakow_ostra_ wyzerka.html.

Dumanowski, Jarosław, Dorota Dias-Lewandowska, and Marta Sikorska. 2016. *Staropolskie przepisy kulinarne. Receptury rozproszone z XVI-XVIII w. Źródła drukowane* [Old Polish recipes: Dispersed recipes from the 16th-18th centuries: Printed sources]. Warszawa: Muzeum Pałacu Króla Jana III w Wilanowie.

Dumanowski, Jarosław, and Magdalena Kasprzyk-Chevriaux. 2019. *Kapłony i szczeżuje. Opowieść o zapomnianej kuchni polskiej* [Capons and duck mussels: A story of forgotten Polish cuisine]. Wołowiec: Czarne.

Dunn, Elizabeth C. 2004. *Privatizing Poland: Baby Food, Big Business, and the Remaking of Labor.* Ithaca: Cornell University Press.

Dürrschmidt, Jörg, and York Kautt, eds. 2019. *Globalized Eating Cultures: Mediation and Mediatization.* Cham: Palgrave Macmillan.

Dyda, Konrad. 2020. "Economic Arguments and Legal Regulations on Ritual Slaughter in Poland." *Estudio Eclesiásticos* 95(375): 955–97.

Dymek, Marta. 2020. *Jadłonomia po polsku* [Foodonomy in Polish]. Warszawa: Wydawnictwo Marginesy.

Easton, Adam. 2018. "Bialowieza Forest: Poland Broke EU law by Logging." *BBC,* April 17, 2018. https://www.bbc.com/news/world-europe-43795166.

El-Sheikha, A. F. 2022. "Why Fermented Foods are the Promising Food Trends in the Future?" *Current Research in Nutrition and Food Science* 10(3). http://dx.doi.org/10.12944/CRNFSJ.10.3.1.

Emontspoola, Julie, and Carina Georgi. 2017. "A Cosmopolitan Return to Nature: How Combining Aestheticization and Moralization Processes Expresses Distinction in Food Consumption." *Consumption Markets & Culture* 20(4): 306–328.

Eris, Irena, n.d. *Tasty Stories.* http://www.drirenaeristastystories.com.

Escobar, Arturo. 2018. *Designs for the Pluriverse: Radical Interdependence, Autonomy, and the Making of Worlds.* Durham: Duke University Press.

European Commission. n.d. Farming Income Support. https://agridata.ec.europa.eu/extensions/DashboardIndicators/FarmIncome.html?select=EU27_FLAG,1.

European Union. 2020. Agriculture, Forestry and Fishery Statistics. Luxembourg: Publications Office of the European Union.

FAO. n.d. Faostat: Poland. https://www-fao-org.proxy.library.nyu.edu/faostat/en/#country/173.

Fatyga, Barbara. 1999. *Dzicy z naszej ulicy: Antropologia kultury młodzieżowej.* Warszawa: Uniwersytet Warszawski, Ośrodek Badań Młodzieży.

Fehérváry, Krisztina. 2013. *Politics in Color and Concrete: Socialist Materialities and the Middle Class in Hungary.* Bloomington: Indiana University Press.

Ferguson, Priscilla Parkhurst. 1998. "A Cultural Field in the Making: Gastronomy in 19th-Century France." *American Journal of Sociology* 104(3): 597–641.

Ferrant, Coline. 2018. "Class, Culture, and Structure: Stratification and Mechanisms of Omnivorousness." *Sociology Compass* 12(7). https://doi.org/10.1111/soc4.12590.

Figurska, Jolanta, Anthony Peterson, and Laura Galang. 2023. *Food Processing Sector Report: Poland.* Washington, DC: USDA.

Fine, Gary A. 1996. *Kitchens: The Culture of Restaurant Work.* Berkeley: University of California Press.

Finnis, Elizabeth, ed. 2012. *Reimagining Marginalized Foods: Global Processes, Local Places.* Tucson: University of Arizona Press.

Fishbone, Doug. 2002. "The Banana Project." *Gastronomica* 2(3): 64–67.

Food Network. 2018a. "Makłowicz w Polsce—Wokół Wolsztyna." Video file, 27:10. Player.pl. https://player.pl/playerplus/programy-online/maklowicz-w-polsce-odcinki,14060/odcinek-1,S01E01,115560.

Food Network. 2018b. "Makłowicz w Polsce—Wielkopolski porządek." Video file, 20:30. Player.pl. https://player.pl/playerplus/programy-online/maklowicz-w-polsce-odcinki,14060/odcinek-2,S01E02,115561.

Fruton, Joseph S. 2006. *Fermentation: Vital or Chemical Process?* Boston: Brill.

Frye, Joshua, and Michael Bruner. 2012. *The Rhetoric of Food: Discourse, Materiality, and Power.* New York: Routledge.

Fundacja Polskiego Godła Promocyjnego. n.d. *Teraz Polska.* https://terazpolska.pl.

Furrow, Dwight. 2016. *American Foodie: Taste, Art, and the Cultural Revolution.* Lanham: Rowman & Littlefield Publishers.

Gal, Susan. 2013. "Tastes of Talk: Qualia and the Moral Flavor of Signs." *Anthropological Theory* 13(1–2): 31–48.

Galent, Marcin, and Paweł Kubicki. 2012. "New Urban Middle Class and National Identity in Poland." *Polish Sociological Review* 179: 385–400.

Gdula, Maciej, and Przemysław Sadura, eds. 2012. *Style życia i porządek klasowy w Polsce* [Lifestyles and class order in Poland]. Warszawa: Wydawnictwo Naukowe Scholar.

Gessen, Masha. 2021. "The Historians Under Attack for Exploring Poland's Role in the Holocaust." *The New Yorker,* March 26, 2021. https://www.newyorker.com /news/our-columnists/the-historians-under-attack-for-exploring-polands-role-in-the-holocaust.

Ghodsee, Kristen, and Mitchell Orenstein. 2021. *Taking Stock of Shock: Social Consequences of the 1989 Revolutions.* Oxford: Oxford Academic.

Gibas, Petr, and Irena Boumová. 2020. "The Urbanization of Nature in a (Post) Socialist Metropolis: An Urban Political Ecology of Allotment Gardening." *International Journal of Urban and Regional Research* 44(1): 18–37.

Giesbers, Noortje. 2021. *The Joy of Fermentation: The Underlying Motivations for Home-Fermentation in the Netherlands.* Msc. Food Technology Thesis, Wageningen University. https://edepot.wur.nl/556874.

Gille, Zsuzsa. 2017. "Introduction: From Comparison to Relationality." *Slavic Review* 76(2): 285–90.

Gomóła, Anna. 2011. "Tradycyjna kuchnia i dyskurs gastronomiczny" [Traditional cuisine and gastronomic discourse]. In *Tradycja w kontekstach kulturowych* [Traditions in cultural contexts], edited by Jan Adamowski and Marta Wójcicka, 4:177–186. Lublin: Wydawnictwo UMCS.

Gomułka, Stanisław. 2016. "Poland's Economic and Social Transformation 1989–2014 and Contemporary Challenges." *Central Bank Review* 16(1): 19–23.

Gomez, Marie-Léandre, and Isabelle Bouty. 2011. "The Emergence of an Influential Practice: Food for Thought." *Organization Studies* 32(7): 921–940.

Gorlach, Krzysztof, and Zbigniew Drąg. 2021. *Think Locally, Act Globally: Polish Farmers in the Global Era of Sustainability and Resilience.* Kraków: Jagiellonian University Press.

Gorlas, Magdalena. 2014. "Przysmak sentymentalny" [A sentimental delicacy]. *Kuchnia,* August 2014, 74–76.

Goszczyński, Wojciech. 2023. *Idylle, Hybrydy i Heterotopie: Wiejskość i jedzenie w alternatywnych sieciach żywieniowych* [Idylls, hybrids and heterotopias: Rurality and food in alternative food networks]. Warszawa: Instytut Rozwoju Wsi i Rolnictwa Polskiej Akademii Nauk.

Goszczyński, Wojciech, and Ruta Śpiewak. 2024. "The Dark Side of the Bun: Endo and Exogenous Class Exclusions in Polish Alternative Food Networks." *Food, Culture & Society* 26(5): 1107–1133.

Goszczyński, Wojciech, Ruta Śpiewak, Aleksandra Bilewicz, and Michał Wróblewski. 2019. "Between Imitation and Embeddedness: Three Types of Polish Alternative Food Networks." *Sustainability* 11(24): 1–19.

Goszczyński, Wojciech, Michał Wróblewski, and Anna Wójtewicz. 2018. "Jakość w polskich alternatywnych sieciach żywnościowych: Analiza praktyk społecznych" [Quality in Polish alternative food chains: Analysis of social practices]. *Studia Socjologiczne* 1(228): 134–170.

Grabowska-Lusińska, Izabela, and Marek Okólski. 2009. *Emigracja ostatnia?* [The last emigration?] Warszawa: Scholar.

Gracjasz, Alexandra. 2024. *In Transformation: Trust, Participation, and New Socialities around Collective Food Procurement Networks in Gdańsk*. PhD diss., Universiteit Leiden.

Gracjasz, Aleksandra, and Cristina Grasseni. 2020. "Food-Gifting in Gdańsk: Between Food Not Bombs and Food Banks." *Ethnologia Polona* 41: 33–50.

Grasseni, Cristina. 2017. *The Heritage Arena: Reinventing Cheese in the Italian Alp*. New York-Oxford: Berghahn Books.

Gruber, Ruth. 2009. "Virtual Judaism." *Jewish Quarterly* 56(2): 22–25.

Grudzińska-Gross, Irena, and Iwa Nawrocki, eds. 2016. *Poland and Polin: New Interpretations in Polish-Jewish Studies*. Frankfurt am Main: Peter Lang.

Gruszczyński, Arkadiusz, and Michał Wojtczuk. 2023. "Joe Biden w Warszawie. Czy tak jak Trzaskowskiego prawica oskarży go o plany wprowadzenia wegedyktatury? Ba. Już to zrobiła" [Joe Biden in Warsaw. Will the right-wing accuse him, like Trzaskowski, of plans to introduce vegedictatorship? Bah. She already did it]. *Wyborcza.pl*, February 21, 2023. https://warszawa.wyborcza.pl/warszawa/7,54420,29483251, rafal-trzaskowski-zabroni-nam-jesc-miesa-a-nad-amerykanskim.html.

Gulczyńska, Hanna, and Mirosława Jastrząb-Mrozicks. 1994. "Wartość wykształcenia a dążenia edukacyjne" [The value of education and educational aspirations]. *Nauka i Szkolnictwo Wyższe* 2(4): 57–74.

Gunn, Wendy, Ton Otto, and Rachel Charlotte Smith. 2013. *Design Anthropology: Theory and Practice*. London: Bloomsbury Academic.

Gvion, Liora. 2009. "Narrating Modernity and Tradition: The Case of Palestinian Food in Israel." *Identities* 16(4): 391–413.

Hackett, Anna. 2023. "Unprecedented Herd of 170 Bison Spotted in Poland." *Notes from Poland*, January 20. https://notesfrompoland.com/2023/01/20/unprecedented-herd-of-170-bison-spotted-in-poland.

Halawa, Mateusz. 2015. "In New Warsaw: Mortgage Credit and the Unfolding of Space and Time." *Cultural Studies* 29(5–6): 707–732.

Halawa, Mateusz, and Fabio Parasecoli. 2019. "Eating and Drinking in Global Brooklyn." *Food, Culture & Society* 22(4): 387–406.

Hannerz, Ulf. 1990. "Cosmopolitans and Locals in World Culture." *Theory, Culture & Society* 7(2–3): 237–251.

Hannerz, Ulf. 2006. "Studying Down, Up, Sideways, Through, Backwards, Forwards, Away and at Home: Reflections on the Field Worries of an Expansive Discipline." In *Locating the Field: Space, Place and Context in Anthropology*, edited by Simon Coleman and Peter Collins, 23–42. New York: Routledge.

Harkness, Nicholas. 2015. "The Pragmatics of Qualia in Practice." *Annual Review of Anthropology* 44(1): 573–589.

Harris, Deborah A., and Rachel Phillips. 2021. "What's Better Than a Biscuit?: Gourmetization and the Transformation of a Southern Food Staple." *Food and Foodways* 29(3): 243–263.

Herzfeld, Michael. 1997. *Cultural Intimacy: Social Poetics and the Real Life of States, Societies, and Institutions*. New York: Routledge.

Ho, Hao-Tzu. 2020. "Cosmopolitan Locavorism: Global Local-Food Movements in Postcolonial Hong Kong." *Food, Culture & Society* 23(2): 137–154.

Hobsbawn, Eric. 1983 "Introduction: Inventing Tradition." In *The Invention of Tradition*, edited by Eric Hobsbawm and Terence Ranger, 1–14. Cambridge: Cambridge University Press.

Hollows, Joanne. 2022. *Celebrity Chefs, Food Media and the Politics of Eating*. London: Bloomsbury.

Horolets, Anna. 2006. Obrazy Europy w polskim dyskursie publicznym [Images of Europe in Polish public discourse]. Kraków: Universitas.

Horolets, Anna. 2013. *Konformizm, bunt, nostalgia: Turystyka niszowa z Polski do krajów byłego ZSRR* [Conformism, rebellion, nostalgia: Niche tourism from Poland to the countries of the former USSR]. Kraków: Universitas.

Hryciuk, Renata, and Katarzyna Król. 2020. "Introduction: The Cultural Politics of Food and Eating in Poland and Beyond." *Ethnologia Polona* 41: 5–11.

Huigen, Siegfried, and Dorota Kołodziejczyk. 2023. *East Central Europe Between the Colonial and in the Postcolonial in the Twentieth Century*. Cham, Switzerland: Palgrave Macmillan.

Iglicka, Krystyna. 2000. "Mechanisms of Migration from Poland before and during the Transition Period." *Journal of Ethnic and Migration Studies* 26(1): 61–73.

Ingall, Andrew. 2003. "Making a Tsimes, Distilling a Performance: Vodka and Jewish Culture in Poland Today." *Gastronomica* 3(1): 22–27.

Ingold, Tim. 2007. "Materials against Materiality." *Archeological Dialogues* 14(1): 1–16.

Jacobs, Adrianne K. 2022. "An Empire in Aspic: Popularizing National Cuisines in Late Soviet Russia." *The Soviet and Post-Soviet Review* 50(1): 8–39.

Jakubiuk, Joanna. 2018. *Ziemniak* [The potato]. Warszawa: Edipresse.

Jakubowska, Longina. 1990. "Political Drama in Poland: The Use of National Symbols." *Anthropology Today* 6(4): 10–13.

James, Deborah. 2014. *Money from Nothing: Indebtedness and Aspiration in South Africa*. Stanford: Stanford University Press.

James, Deborah. 2019. "New Subjectivities: Aspiration, Prosperity and the New Middle Class." *African Studies* 78(1): 33–50.

Janicka, K., and K. Słomczyński. (2014). "Struktura społeczna w Polsce: Klasowy wymiar nierówności" [Social structure in Poland: The class dimension of inequality]. *Przegląd Socjologiczny* 2: 55–72.

Jarecka, Urszula, and Anna Wieczorkiewicz. 2014. *Terytoria smaku: Studia z antropologii i socjologii jedzenia* [Territories of taste: Studies in anthropology and sociology of food]. Warszawa: IFiS PAN.

Jarosz, Dariusz. 2014. "The Collectivization of Agriculture in Poland: Causes of Defeat." In *The Collectivization of Agriculture in Communist Eastern Europe: Comparison and Entanglements*, edited by Arnd Bauerkämper and Constantin Iordachi, 113–139. Vienna: Central European University Press.

Jarosz, Dariusz. 2019. "Mięso" [Meat]. *Polska 1944/45—1989* 17: 313–330.

Jasarevic, Larisa. 2015. "The Thing in a Jar: Mushrooms and Ontological Speculations in Post-Yugoslavia." *Cultural Anthropology* 30(1): 36–64.

Jastrzębiec-Witowska, Anna. 2023. "Food Solidarity Battles: The Case of Poland After the Russian Aggression on Ukraine." *Studia Europejskie* 4: 153–171.

Jaźwiński, Piotr, and Jan Kunert. 2023. "'Lokalna półka', czyli jak PiS już to planował i dlaczego nic z tego nie wyszło" ['Local shelf', or how PiS already planned it and why nothing came of it]. *Konkret24*, September 8, 2023. https://konkret24.tvn24.pl/polska/wybory-parlamentarne-2023-lokalna-polka-czyli-jak-pis-juz-to-planowal-i-dlaczego-nic-z-tego-nie-wyszlo-st7333260.

Jeronimo Martins Polska S.A. 2021. *Kuchnia ŚródziemnoPOLSKA. Codziennie smacznie i zdrowo* [Mediterranean POLISH cuisine. Tasty and healthy everyday]. Kostrzyn: Jeronimo Martins Polska S.A.

Jędruch, Jacek. 1998. *Constitutions, Elections, and Legislatures of Poland, 1493–1977: A Guide to Their History*. New York: Hippocrene Books.

Jehlička, Petr. 2007. "Stories Around Food, Politics and Change in Poland and the Czech Republic." *Transactions of the Institute of British Geographers* 32(3): 395–410.

Jehlička, Petr, Miķelis Grīviņš, Oane Visser, and Bálint Balázs. 2020. "Thinking Food like an East European: A Critical Reflection on the Framing of Food Systems." *Journal of Rural Studies* 76: 286–95.

Jochnowitz, Eve. 2004. "Flavors on Memory: Jewish Food as Culinary Tourism in Poland." In *Culinary Tourism*, edited by Lucy Long, 97–113. Lexington: University Press of Kentucky.

Joffe, Julia. 2012. "The Borscht Belt: Rediscovering Russia's Lost Culinary Heritage." *The New Yorker,* April 16, 2012. https://www.newyorker.com/magazine/2012/04/16/the-borscht-belt.

Johnston, Josée, and Shyon Baumann. 2010. *Foodies: Democracy and Distinction in the Gourmet Foodscape*. New York: Routledge.

Julier, Alice. 2013. *Eating Together: Food, Friendship, and Inequality*. Urbana: University of Illinois.

Jung, Yuson, Jacob A. Klein, and Melissa Caldwell, eds. 2014. *Ethical Eating in the Postocialist and Socialist World*. Los Angeles: University of California Press.

Just, Thomas. 2015. "Public Diplomacy and Domestic Engagement: The Jewish Revival in Poland." *Place Branding and Public Diplomacy* 11: 263–275.

Kaczyński, Jarosław. 2019. "Jarosław Kaczyński w rozmowie o życiu, rodzinie i prywatnych pasjach" [Jarosław Kaczyński in a conversation about life, family and private passions]. *Pytanie na śniadanie,* May 13, 2019. https://pytanienasniadanie .tvp.pl/42603220/jaroslaw-kaczynski-o-zyciu-rodzinie-i-milosci-do-zwierzat.

KAIEN, RS, ASL. 2014. "Rosjanie zmuszą Putina do zniesienia embarga na jabłka" [The Russians will force Putin to lift the apple embargo]. *TVP Info,* July 31, 2014. https://www.tvp.info/16263618/rosjanie-zmusza-putina-do-zniesienia-embarga-na-jablka.

Kalb, Don. 2009. "Headlines of Nationalism, Subtexts of Class: Poland and Popular Paranoia, 1989–2009." *Anthropologica* 51(2): 289–300.

Kancelaria Prezesa Rady Ministrów. 2019. "The National Institute of Polish Rural Culture and Heritage Is Being Established." *premier.gov.pl,* April 16, 2019. https://archiwum.premier.gov.pl/en/news/news/the-national-institute-of-polish-rural-culture-and-heritage-is-being-established.html.

Karpińska, Grażyna Ewa. 2013. "Tradycje kulinarne na 'Szlaku łaknienia'" [Culinary traditions on the 'Appetite Trail']. In *Nie tylko o wsi: Szkice humanistyczne dedykowane Profesor Marii Wieruszewskiej-Adamczyk* [Not only about the countryside: Humanities sketches dedicated to Professor Maria Wieruszewska-Adamczyk], edited by Damian Kasprzyk, 315–332. Łódź: Ed. D. Kasprzyk.

Karpińska, Grażyna Ewa. 2014. "Jak to z produktem regionalnym bywa, czyli o głodzie tradycji we współczesnym świecie" [As it happens with a regional product, i.e. hunger for tradition in the modern world]. In *Głód: Skojarzenia, metafory, refleksje* [Hunger: Associations, metaphors, reflections], edited by Katarzyna Łeńska-Bąk and Magdalena Sztandara, 291–304. Opole: Wydawnictwo Uniwersytetu Opolskiego.

Karski, Jan. 2014. *The Great Powers and Poland: From Versailles to Yalta.* Lanham, MD: Rowman & Littlefield.

Kasprzyk-Chevriaux, Magdalena. 2015. "Robert Trzópek." *Culture.pl,* March 2015. https://culture.pl/en/artist/robert-trzopek.

Katz, Sandor. 2003. *Wild Fermentation: The Flavor, Nutrition, and Craft of Live-Culture Foods.* White River Junction, VT: Chelsea Green Publishing.

Katz, Sandor. 2012. *The Art of Fermentation.* White River Junction, VT: Chelsea Green Publishing.

Katz, Sandor. 2021. *Sandor Katz's Fermentation Journeys: Recipes, Techniques, and Traditions from around the World.* White River Junction, VT: Chelsea Green Publishing.

Kawczyńska, Marta. 2019. "Minister Ardanowski chce, aby bobry były jadalne. Makłowicz: Czegoś równie ohydnego w życiu nie jadłem" [Minister Ardanowski wants beavers to be edible. Makłowicz: I haven't eaten anything so hideous in my life]. *dziennik.pl,* June 7, 2019. https://wiadomosci.dziennik.pl/polityka/artykuly/599716,ardanowski-bobry-afrodyzjak-zubry-maklowicz.html.

Keep Freedom Unlocked. 2019. "How Bananas Came to Symbolise Freedom in Poland." YouTube, December 4, 2019. https://www.youtube.com/watch?v=ZovA9wFI_ms.

Kjellberg, Hans, and Alexandre Mallard. 2013. "Valuation Studies? Our Collective Two Cents." *Valuation Studies* 1(1): 11–30.

Kleśta-Nawrocka, Aleksandra. 2016. *Kucharz doskonały: Historyczno-kulturowy fenomen kuchni staropolskiej* [The perfect cook: The historical and cultural phenomenon of Old Polish cuisine]. Warszawa: Polskie Towarzystwo Historyczne.

Kleśta-Nawrocki, Rafał, and Aleksandra Kleśta-Nawrocka. 2017. "Między lokalnym iwentem a turystycznym megaiwentem kulinarnym" [Between local events and touristic culinary megaeventos]. *Przygody Festiwalu Smaku w Grucznie. Czas Kultury* 192(1): 92–98.

Klesyk, Łukasz. 2012. "Ocena subiektywna" [Subjective assessment]. *Kuchnia,* August 2012, 83.

Kochanowski, Jerzy. 2010. *Tylnymi drzwiami: Czarny rynek w Polsce 1944–1989* [Through the back door: Black market in Poland 1944–1989]. Warszawa: W.A.B.

Koczanowicz, Dorota. 2022. *The Aesthetics of Taste: Eating Within the Realm of Art.* Leiden: Brill.

Koenig, Leah. 2019. "Jewish Food Returns to Warsaw." *tabletmag.com,* December 26, 2019. https://www.tabletmag.com/sections/food/articles/jewish-food-returns-to-warsaw.

Koenker, Diane P. 2018. "The Taste of Others: Soviet Adventures in Cosmopolitan Cuisines." *Kritika: Explorations in Russian and Eurasian History* 19(2): 243–272.

Kolberg, Oskar. 1857–1890. *Lud: Jego zwyczaje, sposób życia, mowa, podania, przysłowia, obrzędy, gusła, zabawy, pieśni, muzyka i tańce* [The country people. Their customs, way of life, speech, legends, proverbs, rituals, witchcraft, games, songs, music and dances]. Warszawa, w drukarni Jana Jaworskiego.

Kolondra, Paulina. 2014. "Zbieramy chrust" [We collect brushwood]. *Kuchnia,* February 2014, 4–5.

Kończal, Kornelia. 2021. "Mnemonic Populism: The Polish Holocaust Law and Its Afterlife." *European Review* 29(4): 457–469.

Kopczyńska, Ewa. 2014. "Stare i nowe smaki lokalnego wina: o lubuskiej winorośli, winnicach i winiarzach" [Old and new flavors of local wine: About Lubuskie vines, vineyards and winemakers]. In *Terytoria smaku. Studia z antropologii i socjologii jedzenia*, edited by U. Jarecka and A. Wieczorkiewicz, 133–152. Warszawa: Wydawnictwo IFiS PAN.

Kopczyńska, Ewa. 2017. "Economies of Acquaintances: Social Relations during Shopping at Food Markets and in Consumers' Food Cooperatives." *East European Politics and Societies: and Cultures* 31(3): 637–658.

Kopczyńska, Ewa. 2018. "How Food Fears Frame Criticisms of the Food System: A Case Study of Customers of Farmers' Market." *Studia Humanistyczne AGH* 17(2): 79–96.

Kopczyńska, Ewa. 2021. *Jedzenie i inne rzeczy: Antropologia zmiany w systemach żywnościowych* [Food and other things: The anthropology of change in food systems]. Kraków: Wydawnictwo Uniwersytetu Jagiellońskiego.

Kopczyńska, Ewa, and Katarzyna Zielińska. 2016. "Feeding the Body, Feeding the Gender: Dietary Choices of Men and Women in Poland." *East European Politics and Societies* 30(1): 147–168.

Kopczyńska, Ewa, and Agata Bachórz. 2018. "Food Fears, Food Distrust and Food Exclusion in One Postsocialist Culture and Beyond." *Studia Humanistyczne AGH* 17(2): 7–13.

Koper, Anna, and Philip Blenkinsop. 2024. "EU Eyes Easing Green Rules on Farmers to Defuse Protests." Reuters, May 15, 2024. https://www.reuters.com/world /europe/eu-plan-ease-farmers-fallow-land-requirement-stalls-detail-2024–03–15.

Korkosz, Michał. 2020a. *Fresh from Poland: New Vegetarian Cooking from the Old Country*. New York City: The Experiment.

Korkosz, Michał. 2020b. *Rozkoszne: Wegetariańska uczta z polskimi smakami* [Delicious: A vegetarian feast with Polish flavors]. Kraków: Wydawnictwo Otwarte.

Korkosz, Michał. 2023. *Polish'd: Modern Vegetarian Cooking from Global Poland*. New York City: The Experiment.

Korkosz, Michał. 2023b. *Nowe rozkoszne. Polskie przepisy, które ekscytują* [New delightful Polish recipes that excite]. Warszawa: Wydawnictwo Buchmann.

Korycki, Kate. 2017. "Memory, Party Politics, and Post-Transition Space: The Case of Poland." *East European Politics, Societies: and Cultures* 31(3): 518–544.

Koryś, Piotr. 2018. *Poland from Partitions to EU Accession: A Modern Economic History, 1772–2004*. Cham: Palgrave Macmillan.

Koselleck, Reinhart. 2004. *Futures Past: On the Semantics of Historical Time*. New York: Columbia University Press.

Kovács, Eszter Krasznai, Agata Bachórz, Natasha Bunzl, Diana Mincyte, Fabio Parasecoli, Simone Piras, and Mihai Varga. 2022. "The War in Ukraine and Food Security in Eastern Europe." *Gastronomica* 22 (3): 1–7.

Kowalczyk, Grzegorz. 2023. "Lokalna półka? Rolnicy wskazują na 'pułapki' obietnicy PiS" [The local shelf? Farmers point to the 'pitfalls' of PiS's promise]. *Business Insider*. September 7, 2023. https://businessinsider.com.pl/gospodarka /lokalna-polka-pomysl-dobry-ale-rolnicy-o-konkrecie-pis/vn6736w.

Kowalska, Dorota. 2014. "Akcja 'Jedz jabłka na złość Putinowi' chwyciła. Sadowników wspierają gwiazdy i zwykli Polacy" [The action 'Eat apples to spite Putin' took hold. Growers are supported by stars and ordinary Poles]. *Polska Times,* August 4, 2014. https://polskatimes.pl/akcja-jedz-jablka-na-zlosc-putinowi-chwycila-sadownikow-wspieraja-gwiazdy-i-zwykli-polacy/ar/3528955.

Krajewski, Marek. 2013. "W kierunku relacyjnej koncepcji uczestnictwa w kulturze" [Towards the relational concept of participation in culture]. *Kultura i Społeczeństwo* 1: 29–67.

Krastev, Ivan, and Stephen Holmes. 2020. *The Light That Failed: Why the West Is Losing the Fight for Democracy?* New York: Pegasus Books.

Krzyżanowski, Piotr. 2012. "Kurpiów groch z kapustą" [Kurpie peas with cabbage]. *Kuchnia,* August 2012, 30–36.

Kuchnia. 2012. "Cook It Raw." November 2012, 46–48.

Kucia, Monika. 2021. *Food: Generations*. Prelude, Kultur Symposium Weimar 2021. https://www.youtube.com/watch?v=F9KDLpoMWlM.

Kuisz, Jarosław. 2023. *The New Politics of Poland : A Case of Post-Traumatic Sovereignty*. Manchester: Manchester University Press.

Kukołowicz, Paula. 2019. *Klasa średnia w Polsce: Czy istnieje polski self-made man?* [The middle class in Poland: Does a Polish self-made man exist?] Warszawa: Polski Instytut Ekonomiczny.

Kundera, Milan. 1984. "The Tragedy of Central Europe." *The New York Review of Books* 31(7): 33–38.

Kurczewski, Jacek, ed. 2004. *Umowa o kartki* [The agreement on ration cards]. Warszawa: Trio.

Kuroń, Jakub. 2013. *Kuroniowie przy stole* [The Kurońs at the table]. Warszawa: Czarna Owca.

Kuropatnicki, Andrzej, Fabio Parasecoli, and Jarosław Dumanowski. 2020. *The Power of Taste: Europe at the Royal Table*. Warszawa: Museum of King Jan III's Palace at Wilanów.

Kuus, Merje. 2004. "Europe's Eastern Expansion and the Reinscription of Otherness in East-Central Europe." *Progress in Human Geography* 28(4): 472–489.

Kwaśniewski, Krzysztof. 1997. "Społeczne rozumienie relacji kresów i terytorium narodowego" [Social understanding of the relationship between borderlands and national territory]. In *Kresy—pojęcie i rzeczywistość* [Borderlands—concept and reality], edited by Kwiryna Handke, 63–83. Warszawa: Slawi-styczny Ośrodek Wydawniczy.

Kwiatkowski, Piotr. 2008. *Pamięć zbiorowa społeczeństwa polskiego w okresie transformacji* [The collective memory of Polish society in the period of transformation]. Warszawa: Instytut Studiów Politycznych Polskiej Akademii Nauk PAN, Wydawnictwo Naukowe Scholar.

Lagrue, Mary Claire. 2021. "One Year Later: How the Pandemic Changed Home Cooking." *All Recipes,* March 16, 2021. https://www.allrecipes.com/longform/coronavirus-cooking-and-grocery-shopping-one-year-later.

Lahne, Jacob. 2016. "Sensory Science, the Food Industry, and the Objectifiction of Taste." *Anthropology of Food* 10. http://aof.revues.org/7956.

Lane, Christel, and M. Pilar Opazo. 2023. "Constructing Global Tastes: A Comparison of Two Cultural Intermediaries in the Field of High-End Cuisine." *Food, Culture & Society* 27(2): 479–505.

Latour, Bruno. 2008. "A Cautious Prometheus? A Few Steps Toward a Philosophy of Design." In *Networks of Design*, edited by Fiona Hackney, Jonathan Glynne, and Viv Minto, 2–10. Penryn: University College Falmouth.

LeBesco, Kathleen, and Peter Naccarato, eds. 2008. *Edible Ideologies: Representing Food and Meaning*. Albany: State University of New York Press.

Leer, Jonatan, and Karen Klitgaard Povlsen, eds. 2018. *Food and Media: Practices, Distinctions and Heterotopias*. London: Routledge.

Leer, Jonatan, and Stinne Gunder Strøm Krogager, eds. 2021. *Research Methods in Digital Food Studies*. New York: Routledge.

Lemnis, Maria, and Henryk Virty. 1979. *Old Polish Traditions in the Kitchen and at the Table*. New York: Hippocrene.

Lepak, Keith J. 1989. "Prelude to Crisis: Leadership Drift in Poland in the 1970s." *Studies in Comparative Communism* 22(1): 11–22.

Lepczyński, Krzysztof. 2021. "Ideologia klasy średniej: od modernizacyjnego projektu do niespełnionej obietnicy" [Middle-class ideology: from a modernizing project to an unfulfilled promise]. *Studia Socjologiczne* 4: 5–31.

Lewando, Fania. 2020. *Dietojarska kuchnia żydowska* [Dietoyar Jewish cuisine]. Kraków: Znak Literova.

Leśniewski, Krzysztof. 2016. *Kuchnia Pałucka*. Bydgoszcz: Wydawnictwo Gaj.

Leszczyński, Adam. 2017. *No dno po prostu jest Polska: Dlaczego Polacy tak bardzo nie lubią swojego kraju i innych Polaków* [Well, the bottom is simply Poland: Why Poles dislike their country and other Poles so much]. Warszawa: Grupa Wydawnicza Foksal.

Lewicki, Mikołaj, and Adrianna Drozdowska. 2017. "'Słoiki' i warszawiacy: klasowe wojny o Warszawę [Jars and Varsovians: class wars for Warsaw]." In *Klasy w Polsce: Teorie, dyskusje, badania, konteksty* [Classes in Poland: Theories, discussions, research, contexts], edited by Maciej Gdula and Michał Sutowski, 93–161. Warszawa: Wydawnictwo Krytyki Politycznej.

Lukowski, Jerzy, and Hubert Zawadzki. 2019. *A Concise History of Poland*. Cambridge: Cambridge University Press.

Łuczaj, Łukasz. n.d. The Wild Food. https://www.youtube.com/@thewildfoodlukaszluczaj1321.

Łuczaj, Łukasz. 2018. *Dzika kuchnia* [Wild cuisine]. Warszawa: Nasza Księgarnia.

Łuczaj, Łukasz. 2020. *Sex in Nature: A Guide to Making Love in Forests and Meadows*. Self-published.

Łuczaj, Łukasz. 2021. *Foraging in Eastern Europe: Wild Edible Plants in Polish Traditional Cuisine*. Pietrusza Wola: Self-published.

Łuczaj, Łukasz, and Zofia Nieroda. 2011. "Collecting and Learning to Identify Edible Fungi in Southeastern Poland: Age and Gender Differences." *Ecology of Food and Nutrition* 50(4): 319–336.

Łuczaj Łukasz, Andrea Pieroni, Javier Tardío, Manuel Pardo-de-Santayana, Renata Sõukand, Ingvar Svanberg, and Raivo Kalle. 2012. "Wild Food Plant Use in 21st-Century Europe: The Disappearance of Old Traditions and the Search for New Cuisines Involving Wild Edibles." *Acta Societatis Botanicorum Poloniae* 81(4): 359–370.

Łuczaj, Łukasz, Jarosław Dumanowski, Cecylia Marszałek, and Fabio Parasecoli. 2023. "Turmeric and Cumin Instead of Stock Cubes: An Internet Survey of Spices and Culinary Herbs Used in Poland Compared with Historical Cookbooks and Herbals." *Plants* 12: 591. https://doi.org/10.3390/plants12030591.

Maciuła-Ziomek, Agnieszka. 2023. "Straganom w Polsce nadal dobrze się wiedzie [Staganom in Poland is still doing well]." *Strefa Buznesu.pl*, July 29, 2023. https://

strefabiznesu.pl/straganom-w-polsce-nadal-dobrze-sie-wiedzie-polacy-uwielbi-aja-zakupy-na-targowiskach-dlugi-tej-branzy-sa-wyraznie-nizsze/ar/c3–17755793 #bazary-odwiedza-wiekszosc-polakow.

Maćkiewicz, Barbara, Magdalena Szczepańska, Ewa Kacprzak, and Runrid Fox-Kämper. 2021. "Between Food Growing and Leisure: Contemporary Allotment Gardeners in Western Germany and Poland." *Die Erde—Journal of the Geographical Society of Berlin* 152(1): 33–50.

Makharadze, Ana. 2020. "Cooking Up National Identity: Cookbooks and Social Transformation in Georgia." Master's thesis, Central European University, Budapest.

Makro. 2018. *One Hundred Recipes for One Hundred Years of Independence (1918–2018)*. Warsaw: Makro.

Malinowska, Mirosława. 2016. "Targowiska w Polsce: Schyłek czy rozkwit?" *Studia Ekonomiczne. Zeszyty Naukowe Uniwersytetu Ekonomicznego w Katowicach* 302: 109–122.

Manzini, Enzo. 2019. *Politics of the Everyday*. London: Bloomsbury.

Mapes, Gwynne. 2021. *Elite Authenticity: Remaking Distinction in Food Discourse*. New York: Oxford University Press.

Mark, James, Bogdan C. Iacob, Tobias Rupprecht, and Ljubica Spaskovska. 2019. *1989: A Global History of Eastern Europe*. Cambridge: Cambridge University Press.

Matijevic, Petra, and Zofia Boni. 2019. "Losing Appetite for the EU? Tensions around Food in Central and Eastern Europe." *Appetite* 140: 305–308.

Matta, Raúl. 2019. "Celebrity Chefs and the Limits of Playing Politics from the Kitchen." In *Globalized Eating Cultures*, edited by Jörg Dürrschmidt and York Kautt, 183–201. Cham: Palgrave Macmillan.

Mazurek, Małgorzata. 2010. *Społeczeństwo kolejki: O doświadczeniach niedoboru 1945–1989* [The queue society: On the experiences of scarcity 1945–1989]. Warszawa: Trio.

Merlak, Hanna. 2019. *Żydzi od kuchni: Opowieści wokół rodzinnego stołu* [Jews from the kitchen: Stories around the family table]. Kraków: Austeria.

Menendez-Roche, Marc. 2025. "Poland Officially Surpasses US: Zloty Takes the Lead over US minimum wage!" *Euroweekly News*, January 4, 2025. https://euroweeklynews.com/2025/01/04/poland-pays-more-than-the-us-zloty-takes-the-lead-over-us-minimum-wage.

Menu Wolności. n.d. "Menu Wolności" [Menu of freedom]. Facebook page. https://www.facebook.com/menuwolnosci.

Menu Wolności. 2019. http://www.menuwolnosci.pl. Accessed May 15, 2019.

Messeni Petruzzelli, Antonio, and Tommaso Savino. 2014. "Search, Recombination, and Innovation: Lessons from Haute Cuisine." *Long Range Planning* 47(4): 224–238.

Mętrak-Ruda, Natalia. 2023. "Sour Tastes: Pickling & Fermentation in Polish Cuisine." Culture,pl, April 25 2023. https://culture.pl/en/article/sour-tastes-pickling-fermentation-in-polish-cuisine-plus-a-recipe.

Mientkiewicz, Gieno and Zbigniew Kmieć. 2020. *Proklamacja ustanowienia dnia twarogu* [Proclamation establishing cottage cheese day]. https://www.facebook.com/photo.php?fbid=3607573995919970&id=%204980600935380058&set%20=%20a.524345524242848.

Mikos, Augustyn. 2024. "While Europe's Green Backlash Grows, Poland Tells Different Story." *Climate Home News,* February 5, 2024. https://www.climatechangenews.com/2024/02/05/while-europes-green-backlash-grows-poland-protects-its-forests.

Milewska, Monika. 2022. *Ślepa kuchnia. Jedzenie i ideologia w PRL* [Blind kitchen: Food and ideology in the Polish People's Republic]. Warszawa: Państwowy Instytut Wydawniczy.

Miller, Jeffrey, and Jonathan Deutsch. 2009. *Food Studies: An Introduction to Research Methods.* Oxford: Berg.

Mincyte, Diana. 2011. "Subsistence and Sustainability in Post-industrial Europe: The Politics of Small-Scale Farming in Europeanising Lithuania." *Sociologia Ruralis* 51(2): 101–118.

Mincyte, Diana. 2012. "How Milk Does the World Good: Vernacular Sustainability and Alternative Food Systems in Post-Socialist Europe." *Agriculture and Human Values* 29(1): 41–52.

Ministerstwo Rolnictwa i Rozwoju Wsi. n.d. Lista produktów tradycyjnych [List of traditional products]. https://www.gov.pl/web/rolnictwo/lista-produktow-tradycyjnych12.

Ministerstwo Rolnictwa i Rozwoju Wsi. 2018. *Katalog: Poznaj Dobra Żywność* [Catalog: Get to know good food]. Warszawa: Ministerstwo Rolnictwa i Rozwoju Wsi.

Ministerstwo Rolnictwa i Rozwoju Wsi. 2019. "Kanon kuchni polskiej—zapraszamy do konsultacji" [The canon of Polish cuisine—we invite you a consultation].Gov.pl,September2,2019.https://www.gov.pl/web/rolnictwo/kanon-kuchni-polskiej—zapraszamy-do-konsultacji.

Mische, Ann. 2009. "Projects and Possibilities: Researching Futures in Action." *Sociological Forum* 24(3): 694–704.

Modelski, Łukasz. 2015. "Bóbr to nie tylko wigilijna ryba" [The beaver is not only a Christmas Eve fish]. *Droga przez mąkę* (radio show), December 13, 2015. https://reportaz.polskieradio.pl/artykul/1557104.

Mokrzycki, Edmund. 2002. "New Middle Class." In *Culture, Modernity and Revolution: Essays in Honour of Zygmunt Bauman,* edited by Richard Kilminster and Ian Varcoe, 184–201. London: Taylor & Francis.

Mol, Annemarie. 2021. *Eating in Theory.* Durham, NC: Duke University Press.

money.pl. 2023. "Zwrot w Brukseli ws. ukraińskiego zboża? Minister: mamy przecieki" [A turnaround in Brussels regarding Ukrainian grain? Minister: we have leaks]. *Money.pl,* September 15, 2023. https://www.money.pl/gospodarka/polska-dopiela-swego-ws-importu-ukrainskiego-zboza-minister-zdradza-date-6941734339893952a.html.

Moor, Liz. 2012. "Beyond Cultural Intermediaries? A Socio-Technical Perspective on the Market for Social Interventions." *European Journal of Cultural Studies* 15(5): 563–580.

Mroczkowska, Joanna. 2016. *Polityka smaku: Rola jedzenia w tworzeniu, podtrzymywaniu i negocjowaniu więzi społecznych i rodzinnych w Dąbrowie Białostockiej i okolicach* [The politics of taste: The role of food in creating, maintaining and negotiating social and family ties in Dąbrowa Białostocka and its vicinity]. PhD diss, Uniwersytet Warszawski.

Mroczkowska, Joanna. 2018. "Podlaski 'słoik'—Mobilna grupa społeczna i mobilne medium tożsamości lokalnej" [Podlaski 'Jar'—A mobile social group and a mobile medium of local identity]. *Studia Socjologiczne* 4(231): 77–102.

Mroczkowska, Joanna. 2019. "Pork Politics: The Scales of Home-Made Food in Eastern Poland." *Appetite* 140: 223–230.

Müller, Martin. 2019. "Goodbye, Postsocialism!" *Europe-Asia Studies* 71: 1–18.

Munn, Nancy. 1986. *The Fame of Gawa: A Symbolic Study of Value Transformation in a Massim (Papua New Guinea) Society.* Cambridge: Cambridge University Press.

Muraszko, Małgorzata. 2019. "Kiedy zachorowała na nowotwór, zainteresowała się kiszonkami. Dziś kisi na pełen etat [When she fell ill with cancer, she became interested in pickles. Today, she works full-time]." *Wyborcza.pl,* October 19, 2019. https://www.wysokieobcasy.pl/wysokie-obcasy/7,53667,25310782,zachorowala-na-nowotwor-po-chorobie-zajela-sie-kiszonkami.html.

Musidłowska, Maryla. 2021. *Boker Tov: JCC Warsaw Kosher Vegetarian Recipes And Stories.* Kraków: Austeria.

Myles, Colleen, ed. 2020. *Fermented Landscapes: Lively Processes of Socio-Environmental Transformation.* Lincoln: University of Nebraska Press.

Naccarato, Peter, and Kathleen LeBesco. 2012. *Culinary Capital.* London: Berg.

Nader, Laura. 1972. "Up the Anthropologist: Perspectives Gained from Studying Up." In *Reinventing Anthropology,* edited by Dell Hyms, 284–311. New York: Random House.

Nagengast, Marian Carole. 1982. "Polish Peasants and the State." *Dialectical Anthropology* 7(1): 47–66.

Nazaruk, Igor. 2013. "Pan Sandacz słyszy ryby" [Mr. Zander hears the fish]. *Kuchnia,* July 2013, 43.

Nazaruk, Igor. 2014. "W tym właśnie sęk" [Here's the point]. *Kuchnia,* January 2014, 65.

Negus, Keith. 2002. "The Work of Cultural Intermediaries and the Enduring Distance between Production and Consumption." *Cultural Studies* 16(4): 501–515.

Nestle, Marion. 2010. "Writing the Food Studies Movement." *Food, Culture & Society* 13(2): 161–70.

Netczuk, Łukasz K. 2016. *Historia ogrodnictwa i ruchu działkowego na ziemiach polskich: Zarys problematyki badań i studiów źródłowych* [History of horticulture and allotments in Poland: Outline of research and source studies]. Warszawa: Krajowa Rada Polskiego Związku Działkowców.

Niedźwiecki, Konrad. 2019. "'Bobrzyna.' Największy polski gryzoń jest nie lada przysmakiem" [Beaver meat: The largest Polish rodent is a real delicacy]. *WP Finanse,* May 19, 2019. https://finanse.wp.pl/bobrzyna-najwiekszy-polski-gryzon-jest-nie-lada-przysmakiem-6381901670844033a.

Nizinkiewicz, Jacek. 2017. "Friszke: Samobójcza polityka historyczna PiS" [Friszke: PiS's suicidal historical policy]. *Rzeczpospolita,* September 10, 2017, https://www.rp.pl/Polityka/309109944-Friszke-Samobojcza-polityka-historyczna-PiS.html.

Nogaś, Michał. 2020. "Przepraszam za to, co przez lata pisałam o gotowaniu fasoli. Myliłam się" [I apologize for what I have written over the years about cooking beans. I was wrong]. *Gazeta Wyborcza,* June 6, 2020. https://wyborcza.pl/7,75410, 26006684,chlop-wchodzi-na-salony.html.

Nowak, Krystian. 2020. *Kebabistan: Rzecz o Polskim Daniu Narodowym.* Warszawa: Krytyka Polityczna.

Nowicka-Franczak, Magdalena. 2018. "Was Another Modernisation Possible? Liberal and Leftist Critique of the Transformation in the Public Debate in Poland." *Polish Sociological Review* 3: 321–343.

Ocejo, Richard E. 2017. *Masters of Craft: Old Jobs in the New Urban Economy.* Princeton. Princeton University Press.

Ochman, Paweł. 2020. *Roślinna kuchnia regionalna* [Vegetarian regional cooking]. Warszawa: Marginesy.

O'Connor, Justin. 2015. "Intermediaries and Imaginaries in the Cultural and Creative Industries." *Regional Studies* 49(3): 374–387.

Okólski, Marek. 2021. "The Migration Transition in Poland: Central and Eastern European." *Migration Review* 10(2): 151–169.

Oleksiuk, Inga, and Agnieszka Werenowska. 2018. "Geographical Indications and Traditional Specialities: Case Study of Poland." *Problems of World Agriculture* 18(3): 229–237.

Olewicz, Agata. 2013. "Sprawdzony Smak: Kulki owsiane" [Proven Taste: Oat balls]. *Przyślij przepis*, February 2013, 37.

Olszanka, Paulina. 2022. "Eating Our Way to Authenticity: Polish Food Culture & the Post-Socialist 'Transformation'." *Social Sciences* 11(2): 44.

Oltermann, Philip. 2014. "Poland Takes the Bite Out of Russian Apple Ban." *The Guardian,* July 31, 2014. https://www.theguardian.com/world/2014/jul/31/poland-takes-bite-out-russian-apple-ban.

Omachel, Radosław. 2019. "Polacy jedzą go zdecydowanie za dużo: Ale już wkrótce to się zmieni, a mięso stanie się towarem luksusowym" [Poles eat far too much of it: But that will soon change and meat will become a luxury commodity]. *Newsweek Polska,* July 7, 2019. https://www.newsweek.pl/polska/spoleczenstwo/spozycie-miesa-w-polsce-spadlo-o-ponad-2-procent-czy-mieso-stanie-sie-towarem/kzygjfs.

Orstrander, Suran A. 1993. "'Surely You Are Not in This Just to Be Helpful': Access, Rapport, and Interviews in Three Studies of Elites." *Journal of Contemporary Ethnography* 22(1): 7–27.

Ortner, Sherry B. 2016. "Dark Anthropology and its Others." *HAU: Journal of Ethnographic Theory* 6(1): 47–73.

Ost, David. 2005. *The Defeat of Solidarity: Anger and Politics in Postcommunist Europe*. Ithaca, NY: Cornell University Press.

PAP. 2016. "Waszczykowski w niemieckiej gazecie: Nie chcemy świata złożonego z rowerzystów i wegetarian" [Waszczykowski in a German newspaper: We don't want a world made up of cyclists and vegetarians]. *Newsweek Polska*, January 3, 2016. https://www.newsweek.pl/polska/witold-waszczykowski-wywiad-dla-bild-rowerzysci-i-wegetarianie/88ojm5h.

Paprot-Wielopolska, Aleksandra. 2018. *Żuławy i Powiśle: kreowanie tożsamości lokalnych i regionalnych po 1989 roku* [Żuławy and Powiśle regions: Creating local and regional identities after 1989]. Warszawa: Wydawnictwo Naukowe Scholar.

Parasecoli, Fabio. 2008. *Bite Me: Food in Popular Culture*. Oxford: Berg.

Parasecoli, Fabio. 2016. "Starred Cosmopolitanism: Celebrity Chefs, Documentaries, and the Circulation of Global Desire." *Semiotica* 211: 315–340.

Parasecoli, Fabio. 2017. *Knowing Where It Comes From: Labeling Traditional Food to Compete in a Global Market*. Iowa City: Iowa University Press.

Parasecoli, Fabio. 2018. "Food, Design, Innovation: From Professional Specialization to Citizens' Involvement." In *Handbook of Food and Popular Culture*, edited by Kathleen LeBesco and Peter Naccarato, 155–168. London: Bloomsbury.

Parasecoli, Fabio. 2022. *Gastronativism: Food, Identity, Politics*. New York City: Columbia University Press.

Parasecoli, Fabio, and Mateusz Halawa, eds. 2021. *Global Brooklyn: Designing Food Experiences in World Cities*. London: Bloomsbury Academic.

Parker, Christine Susan. 2003. "History Education Reform in Post-Communist Poland, 1989–1999: Historical and Contemporary Effects on Educational Transition." PhD diss., The Ohio State University.

Parkhurst Ferguson, Priscilla. 2004. *Accounting for Taste: The Triumph of French Cuisine*. Chicago: University of Chicago Press.

Parham, Susan. 2012. *Market Place: Food Quarters, Design and Urban Renewal in London*. Newcastle upon Tyne: Cambridge Scholars Publishing.

Pawlikowska-Piechotka, Anna. 2010. *Tradycja Ogrodów Działkowych w Polsce*. Gdynia: Wydawnictwo Novae Res.

Paxson, Heather. 2008. "Post-Pasteurian Cultures: The Microbiopolitics of Raw-Milk Cheese in the United States." *Cultural Anthropology* 23(1): 15–47.

Pellerano, Joana A., and Viviane Riegel. 2017. "Food and Cultural Omnivorism: A Reflexive Discussion on Otherness, Interculturality and Cosmopolitanism." *International Review of Social Research* 7(1): 13–21.

Peterson, Richard A., and Roger M. Kern. 1996. "Changing Highbrow Taste: From Snob to Omnivore." *American Sociological Review* 61(5): 900–907.

Phillipov, Michelle. 2017. *Media and Food Industries: The New Politics of Food*. Cham: Springer International Publishing AG.

Pickering, Michael, and Emily Keightley. 2006. "The Modalities of Nostalgia." *Current Sociology* 54(6): 919–940.

Pikuła, Rafał. 2023. "Talerz pychy i pogardy: Jak PiS próbował wystraszyć Polaków zakazem jedzenia mięsa" [A plate of pride and contempt: How PiS-party tried to scare Poles with a ban on eating meat]. *Wyborcza.biz,* February 20, 2023. https://wyborcza.biz/biznes/7,179195,29481638,drogi-talerz-pis-miesne-dania-ktorymi-lansuja-sie-politycy.html.

Piotrowski, Grzegorz, ed. 2024. *Kuchnia (w) PRL* [Cuisine in (of) the Polish People's Republic]. Gdańsk: Europejskie Centrum Solidarności/European Solidarity Center.

Polanyi, Karl. 1957. "The Economy as Instituted Process." In *Trade and Market in the Early Empires,* edited by Karl Polanyi, Conrad Arensberg, and Harry Pearson, 243–70. New York: Free Press.

Polányi, Michael. 1962. *Personal Knowledge: Towards a Post-Critical Philosophy.* London: Routledge and Kegan Paul.

Polish Cultural Institute in New York. 2020. *Polish Cuisine: Fermentation by Aleksander Baron.* https://www.youtube.com/watch?v=PAO9rkdo_ZM.

Polonia Christiana. 2018. "Robak na talerzu: kuchenne rewolucje" [Bug on the plate: a culinary revolution] (magazine cover). March-April 2018. https://www.ksiegarnia.poloniachristiana.pl/produkt,polonia-christiana-nr-61,594.html.

Porter-Szücs, Brian. 2014. *Poland in the Modern World: Beyond Martyrdom.* Chichester: John Wiley & Sons.

Poulain, Jean-Pierre. 2011. "La gastronomisation des cuisines de terroir: sociologie d'un retournement de perspective." In *Transmettre, quel(s) patrimoine(s)?—Autour du patrimoine culturel immatériel,* edited by Nicolas Adell and Yves Pourcher, 239–248. Paris: Michel Houdiard éditeur.

Proctor, Robert, and Londa L. Schiebinger. 2008. *Agnotology: The Making and Unmaking of Ignorance.* Stanford: Stanford University Press.

Przymuszała, Lidia, and Dorota Świtała-Trybek. 2021. *Leksykon Dziedzictwa Kulinarnego Śląska* [Lexicon of Silesian culinary heritage]. Opole: Uniwersytet Opolski.

Pszczelarium. n.d. *Tworzymy pszczelarstwo miejskie w Polsce od 2013* [We have been creating urban beekeeping in Poland since 2013]. https://pszczelarium.pl/pages/o-nas.

Ptak, Alicja. 2022b. "Supermarket Introduces Bilingual Polish-Silesian Signs," *Notes from Poland,* December 28, 2022, https://notesfrompoland.com/2022/12/28/supermarket-introduces-bilingual-polish-silesian-signs.

Ptak, Alicia. 2024. "Majority of Poles Now Favour Ending War Even at Cost of Ukraine Losing Territory or Independence." *Notes from Poland,* December 20, 2024, https://notesfrompoland.com/2024/12/20/majority-of-poles-now-favour-ending-war-even-at-cost-of-ukraine-losing-territory-or-independence.

Puzio, Małgorzata. 2023. "Number of Vineyards in Poland 2023, by Voivodeship." *Statista.com,* April 4, 2023. https://www.statista.com/statistics/1137348/poland-number-of-vineyards-by-voivodeship.

Quave, Cassandra L., and Andrea Pieroni. 2014. "Fermented Foods for Food Security and Food Sovereignty in the Balkans: A Case Study of the Gorani People of Northeastern Albania." *Journal of Ethnobiology* 34(1): 28–43.

Rakowiecka, Agata. 2018. "75 years after the Warsaw Ghetto Uprising, Poland's Jews Are Not Giving Up." *CNN.com,* April 19, 2018. https://www.cnn.com/2018/04/19/opinions/warsaw-uprising-anniversary-opinion-rakowiecka/index.html.

Ray, Krishnendu. 2016. *The Ethnic Restaurateur.* London: Bloomsbury.

Reuters. 2021. "Poland to Resume Some Logging in Ancient Bialowieza Forest." March 9, 2021. https://www.reuters.com/business/environment/poland-resume-some-logging-ancient-bialowieza-forest-2021-03-09.

Richie, Alexandra. 2013. *Warsaw 1944: Hitler, Himmler, and the Warsaw Uprising.* New York: Farrar, Straus and Giroux.

Ries, Nancy. 2009. "Potato Ontology: Surviving Postsocialism in Russia." *Cultural Anthropology* 24(2): 181–212.

Rancew-Sikora, Dorota. 2009. *Sens polowania. Współczesne znaczenia tradycyjnych praktyk na przykładzie dyskursu łowieckiego* [The meaning of hunting. Contemporary meanings of traditional practices on the example of hunting discourse]. Warszawa: Wydawnictwo Naukowe.

Robinson, Matthew. 2019. "Protesters Stage 'Eat-In' as Polish Gallery Plans to Ditch Video Installation of Woman Eating Banana." *CNN,* April 30, 2019. https://www.cnn.com/style/article/poland-banana-protest-warsaw-natalia-ll-intl-scli/index.html.

Rogacin, Kacper. 2019. "Prof. Jarosław Dumanowski, historyk kuchni: W dawnych czasach za afrodyzjak uważano nie ogon, a jądra bobra" [Prof. Jarosław Dumanowski, food historian: In the old days, not the tail, but the beaver testicles were considered an aphrodisiac]. *Polska Times,* June 7, 2019. https://polskatimes.pl/prof-jaroslaw-dumanowski-historyk-kuchni-w-dawnych-czasach-za-afrodyzjak-uwazano-nie-ogon-a-jadra-bobra/ar/c1-14194001.

Rössel, Jörg, and Julia H. Schroedter. 2015. "Cosmopolitan Cultural Consumption: Preferences and Practices in a Heterogenous, Urban Population in Switzerland." *Poetics* 50: 80–95.

Rousseau, Jean-Jacques. 1985. *The Government of Poland.* Trans. Willmoore Kendall. Indianapolis: Hackett.

Rousseau, Signe. 2012. *Food and Social Media: You Are What You Tweet.* Lanham, MD: AltaMira Press.

Rzhevkina, Anna. 2022. "Poland Among Europe's Leaders in Kosher and Halal Meat, Despite Uncertainty around Ritual Slaughter." *NotesfromPoland.com,* February 21, 2022. https://notesfrompoland.com/2022/02/21/poland-among-europes-leaders-in-kosher-and-halal-meat-despite-uncertainty-around-ritual-slaughter.

Rowiński, Rafał, Andrzej Dąbrowski, and Tomasz Kostka. 2015. "Gardening as the Dominant Leisure Time Physical Activity (LTPA) of Older Adults from a Post-Communist Country: The Results of the Population-Based PolSenior Project from Poland." *Archives of Gerontology and Geriatrics* 60(3): 486–491.

Salon24. 2019. "Kaczyński w 'Pytaniu na śniadanie': Opowiedział o matce, kotach i jedzeniu" [Kaczyński in 'Question for Breakfast': He talks about his mother, cats and food]. May 13, 2019. https://www.salon24.pl/newsroom/955533,kaczynski-w-pytaniu-na-sniadanie-opowiedzial-o-matce-kotach-i-jedzeniu.

Sas, Adriana. 2023. "Agriculture in Poland—Statistics & Facts." *Statista,* December 21, 2023. https://www.statista.com/topics/11324/agriculture-in-poland.

Sax, David. 2015. *The Tastemakers: A Celebrity Rice Farmer, a Food Truck Lobbyist, and Other Innovators Putting Food Trends on Your Plate*. New York: PublicAffairs.

Scott, E. R. 2012. "Edible Ethnicity How Georgian Cuisine Conquered the Soviet Table." *Kritika: Explorations in Russian and Eurasian History* 13(4): 831–858.

Selwyn, Tom. 1996. "Introduction." In *The Tourist Image: Myths and Myth Making in Tourism*, edited by Tom Selwyn, 1–32. Chichester: Wiley.

Sennett, Richard. 2008. *The Craftsman*. United Kingdom: Penguin.

Shkodrova, Albena. 2018. "From Duty to Pleasurein the Cookbooks of Communist Bulgaria: Attitudes to Food in the Culinary Literature for Domestic Cooking Released by the State-Run Publishers between 1949 And 1989." *Food, Culture & Society* 21(4): 468–487.

Shkodrova, Albena. 2021. *Communist Gourmet: The Curious Story of Food in the People's Republic of Bulgaria*. Vienna: Central European University Press.

Sikorska, Marta. 2019. *Smak i tożsamość: Polska i niemiecka literatura kulinarna w XVII wieku* [Taste and identity: Polish and German culinary literature in the 17th century]. Warszawa: Muzeum Pałacu Króla Jana III w Wilanowie.

Słomczyński, Kazimierz, Irina Tomescu-Dubrow, and Joshua K. Dubrow. 2018. "Polish Sociology and Investigations into Social Class and Stratification, 1945–2015." In *Dynamics of Class and Stratification in Poland*, edited by Irina Tomescu-Dubrow, Kazimierz M. Słomczyński, Henryk Domański, Joshua Kjerulf Dubrow, Zbigniew Sawiński, and Dariusz Przybysz, 13–38. Central European University Press.

Smith, Joe, and Petr Jehlička. 2007. "Stories around Food, Politics and Change in Poland and the Czech Republic." *Transactions of the Institute of British Geographers* 32(3): 395–410.

Smith, Joe, and Petr Jehlička. 2013. "Quiet Sustainability: Fertile Lessons from Europe's Productive Gardeners." *Journal of Rural Studies* 32: 148–157.

Smith, Rachel Charlotte, Kasper Tang Vangkilde, Mette Gislev Kjærsgaard, Ton Otto, Joachim Alse, and Thomas Binder, eds. 2016. *Design Anthropological Futures*. London: Bloomsbury Academic.

Smith Maguire, Jennifer, and Julian Matthews. 2014. *The Cultural Intermediaries Reader*. Thousand Oaks, CA: Sage.

Smołucha, Janusz. 2023. "Incidenza delle tradizioni romane sulla cultura della tavola nella Polonia del passato." In *Perché la Polonia? Conferenze 147*. Roma: Accademia Polacca Roma.

Snyder, Timothy. 2003. *The Reconstruction of Nations: Poland, Ukraine, Lithuania, Belarus, 1569–1999*. New Haven: Yale University Press.

Sosnowska, Anna. 2004. *Zrozumieć zacofanie: spory historyków o Europę Wschodnią (1947–1994)*. [Understanding backwardness: Historians' arguments about Eastern Europe (1947–1994)]. Warszawa: Wydawnictwo Trio.

Sõukand, Renata, Andrea Pieroni, Marianna Biró, Andrea Dénes, Yunus Dogan, Avni Hajdari, Raivo Kalle, Benedict Reade, Behxhet Mustafa, Anely Nedelcheva, Cassandra L. Quave, and Łukasz Łuczaj. 2015. "An Ethnobotanical Perspective on Traditional Fermented Plant Foods and Beverages in Eastern Europe." *Journal of Ethnopharmacology* 170: 284–296.

Sõukand, Renata, Natalyia Stryamets, Michele Filippo Fontefrancesco, and Andrea Pieroni. 2020. "The Importance of Tolerating Interstices: Babushka Markets in Ukraine and Eastern Europe and Their Role in Maintaining Local Food Knowledge and Diversity." *Heliyon* 6(1): e03222.

Spackman, Christy, and Gary Burlingame. 2018. "Sensory Politics: The Tug-of-War between Potability and Palatability in Municipal Water Production." *Social Studies of Science* 48(3): 350–71.

Spackman, Christy, and Jacob Lahne. 2019. "Sensory Labor: Considering the Work of Taste in the Food System." *Food, Culture & Society* 22(2): 142–151.

Stacul, Jaro. 2018. "Redeveloping History in Postsocialist Poland." *Focaal—Journal of Global and Historical Anthropology* 81 (2018): 72–85.

Stasik, Agata. 2018. "Praktykowanie nielegalności: Ekonomia śliwowicy łąckiej" [Practicing illegality: Economics of Łącko plum brandy]. *LUD. Organ Polskiego Towarzystwa Ludoznawczego* 102: 279–299.

Stańczak-Wiślicz, Katarzyna. 2020. "Eating Healthy, Eating Modern: The 'Urbanization' of Food Tastes in Communist Poland (1945–1989)." *Ethnologia Polona* 41: 141–162.

Statistics Poland [Główny Urząd Statystyczny]. 2022. *Internal Market in 2021.* Warszawa: GUS.

Statistics Poland [Główny Urząd Statystyczny]. 2023. *Agricultural Census.* Warsaw: GUS.

Statistics Poland [Główny Urząd Statystyczny]. 2024. *Population.* Warsaw: GUS.

Stegner, Tadeusz. 2003. "'Heretyckie jadło' czyli o polsko-niemieckich relacjach kulinarnych w XIX i na początku XX wieku" [Heretic food or the Polish-German culinary relationships in the nineteenth and at the beginning of the twentieth century]. In *W kuchni i za stołem: Dystanse i przenikanie kultur* [In the kitchen and at the table: Distances and the penetration of cultures], edited by Tadeusz Stegner. Gdańsk: Arche.

Stola, Dariusz. 2010. *Kraj bez wyjścia: Migracje z Polski 1949–1989* [A country with no exit: Migrations from Poland in 1949–1989]. Warszawa: IPN.

Straczuk, Justyna. 2013. *Cmentarz i stół: Pogranicze prawosławno-katolickie w Polsce i na Białorusi* [The graveyard and the table: The Catholic and Orthodox borderland in Poland and Belarus]. Toruń: Wydawnictwo Naukowe Uniwersytetu Mikołaja Kopernika.

Straczuk, Justyna. 2016a. *Modernizacja wzorów żywienia w PRL wobec wiedzy potocznej i codziennych praktyk* [Modernization of dietary patterns in the Polish People's Republic in the light of common knowledge and everyday practices]. In *Przemiany kulturowe we współczesnej Polsce: ramy, właściwości, epizody* [Cultural transformations in contemporary Poland: framework, features, episodes], edited by Joanna Kurczewska with Marta Karkowska, 200–211. Warszawa: IFiS PAN.

Straczuk, Justyna. 2016b. "Smak trwania, smak zmiany. Preferencje i praktyki jedzeniowe Polaków w kontekście zmiany społecznej" [The taste of duration, the taste of change: Poles' eating preferences and practices in the context of social change]. *Studia Socjologiczne* 222(3): 31–50.

Stroe, Monica. 2018. "Preserves Exiting Socialism: Authenticity, Anti-Standardization and Middle Class Consumption in Postsocialist Romania." In *Approaching Consumer Culture: Global Flows and Local Contexts*, edited by Evgenia Krasteva-Blagoeva, 147–180. Springer.

Strong, Jeremy. 2011. *Educated Tastes: Food, Drink, and Connoisseur Culture*. Lincoln: University of Nebraska Press.

Sulima, Roch. 2000. *Antropologia codzienności* [Anthropology of the everyday]. Kraków: Wydawnictwo Uniwersytetu Jagiellońskiego, Kraków.

Svašek, Maruška. 2006. *Postocialism: Politics and Emotions in Central and Eastern Europe*. Oxford: Berghahn.

Szczurek, Małgorzata, and Magdalena Zych, eds. 2012. *Dzieło-działka* [Work of art-allotment garden]. Kraków: Muzeum Etnograficzne im. Seweryna Udzieli w Krakowie [The Seweryn Udziela Ethnographic Museum of Kraków].

Szlendak, Tomasz, Jacek Nowiński, Krzysztof Olechnicki, Arkadiusz Karwacki, and Wojciech Józef Burszta, eds. 2012. *Dziedzictwo w akcji. Rekonstrukcja historyczna jako sposób uczestnictwa w kulturze* [Heritage in action: Historical reconstruction as a mode of cultural participation]. Warszawa: Narodowe Centrum Kultury.

Szlendak, Tomasz, and Krzysztof Olechnicki. 2014. "Megaceremoniały i subświaty: O potransformacyjnych przemianach uczestnictwa Polaków w kulturze" [Megaceremonials and sub-worlds: On the post-transformation changes in the participation of Poles in culture]. *Ruch Prawniczy, Ekonomiczny i Socjologiczny* 76(2): 293–308.

Szpociński, Andrzej. 2004. "Współczesne społeczeństwo polskie wobec przeszłości" [Contemporary Polish society in the face of the past]. In *Różnorodność procesów zmian: Transformacja niejedno ma imię* [A variety of change processes: Transformation has many names], edited by Andrzej Szpociński, 151–179. Warszawa: Instytut Studiów Politycznych Polskiej Akademii Nauk.

Szumilas, Hannah. 2014. "Allotment Gardens in Former Eastern Bloc Countries—A Comparative Study of Spatial Policy in Tallinn and Warsaw." *Annals of Warsaw University of Life Sciences—SGGW Horticulture and Landscape Architecture* 35: 39–51.

Szydłowska, Agata, 2018. *Od solidarycy do TypoPolo: Typografia a tożsamości zbiorowe w Polsce po roku 1989* [From Solidarity to TypoPolo: Typography and collective identities in Poland after 1989]. Wrocław: Zakład Narodowy im. Ossolińskich.

Szymanderska, Hanna. 2013. *Kuchnia polska: Potrawy regionalne* [Polish cuisine: Regional dishes]. Warszawa: Świat Książki.

Svejenova, Silviya, Carmelo Mazza, and Marcel Planellas. 2007. "Cooking Up Change in Haute Cuisine: Ferran Adria as an Institutional Entrepreneur." *Journal of Organizational Behaviour* 28(5): 539–561.

Świrek, Krzysztof. 2023. "Klasy społeczne w dyskursie publicznym: klasa średnia i pasaże polskiej polityczności" [Social classes in public discourse: The middle class and passages of Polish politicality]. *Przegląd Socjologiczny* 72(4): 83–110.

Świtała-Trybek, Dorota. 2007. "Święto kartofla, żymloka i pstrąga, czyli o kulinarnych imprezach plenerowych" [The feast of potato, slug and trout, i.e. about culinary outdoor events]. In *Pokarmy i jedzenie w kulturze. Tabu, dieta, symbol* [Foods and eating in culture: Taboo diet symbol], edited by Katarzyna Łeńska-Bąk, 339–350. Opole: Wydawnictwo Uniwersytetu Opolskiego.

Szelągowska, Grażyna. 2004. "Ziemniaki w tradycyjnym pożywieniu ludowym" [Potatoes in traditional folk food]. *Lud* 88: 251–274.

Szromba-Rysowa, Zofia. 1978. *Pożywienie ludności wiejskiej na Śląsku* [Food for the rural population in Silesia]. Wrocław: Zakład Narodowy im. Ossolińskich.

Szyszko, Jan. 2019. "Podwójna jakość produktów w Unii jest faktem" [The double quality of products in the European Union is a fact]. *Polityka,* June 15, 2019. https://www.polityka.pl/tygodnikpolityka/rynek/1797928,1,podwojna-jakosc-produktow-w-unii-jest-faktem.read.

Tarkowska, Elżbieta. 2013. "Collective Memory, Social Time and Culture: The Polish Tradition in Memory Studies." *Polish Sociological Review* 183(3): 281–296.

Teffer, Peter. 2019. "EU Study: No Evidence of 'East vs West' Food Discrimination." *EU Observer,* June 24, 2019. https://euobserver.com/political/145251.

Tilles, Daniel. 2019. "Warsaw Ranked Sixth Most Vegan-Friendly City in the World." *Notes from Poland,* December 5, 2019. https://notesfrompoland.com/2019/12/05/warsaw-named-sixth-most-vegan-friendly-city-in-the-world.

Tilles, Daniel. 2022. "Poland to Become European Kimchi Hub with New South Korean Factory." *Notes from Poland,* November 8, 2022. https://notesfrompoland.com/2022/11/08/poland-to-become-european-kimchi-hub-with-new-south-korean-factory.

Todorova, Maria, and Zsuzsa Gille, eds. 2010. *Post-Communist Nostalgia.* New York: Berghahn.

Tomescu-Dubrow, Irina, Kazimierz M. Słomczyński, Henryk Domański, Joshua Kjerulf Dubrow, Zbigniew Sawiński, and Dariusz Przybysz. 2018. *Dynamics of Class and Stratification in Poland.* Vienna: Central European University Press.

Tominc, Ana. 2017. *The Discursive Construction of Class and Lifestyle: Celebrity Chef Cookbooks in Post-Socialist Slovenia.* Amsterdam: John Benjamins.

Tominc, Ana. 2023. "Between the Balkans and Central Europe: Celebrity Chefs, National Culinary Identity and the Post-Socialist Elite in Slovenia." *Food and Foodways* 31(2): 67–89.

Tompkins, Kyla Wazana. 2012. *Racial Indigestion: Eating Bodies in the 19th Century.* New York: New York University Press.

Toplišek, Alen. 2020. "The Political Economy of Populist Rule in Post-Crisis Europe: Hungary and Poland." *New Political Economy* 25(3): 388–403.

Török, Áron, and Attila Jámbor. 2013. "Competitiveness and Geographical Indications: The Case of Fruit Spirits in Central and Eastern European Countries." *Studies in Agricultural Economics* 115: 25–32.

Trandafoiu. Ruxandra. 2014. "'The World on a Plate': Transformed Cosmopolitan Utopia in Food Blog Culture." In *Media and Cosmopolitanism,* edited by Aybige

Yilmaz, Ruxandra Trandafoiu, and Aris Mousoutzanis, 29–50. Lausanne: Peter Lang.

Trubek, Amy. 2009. *The Taste of Place: A Cultural Journey into Terroir.* Berkeley: University of California Press.

Tsigkas, Alexios. 2019. "Tasting Ceylon Tea: Aesthetic Judgment Beyond 'Good Taste.'" *Food, Culture & Society* 22(2): 152–167.

Tymochowicz, Mariola. 2019. *Tradycyjne pożywienie chłopskie na Lubelszczyźnie* [Traditional peasant food in the Lublin region]. Lublin: Wydawnictwo UMCS.

Ulloa, Ana María. 2018. "The Aesthetic Life of Artificial Flavors." *The Senses and Society* 13(1): 60–74.

Ulloa, Ana María. 2019. "The Chef and the Flavorist: Reflections on the Value of Sensory Expertise." *Food, Culture & Society* 22(2): 186–202.

Urbański, Jarosław. 2016. *Społeczeństwo bez mięsa. Socjologiczne i ekonomiczne uwarunkowania wegetarianizmu.* Poznań: Wydawnictwo A+.

Verdery, Katherine. 1996. *What Was Socialism, and What Comes Next?* Princeton: Princeton University Press.

Vezovnik, Andreja, and Ana Tominc. 2019. "Potica: The Leavened Bread That Reinvented Slovenia: Andreja Vezovnik and Ana Tominc." In *The Emergence of National Food*, edited by Atsuko Ichijo, Venetia Johannes, and Roland Ranta, 39–50. London: Bloomsbury.

Wagner, Izabela. 2012. "Selektywna analiza problemu publikacji humanistów i przedstawicieli nauk społecznych w języku angielskim" [Selective analysis of the problem of publishing in English for Polish social and humanities researchers]. *Przegląd Socjologii Jakościowej* 8(1): 166–187.

Walecka, Monika, 2016. *Opowiadania drewnianego stołu. 125 przepisów, jak sprawić przyjemność bliskim i sobie* [Stories of an old table: 125 recipes to please your loved ones and yourself]. Warszawa: Septem.

Walicki, Andrzej. 1978. "Polish Romantic Messianism in Comparative Perspective." スラヴ研究 *(Slavic Studies)* 22: 1–15. http://hdl.handle.net/2115/5067.

Wallerstein, Immanuel. 1974. "The Rise and Future Demise of the World Capitalist System: Concepts for Comparative Analysis." *Comparative Studies in Society and History* 16(4): 387–415.

Walker, Stuart, Martyn Evans, Tom Cassidy, Jeyon Jung, and Amy Twigger Holroyd. 2018. *Design Roots: Culturally Significant Designs, Products, and Practices.* London: Bloomsbury Academic.

Warde, Alan. 1997. *Consumption, Food, and Taste: Culinary Antinomies and Commodity Culture.* Thousand Oaks, CA: Sage.

Warszawski Festiwal Kulinarny. 2017. "O Nowej Kuchni Polskiej—czy w ogóle istnieje?—panel dyskusyjny." YouTube, October 22, 2017. https://www.youtube.com/watch?v=l8LJbsrXrpo.

Wasilewski, Artur. n.d. *Kulinaria żuławskie* [Żuławy cuisine]. n.p.

Weenink, Don. 2008. "Cosmopolitanism as a Form of Capital: Parents Preparing their Children for a Globalizing World." *Sociology* 42(6): 1089–1106.

Węgiel, Anna. 2024. *Wysoce modernistyczna dieta: scjentyzm, futuryzm i inne ideolo-*

gie w dyskursie porady żywieniowej w Polskiej Rzeczypospolitej Ludowej 1970–1979 [A highly modernist diet: scientism, futurism and other ideologies in the discourse of nutritional advice in the Polish People's Republic 1970–1979]. PhD diss., Warszawa: IFIS PAN.

White, Anne. 2015. "Polish Migration to the UK Compared with Migration Elsewhere in Europe: A Review of the Literature." *Social Identities* 22(1): 10–25.

Wight, Ed. 2019. "Polish Vodka Gets 'Protected Status' in Historic EU-China Deal." *The First News*, November 7, 2019. https://www.thefirstnews.com/article /polish-vodka-gets-protected-status-in-historic-eu-china-deal-8543.

Williams-Forson, Psyche. 2006. *Building Houses Out of Chicken Legs: Black Women, Food, and Power.* Chapel Hill: University of North Carolina Press.

Wolff, Larry. 1994. *Inventing Eastern Europe: The Map of Civilization on the Mind of the Enlightenment.* Stanford: Stanford University Press.

Wójcik, Magda. 2014. "Dym o dym" [Smoke on smoke]. *Kuchnia,* April 2014, 74.

Wudyka, Tadeusz. 2016. *Market Economy in Poland: A History.* Alphen aan den Rijn: Wolters Kluwer.

Zadrożyńska, Anna. 2002. *Świętowania polskie: Przewodnik po tradycji* [Polish celebrations: A guide to tradition]. Warszawa: Wydawnictwo Twój Styl.

Zak, Zuza. 2016. *Polska: New Polish Cooking.* London: Quadrille.

Zak, Zuza. 2022. *Pierogi.* London: Quadrille.

Zarycki, Tomasz. 2009. "The Power of the Intelligentsia: The Rywin Affair and the Challenge of Applying the Concept of Cultural Capital to Analyze Poland's Elites." *Theory and Society* 38: 613–648.

Zarycki, Tomasz. 2012. "The Embarrassing Russian Connection: Selective Memory of the Russian Heritage in Contemporary Poland." In *Russia's Identity in International Relations. Images, Perceptions, Misperceptions,* edited by Raymond Taras, 133–148. London: Routledge.

Zarycki, Tomasz. 2014. *Ideologies of Eastness in Central and Eastern Europe.* London: Routledge.

Zarycki, Tomasz, ed. 2016. *Polska jako peryferie* [Poland as periphery]. Warszawa: Wydawnictwo Naukowe Scholar.

Zarycki, Tomasz. 2019. "Modernizacja kulturowa i psychologiczna jako ideologia inteligenckiej hegemonii" [Cultural and psychological modernization as an ideology of the intelligentsia's hegemony]. *Przegląd Socjologiczny* 64(2): 45–68.

Zarycki, Tomasz, Rafał Smoczyński, and Tomasz Warczok. 2017. "The Roots of Polish Culture-Centered Politics: Toward a Non-Purely Cultural Model of Cultural Domination in Central and Eastern Europe." *East European Politics and Societies: And Cultures* 31(2): 360–381.

Zhang, Lu, and Lydia Hanks. 2018. "Online Reviews: The Effect of Cosmopolitanism, Incidental Similarity, and Dispersion on Consumer Attitudes toward Ethnic Restaurants." *International Journal of Hospitality Management* 68 (Supplement C): 115–23.

Zhen, Willa. 2019. *Food Studies: A Hands-On Guide.* London: Bloomsbury Academic.

Zimmerman, Joshua D. 2022. *Jozef Pilsudksi: Founding Father of Modern Poland.* Cambridge, MA: Harvard University Press.

Zubrzycki, Geneviève. 2022. *Resurrecting the Jew: Nationalism, Philosemitism, and Poland's Jewish Revival.* Princeton: Princeton University Press.

Żuk, Piotr, and Paweł Żuk. 2021. "Between Private Property, Authoritarian State and Democracy: Clearing Trees in Cities and Destroying the Białowieża Forest in Poland." *Capitalism Nature Socialism* 32(2): 56–76.

Zukin, Sharon. 2008. "Consuming Authenticity: From Outposts of Difference to Means of Exclusion." *Cultural Studies* 22(5): 724–48.

Zukin, Sharon. 2011. "Reconstructing the Authenticity of Place." *Theory and Society* 40(2): 161–165.

Zuzańska-Żyśko, Elżbieta, and Sławomir Sitek. 2011. "Rola handlu targowiskowego w rozwoju miast: Człowiek w przestrzeni zurbanizowanej" [The role of market trade in the development of cities: Humans in an urbanized space]. In *Człowiek w przestrzeni zurbanizowanej* [Humans in an urbanized space], edited by Maria Soja and Andrzej Zborowski, 271–281. Kraków: Uniwersytet Jagielloński.

Zysiak, Agata. 2017. "Socjalizm jako modernizacja—powojenna historia Polski w perspektywie rewizjonistycznej" [Socialism as modernization: Post-war history of Poland in a revisionist perspective]. *Przegląd Humanistyczny* 2: 135–145.

INDEX

Akademia Inspiracji Makro, 75, 93
alternative food networks, 49–50, 88, 190
Amaro, Wojciech Modest, 95, 97, 140
Andrzejewski, Arek, 70, 152–153
apple, 56, 199
art, food in, 54–55, 172
artisanal products, 3, 29, 36, 40–41, 50, 73, 121, 130, 150, 154, 155, 163, 177–178
authenticity, 6, 15, 16, 70, 73, 92, 98, 127, 131, 145, 168, 182

babka ziemniaczana (savory potato casserole), 63, 103, 116, 124
Baj, Kamil, 88
banana, 54, 172
Barański, Dariusz, 143–144, 146
Baron, Aleksander, 136, 151–152, 174
beaver, 59–60, 136
beekeeping, 88, 160, 166
bison, 59–60
bison grass, 96, 103, 111
Belarus, 6, 26, 103, 120, 135, 182
Bielka-Vescovi, Monika, 161
barszcz (borscht, beetroot soup), 5, 72, 90, 100
Białystok, 102–104
bigos (hunter's stew), 34, 98, 123, 135, 149
blandness, 95, 132, 135, 144, 145, 178
Bosak, Wojtek, 82
border shifts, 29, 31, 109, 116
borderlands (Eastern, *Kresy*), 103, 135, 200
Bydgoszcz, 17, 112, 115

Camastra, Andrea, 134, 201
Capponi Borawska, Tessa, 84, 197
career changer, 12, 16, 39–40, 67, 75, 78–81
carp, 63, 129, 131, 140
Catholicism, 12, 23–24, 28, 36, 37, 55, 60, 61, 127, 130
cebularz lubelski (flatbread), 106–107, 130
Central and Eastern Europe, 3, 13, 27, 28, 46, 49, 52, 106, 133, 180, 183–184, 188, 190
cheese, 39, 116, 130, 155–156
chefs, 2, 3, 7, 10, 25, 43, 59, 66, 75, 85, 98, 120, 131, 140
childhood memories, 67, 71, 122, 144, 153
Christmas Eve (Wigilia), 59, 120, 129, 141
Cichy, Łukasz, 43, 199
class structure (in Poland), 43–44, 76
Cook It Raw, 2, 97
Compendium Ferculorum, 25, 133, 136, 137, 138, 191
Connoisseurship. *See* expertise
conservatism, 14, 34, 55, 181
cookbooks, 2, 6, 25, 27, 58, 84, 100, 123, 173, 190, 198
coping strategies (against food shortages), 6, 32, 33, 51, 130, 150
cosmopolitanism, 2, 8–9, 10, 40–41, 46–48, 83–87, 94, 96, 121, 127, 133, 148, 152, 174, 180
COVID-19, 19, 52, 184, 200
cucumbers, 50, 103, 149, 151
culinary capital, 42, 86, 125, 179
culinary education, 67, 73–76

culinary field, 4, 8, 42, 66–67, 92, 137, 177
culinary tourism, 39, 104, 158
cultural intermediaries, 9, 10–11, 162, 179.
   See also tastemakers
Czekajło, Michał, 78, 147
Czerniecki, Stanisław, 25, 134
czernina duck-blood soup, 63, 90, 124
Czudowski, Tomasz, 79, 86

design, 10, 11, 79, 89, 95, 131, 151, 175
dietary advice, 29, 31
distinction, 46, 48, 50, 158, 190
Dr. Irena Eris Spa, 69, 74, 104
działka (allotment garden), 32, 51, 89, 98
Duda, Tomasz, 7
Dumanowski, Jarosław, 59–60, 62, 112, 127,
   129, 133–134, 190, 201
Duszyński, Rafał, 39–40

elections (2015), 35, 181
elections (2023), 37, 53, 59, 182, 199
elevation (of Polish food), 2, 3, 7, 9, 43, 45,
   89, 95, 105, 117, 146, 176
elites, 9, 36, 41, 45, 70, 137, 183
embeddedness, 92, 147
empire, Poland as, 26, 135
Enlightenment, 7, 26
entrepreneurship, 12, 33, 44, 49, 118, 150,
   158, 166
Epoka restaurant, 36, 138
ethnic structure, 29, 61, 135–136
European Union, 8, 14, 22, 37, 52, 53, 57, 59,
   84, 105, 159; accession to, 8, 82, 84, 85,
   152, 202
Europeanization, 8, 85, 92, 181
expertise, 8, 10, 40, 42, 44, 70, 73, 90, 94,
   126, 147, 156, 158, 165, 179

family, 31, 64, 70–73, 122, 126, 182
farmers, 6, 22, 30, 31, 37, 54, 56, 57, 121, 199
farmers' markets, 2, 50, 52, 143, 166–167
fasting, 24, 57
fermentation, 32, 48, 148–156
fermented (*kiszone*) vegetables, 50, 149–150,
   151, 152, 162
Fiedoruk, Andrzej, 103–104, 200
fieldwork, 17–18
food festivals, 5, 60, 62, 90–91, 137, 164, 173

food markets, 2, 50, 52, 140, 143, 150,
   166–169
food museums, 1, 79, 109–113
food shortages, 29–33, 51, 57, 129, 190, 191
food studies, 17, 189, 193
foodie, 2–3, 41, 42–43, 46, 53, 134, 144, 148,
   179
foraging, 32, 48, 96, 98
foreign food in Poland, 9, 25–26, 31, 34–35,
   40, 46–49, 92, 132, 180, 198
future, 14, 80, 184

Gałązka, Bogdan, 76, 78, 137
Gessler, Magda, 55, 83, 197
Gdańsk, 24, 25, 28, 31, 32, 43, 110, 117, 118,
   133, 151, 170
gentrification, 15, 136, 140, 172
Geographical indications, 105–107, 110, 111,
   155, 185
German heritage, 24, 29, 61, 70, 105, 116
Gierek, Edward, 31–32
Global Brooklyn style, 168, 169
globalization, 45, 48, 49, 92, 147, 177, 180,
   182, 183
Głowacki, Łukasz, 161
Gomułka, Władysław, 30, 31
goose, 63, 69, 72, 115, 134, 175
grandmother (*babcia*), 51, 72, 117, 122, 146
Gręda, Grzegorz, 74, 86, 105, 199

Hala Mirowska market, 140, 167
heritage, 20, 63–64, 189
hierarchies of taste, 8–9, 15, 40, 45, 161
history, 12–13, 104, 111, 182, 190
homemade food, 6, 7, 71, 120, 150, 156, 178
homogeneity, 29, 135
honey, 88–89, 106; honey as mead (*miód
   pitny*), 120
hunting, 60–61, 136

independence, 27–28, 62, 115
inequality (social inequalities), 25, 30, 33,
   35–36, 44, 47, 184, 190
inflation, 19, 37, 46
innovation, 7, 9, 11, 20, 83, 88, 118, 124
Instagram, 18, 43, 56, 138, 171, 179
intelligentsia, 10, 33, 44, 67, 68, 78, 97, 137,
   179, 194

236 · INDEX

intergenerational transmission of culinary knowledge, 121, 122–123
internet, 55, 81, 120, 123
interwar period, 27, 104, 113, 128, 134

Jakubiak, Tomasz, 93, 125, 130
Jakubiuk, Joanna, 2, 4–5, 102
Judaism, 24, 27, 61, 62, 106, 110, 117, 134, 136, 171–176

Kaczyński, Jarosław, 34, 55, 59, 201
kartacze dumplings, 5, 103
karczma restaurants, 52–52, 121
kashrut, 136, 174–176
kasza gryczana (buckwheat groats), 120, 123
kaszanka (blood sausage), 63, 103, 143
Kaszuby, 61, 93, 100, 102, 116
Katz, Sandor, 150–151, 152
kebab, 48–49, 180
kimchi, 46, 152, 180
kiełbasa (sausage), 5, 34, 52, 90, 98, 100, 121, 143, 180
Klorek, Waldemar, 115
Kłosińska, Basia, 79, 174
Komosa, Robert, 162
kompot (fruit beverage), 123, 165
Korkosz, Michał, 6, 58, 198
Kosmala, Justyna, 79, 86, 168, 174
Kraków, 25, 61, 69, 117, 170, 174
Kucia, Monika, 5, 123, 198
kuchnia staropolska (old-style cooking), 31, 53, 104, 201
Kuroń, Jacek, 33–34, 198
Kwiatkowski, Mirosław Jaxa, 83, 85, 159

Łagowski, Tomasz, 72, 75, 79
Łapanowski, Grzegorz, 77
Leśniewski, Krzysztof, 100
list of traditional products (lista produktów tradycyjnych), 101, 107–108
Lithuania, 6, 24, 26, 116, 120, 135
local food, 2, 5, 8, 9, 29, 42, 96, 98
locality, 20, 54, 89, 91–92, 94, 98, 166
Lublin, 23, 39, 70, 106, 130, 137
Łuczaj, Łukasz, 98–99
Łuczywek, Ania, 39–40
Łukawski, Adam, 79, 109
Lwów, 109–110

Majewski, Karol, 164
Makłowicz, Robert, 59, 77, 125, 128, 197, 200
Makro, 62, 75, 93
marketing, 16, 34, 82, 92, 121, 158–159, 201
materiality, 11, 95, 140, 142
meat, 30, 31, 32–33, 57–61, 175–176
media, 18–19, 55, 78, 80, 86, 94, 114, 124–128, 153, 183, 201; foodie approach to, 125; pragmatic approach to, 125, 183
memory, 12, 13, 27, 105, 113, 119, 126, 128, 144, 190
Michelin stars (or Guide), 15, 36, 95–96, 134, 161, 201
milk bars (*bary mleczne*), 7, 130
migration, 8, 10, 14, 31, 46, 47, 74, 84–85; internal, 6, 29, 36, 69–70, 72, 100, 116
middle class, 16, 44, 68, 75, 136, 179, 194
middle classing, 45–46, 145
Mientkiewicz, Gieno, 155–156
Modelski, Łukasz, 78, 134
modernization, 15, 27, 29, 72, 123
Moroz, Artur, 117–118, 200
Museum of King Jan III's Palace, 63, 112, 127, 133, 190
mushrooms, 98, 141, 142, 144, 184

naleśniki (pancakes), 34, 123
nalewka, 120, 148, 163–166
national Polish cuisine, 3, 4, 27, 34, 61–63, 95, 98
nation, 12, 23, 27, 35, 53, 93, 94–95, 114, 126
nationalism, 14, 34, 48, 49, 55, 94, 181, 183
nature, 41, 89, 94–97
New Nordic Cuisine, 2, 41. 96, 97, 99, 101
Niemiec, Marcin, 81, 85, 87
nobility, 25, 26, 60, 136
nostalgia, 8, 31, 72, 93, 128, 135, 154
Nowicki, Maciej, 63, 111, 127, 136, 200

offal, 43, 103, 144, 147
Okrasa, Karol, 134, 197
omnivorism, 8, 9, 46–47, 180, 190
Optiz, Marek, 100, 116
organic food, 2, 11, 49–50
oscypek cheese, 102, 106, 112, 155

pączki (fried pastries), 5, 180
partitions, 26–27, 63, 128

patriotism, 56, 133, 182

periphery (Poland's status as), 8, 12, 21, 25, 45, 53, 87, 180, 184, 187, 191

pierogi, 5, 7, 34, 98, 103, 115, 120, 123, 134, 149, 155, 177

pizza, 48–49, 180

PiS (*Prawo i Sprawiedliwość*), 14, 34–36, 37, 55, 60, 64, 181

placki ziemniaczane (potato latkes), 34, 123, 175

Pławecki, Marcin, 69, 72, 74, 134

placemaking, 20, 92, 97, 99

Podlasie, 5, 102, 111

Polin Museum, 172–173

Polish-Lithuanian Commonwealth, 26, 113, 135, 137

Polish People's Republic (Polska Rzeczpospolita Ludowa), 28–33, 128–131. *See also* socialist regime in Poland

Polish United Workers' Party (Polska Zjednoczona Partia Robotnicza), 30, 131, 201

Polishness, 14, 40, 54, 58, 61, 91, 93, 100, 114, 119, 124, 133, 141, 144, 147, 152, 163, 166, 171, 182

populism, 34, 67

postcolonial syndrome (or complex), 7, 35, 200

postsocialist transformation, 6, 13–14, 33–36, 41, 43, 46, 51, 74, 75, 84, 92, 131, 182, 188, 197

potato, 2, 12, 103

Poznaj Dobrą Żywność (Get to know fine foods), 64, 91

Poznań, 30, 41, 103, 106, 112, 161, 164, 169, 189

powidła plum jam, 102, 120

PRL. *See* Polish People's Republic

Protestants, 24, 61

Pszczelarium, 88–89, 166

Przybysz, Marcin, 137

PZPR. *See* Polish United Workers' Party

recipes, 7, 25, 59, 62, 100, 101, 123, 125, 137, 138

refinement (of Polish food). *See* elevation

regional food, 69, 87, 93, 99–105, 189

restaurant, 19, 28, 36, 120, 157, 183

retail chains, 35, 47, 92, 93, 121, 131, 146, 153, 159, 166, 177–178

revaluation (of Polish food), 1, 8, 9, 23, 43, 111, 113, 147

rogal świętomarciński (pastry), 106, 112

rosół soup, 63, 122, 178

rural population, 14, 16, 22, 25, 31, 36, 50, 57, 71, 82, 189, 198

Russia, 6, 26, 27, 50, 55–57, 120, 128, 182, 183, 198

schabowy (fried pork chop), 34, 42, 43, 49, 58, 61, 98, 130, 144, 178

Scheller, Kurt, 75, 76, 77, 197

self-orientalizing, 41, 96

self-provisioning, 32, 33, 73. *See also* coping strategies

sensoriality (of Polish food), 6, 144–147

sensory categories, 146, 148, 156, 158, 162, 163, 166

sensory politics, 148–149, 156, 158, 162, 163, 174, 176

Sierszuła, Zbigniew, 164–165

Silesia (Śląsk), 23, 93, 100, 102, 200

słoiki (jars), 6, 33, 51, 150

Slow Food, 16, 103, 104, 116, 167

Słupska Kartaczowska, Justyna, 71–72

smalec (ground pork fat), 42, 43, 90

smoked food, 6, 21, 46, 48, 60, 90, 102, 106, 115, 117, 120, 129, 143, 155

social media, 18, 54, 55, 58, 65, 81, 86, 138, 162, 179

social protests, 30, 31, 32, 55

socialist consumerism, 31, 52, 54, 198

socialist regime in Poland, 6, 29–31, 50, 57, 65, 72, 100, 107, 121, 128, 149

Solidarność, 32, 65, 170

soup (Polish), 1, 5, 6, 10, 34, 52, 63, 65, 72, 90, 100, 103, 116, 117, 122, 123, 124, 141–142, 148, 149, 152, 178

sourdough bread, 70–71, 153, 154

spices, 25, 124, 133, 134, 137

Stawicki, Paweł, 66, 199

storytelling, 9, 78, 104, 162

Szkaradzińska, Anna, 118

tastemakers, 9–12, 15–16, 42, 46–48, 50, 61, 66–67, 73, 93, 108, 119, 135, 142, 177, 179, 181

Targ Pietruszkowy, 80, 167

Tatars, 24, 61, 117, 136
Teraz Polska (Poland now), 34, 93
terroir, 97–99, 158
time, 12–14, 23
Tomaszewska-Bolałek, Magdalena, 78
Toruń, 17, 43, 112, 189, 190
tradition, 3, 9, 12–14, 36, 42, 64, 101, 111,
    114, 119–124, 178, 182, 190
Trzópek, Robert, 101–102, 107
twaróg soft cheese, 50, 143, 155–156, 162

Ukraine, 6, 26, 27, 50, 55–57, 110, 116, 120,
    135, 182
urban population, 6, 16, 31, 46, 51, 89, 150,
    166, 171, 198

valuation processes, 15–16, 93, 94, 142, 176
vegetarian, 7, 58, 201
vegan, 7, 36, 58
vodka, 1, 12, 109, 111, 120, 130, 176; vodka
    Museum (Muzeum Wódki), 1, 79,
    109–110; Polish vodka museum (Muz-
    eum Polskiej Wódki), 110–111

Walecka, Monika, 153–154
Warsaw, 27, 28, 32, 36, 47, 58, 59, 70, 89, 147,
    167–169, 189
Welter, Tomasz, 74–75, 199
West, belonging to, 85; borderland with,
    24–25, 133, 135; catching up with, 8, 12,
    47, 83; relationship with, 7–8, 12, 15,
    24–25, 28, 40, 41, 53, 87, 93, 128, 145, 181,
    182, 187, 188, 194; separation from, 4,
    7–8, 49, 180; influenced by, 35, 49, 85,
    121, 152, 168, 180
Wilbrandt, Agnieszka, 69, 71
wine, 25, 82, 87, 101, 156–163, 184, 201
winemakers, 81–83, 87, 158
Wojda, Agata, 75, 77
working class, 9, 16, 36, 42, 57, 80, 144, 188
Wrocław, 69, 71, 78, 147, 167
Wyrobek-Rousseau, Agnieszka, 159–160

Zakwasownia, 79, 151
Żuławy, 100, 105, 116
żurek (fermented rye soup), 1, 10, 72, 117,
    148, 149, 152

CALIFORNIA STUDIES IN FOOD AND CULTURE

Darra Goldstein, Editor

1. *Dangerous Tastes: The Story of Spices,* by Andrew Dalby

2. *Eating Right in the Renaissance,* by Ken Albala

3. *Food Politics: How the Food Industry Influences Nutrition and Health,* by Marion Nestle

4. *Camembert: A National Myth,* by Pierre Boisard

5. *Safe Food: The Politics of Food Safety,* by Marion Nestle

6. *Eating Apes,* by Dale Peterson

7. *Revolution at the Table: The Transformation of the American Diet,* by Harvey Levenstein

8. *Paradox of Plenty: A Social History of Eating in Modern America,* by Harvey Levenstein

9. *Encarnación's Kitchen: Mexican Recipes from Nineteenth-Century California: Selections from Encarnación Pinedo's El cocinero español,* by Encarnación Pinedo, edited and translated by Dan Strehl, with an essay by Victor Valle

10. *Zinfandel: A History of a Grape and Its Wine,* by Charles L. Sullivan, with a foreword by Paul Draper

11. *Tsukiji: The Fish Market at the Center of the World,* by Theodore C. Bestor

12. *Born Again Bodies: Flesh and Spirit in American Christianity,* by R. Marie Griffith

13. *Our Overweight Children: What Parents, Schools, and Communities Can Do to Control the Fatness Epidemic,* by Sharron Dalton

14. *The Art of Cooking: The First Modern Cookery Book,* by the Eminent Maestro Martino of Como, edited and with an introduction by Luigi Ballerini, translated and annotated by Jeremy Parzen, and with fifty modernized recipes by Stefania Barzini

15. *The Queen of Fats: Why Omega-3s Were Removed from the Western Diet and What We Can Do to Replace Them,* by Susan Allport

16. *Meals to Come: A History of the Future of Food,* by Warren Belasco

17. *The Spice Route: A History,* by John Keay

18. *Medieval Cuisine of the Islamic World: A Concise History with 174 Recipes,* by Lilia Zaouali, translated by M. B. DeBevoise, with a foreword by Charles Perry

19. *Arranging the Meal: A History of Table Service in France,* by Jean-Louis Flandrin, translated by Julie E. Johnson, with Sylvie and Antonio Roder; with a foreword to the English-language edition by Beatrice Fink

20. *The Taste of Place: A Cultural Journey into Terroir,* by Amy B. Trubek

21. *Food: The History of Taste,* edited by Paul Freedman

22. *M. F. K. Fisher among the Pots and Pans: Celebrating Her Kitchens,* by Joan Reardon, with a foreword by Amanda Hesser

23. *Cooking: The Quintessential Art,* by Hervé This and Pierre Gagnaire, translated by M. B. DeBevoise

24. *Perfection Salad: Women and Cooking at the Turn of the Century,* by Laura Shapiro

25. *Of Sugar and Snow: A History of Ice Cream Making,* by Jeri Quinzio

26. *Encyclopedia of Pasta,* by Oretta Zanini De Vita, translated by Maureen B. Fant, with a foreword by Carol Field

27. *Tastes and Temptations: Food and Art in Renaissance Italy,* by John Varriano

28. *Free for All: Fixing School Food in America,* by Janet Poppendieck

29. *Breaking Bread: Recipes and Stories from Immigrant Kitchens,* by Lynne Christy Anderson, with a foreword by Corby Kummer

30. *Culinary Ephemera: An Illustrated History,* by William Woys Weaver

31. *Eating Mud Crabs in Kandahar: Stories of Food during Wartime by the World's Leading Correspondents,* edited by Matt McAllester

32. *Weighing In: Obesity, Food Justice, and the Limits of Capitalism,* by Julie Guthman

33. *Why Calories Count: From Science to Politics,* by Marion Nestle and Malden Nesheim

34. *Curried Cultures: Globalization, Food, and South Asia,* edited by Krishnendu Ray and Tulasi Srinivas

35. *The Cookbook Library: Four Centuries of the Cooks, Writers, and Recipes That Made the Modern Cookbook,* by Anne Willan, with Mark Cherniavsky and Kyri Claflin

36. *Coffee Life in Japan,* by Merry White

37. *American Tuna: The Rise and Fall of an Improbable Food,* by Andrew F. Smith

38. *A Feast of Weeds: A Literary Guide to Foraging and Cooking Wild Edible Plants,* by Luigi Ballerini, translated by Gianpiero W. Doebler, with recipes by Ada De Santis and illustrations by Giuliano Della Casa

39. *The Philosophy of Food,* by David M. Kaplan

40. *Beyond Hummus and Falafel: Social and Political Aspects of Palestinian Food in Israel,* by Liora Gvion, translated by David Wesley and Elana Wesley

41. *The Life of Cheese: Crafting Food and Value in America,* by Heather Paxson

42. *Popes, Peasants, and Shepherds: Recipes and Lore from Rome and Lazio,* by Oretta Zanini De Vita, translated by Maureen B. Fant, foreword by Ernesto Di Renzo

43. *Cuisine and Empire: Cooking in World History,* by Rachel Laudan

44. *Inside the California Food Revolution: Thirty Years That Changed Our Culinary Consciousness,* by Joyce Goldstein, with Dore Brown

45. *Cumin, Camels, and Caravans: A Spice Odyssey,* by Gary Paul Nabhan

46. *Balancing on a Planet: The Future of Food and Agriculture,* by David A. Cleveland

47. *The Darjeeling Distinction: Labor and Justice on Fair-Trade Tea Plantations in India,* by Sarah Besky

48. *How the Other Half Ate: A History of Working-Class Meals at the Turn of the Century,* by Katherine Leonard Turner

49. *The Untold History of Ramen: How Political Crisis in Japan Spawned a Global Food Craze,* by George Solt

50. *Word of Mouth: What We Talk About When We Talk About Food,* by Priscilla Parkhurst Ferguson

51. *Inventing Baby Food: Taste, Health, and the Industrialization of the American Diet,* by Amy Bentley

52. *Secrets from the Greek Kitchen: Cooking, Skill, and Everyday Life on an Aegean Island,* by David E. Sutton

53. *Breadlines Knee-Deep in Wheat: Food Assistance in the Great Depression,* by Janet Poppendieck

54. *Tasting French Terroir: The History of an Idea,* by Thomas Parker

55. *Becoming Salmon: Aquaculture and the Domestication of a Fish,* by Marianne Elisabeth Lien

56. *Divided Spirits: Tequila, Mezcal, and the Politics of Production,* by Sarah Bowen

57. *The Weight of Obesity: Hunger and Global Health in Postwar Guatemala,* by Emily Yates-Doerr

58. *Dangerous Digestion: The Politics of American Dietary Advice,* by E. Melanie DuPuis

59. *A Taste of Power: Food and American Identities,* by Katharina Vester

60. *More Than Just Food: Food Justice and Community Change,* by Garrett M. Broad

61. *Hoptopia: A World of Agriculture and Beer in Oregon's Willamette Valley,* by Peter A. Kopp

62. *A Geography of Digestion: Biotechnology and the Kellogg Cereal Enterprise,* by Nicholas Bauch

63. *Bitter and Sweet: Food, Meaning, and Modernity in Rural China,* by Ellen Oxfeld

64. *A History of Cookbooks: From Kitchen to Page over Seven Centuries,* by Henry Notaker

65. *Reinventing the Wheel: Milk, Microbes, and the Fight for Real Cheese,* by Bronwen Percival and Francis Percival

66. *Making Modern Meals: How Americans Cook Today,* by Amy B. Trubek

67. *Food and Power: A Culinary Ethnography of Israel,* by Nir Avieli

68. *Canned: The Rise and Fall of Consumer Confidence in the American Food Industry,* by Anna Zeide

69. *Meat Planet: Artificial Flesh and the Future of Food,* by Benjamin Aldes Wurgaft

70. *The Labor of Lunch: Why We Need Real Food and Real Jobs in American Public Schools,* by Jennifer E. Gaddis

71. *Feeding the Crisis: Care and Abandonment in America's Food Safety Net,* by Maggie Dickinson

72. *Sameness in Diversity: Food and Globalization in Modern America,* by Laresh Jayasanker

73. *The Fruits of Empire: Art, Food, and the Politics of Race in the Age of American Expansion,* by Shana Klein

74. *Let's Ask Marion: What You Need to Know about the Politics of Food, Nutrition, and Health,* by Marion Nestle, in conversation with Kerry Trueman

75. *The Scarcity Slot: Excavating Histories of Food Security in Ghana,* by Amanda L. Logan

76. *Gastropolitics and the Specter of Race: Stories of Capital, Culture, and Coloniality in Peru,* by María Elena García

77. *The Kingdom of Rye: A Brief History of Russian Food,* by Darra Goldstein

78. *Slow Cooked: An Unexpected Life in Food Politics,* by Marion Nestle

79. *Yerba Mate: The Drink That Shaped a Nation,* by Julia J. S. Sarreal

80. *Wonder Foods: The Science and Commerce of Nutrition,* by Lisa Haushofer

81. *Ways of Eating: Exploring Food through History and Culture,* by Benjamin A. Wurgaft and Merry I. White

82. *From Label to Table: Regulating Food in America in the Information Age,* by Xaq Frohlich

83. *Intoxicating Pleasures: The Reinvention of Wine, Beer, and Whiskey after Prohibition,* by Lisa Jacobson

84. *The Quinoa Bust: The Making and Unmaking of an Andean Miracle Crop,* by Emma McDonell

85. *On Hunger: Violence and Craving in America, from Starvation to Ozempic,* by Dana Simmons

86. *The Pierogi Problem: Cosmopolitan Appetites and the Reinvention of Polish Food,* by Fabio Parasecoli, Agata Bachórz, and Mateusz Halawa

Founded in 1893,
UNIVERSITY OF CALIFORNIA PRESS
publishes bold, progressive books and journals
on topics in the arts, humanities, social sciences,
and natural sciences—with a focus on social
justice issues—that inspire thought and action
among readers worldwide.

The UC PRESS FOUNDATION
raises funds to uphold the press's vital role
as an independent, nonprofit publisher, and
receives philanthropic support from a wide
range of individuals and institutions—and from
committed readers like you. To learn more, visit
ucpress.edu/supportus.